HUMAN RESOURCES ADMINISTRATION

A SCHOOL-BASED PERSPECTIVE

Richard E. Smith

EYE ON EDUCATION
6 DEPOT WAY WEST, SUITE 106
LARCHMONT, NY 10538
(914) 833–0551
(914) 833–0761 fax

ISBN 1-883001-44-7

Library of Congress Cataloging-in-Publication Data

Smith, Richard E., 1941–
   Human resources administration : a school-based perspective /
Richard E. Smith.
      p.   cm.
   Includes bibliographical references (p.) and index.
   ISBN 1-883001-44-7
   1. School personnel management--United States.   2. School-based
management--United States.   I. Title.
LB2831.58.S57   1998
371.2'01--dc21   97-22968
                                                                        CIP

10 9 8 7 6 5 4 3

Editorial and production services provided by Richard H. Adin Freelance Editorial Services,
9 Orchard Drive, Gardiner, NY 12525 (914-883-5884)

Published by Eye On Education

THE PRINCIPAL AS STEWARD
By Jack McCall

THE PRINCIPAL'S EDGE
By Jack McCall

INSTRUCTION AND THE LEARNING ENVIRONMENT
By James Keefe and John Jenkins

RESOURCE ALLOCATION
Managing Money and People
By M. Scott Norton and Larry K. Kelly

WRITTEN EXPRESSION
The Principal's Survival Guide
By India Podsen, Charles Allen, Glenn Pethel, and John Waide

WRITTEN EXPRESSION
The Principal's Survival Guide
Disk with Workbook
By India Podsen

HUMAN RESOURCES ADMINISTRATION
A School-Based Perspective
By Richard E. Smith

RESEARCH ON EDUCATIONAL INNOVATIONS 2d ed.
By Arthur K. Ellis and Jeffrey T. Fouts

THE REFLECTIVE SUPERVISOR
A Practical Guide For Educators
By Ray Calabrese and Sally Zepeda

HANDS-ON LEADERSHIP TOOLS FOR PRINCIPALS
By Ray Calabrese, Gary Short, and Sally Zepeda

LEADERSHIP THROUGH COLLABORATION
Alternatives to the Hierarchy
By Michael Koehler and Jeanne C. Baxter

THE SCHOOL PORTFOLIO
A Comprehensive Framework For School Improvement
By Victoria L. Bernhardt

THE ADMINISTRATOR'S GUIDE TO SCHOOL–COMMUNITY RELATIONS
By George E. Pawlas

ORGANIZATIONAL OVERSIGHT
Planning and Scheduling for Effectiveness
By David A. Erlandson, Peggy L. Stark, and Sharon M. Ward

MOTIVATING OTHERS
Creating the Conditions
By David P. Thompson

INTERPERSONAL SENSITIVITY
By John R. Hoyle and Harrison M. Crenshaw

ORAL AND NONVERBAL EXPRESSION
By Ivan Muse

LEADERSHIP
A Relevant and Realistic Role for Principals
By Gary Crow, Joseph Matthews, & Lloyd McCleary

JUDGMENT
Making the Right Calls
By Jim Sweeney and Diana Bourisaw

PROBLEM ANALYSIS
Responding to School Complexity
By Charles M. Achilles, John S. Reynolds, and Susan H. Achilles

ABOUT THE AUTHOR

Richard E. Smith is the chair and associate professor of educational administration in the Graduate School at Seattle Pacific University. He had previously been a high school teacher and coach, elementary school counselor, middle school principal, assistant superintendent, and superintendent. He earned his B.A. in mathematics at Seattle Pacific University and both his M.A. and Ph.D. degrees at the University of Oregon. His main focus and concentration during his career in education has been on human resources functions.

He has written several journal articles, but this is his first book. In addition to teaching, he regularly consults with education and other organizations regarding personnel functions.

ACKNOWLEDGMENTS

The author gratefully acknowledges the competent and diligent work of several graduate students who share the author's interest in human resources issues. These students have visited numerous schools and districts, making this text tightly connected to the best practices of some of the most effective schools. The examples listed as figures and incorporated in the text represent potential solutions to both recurring and new human resources problems. The author appreciates the willingness to share materials by school districts and their best principals.

Ankeny School District, IA
Bainbridge Island School District, WA
Council Bluffs School District, IA
Edmonds School District, WA
Educational Service District
  No. 113, WA
Elk Grove School District, CA
Everett School District, WA
Issaquah School District, WA
Key West School District, FL
Lake Stevens School District, WA
Lake Washington School District, WA
Marysville School District, WA

Mukilteo School District, WA
North Slope Borough School
  District, WA
Oak Harbor School District, WA
Port Angeles School District, WA
Renton School District, WA
Shelton School District, WA
South Kitsap School District, WA
Sumner School District, WA
Wenatchee School District, WA
Westborough School District, WA
West Valley School District, WA

In addition, Dr. Randy Dunn of Southern Illinois University at Carbondale and Dr. Thomas Williams of California State University, Sacramento provided comments and advice on early drafts of this manuscript. Their advice was very helpful and appreciated. Further, Dr. Larry Nyland, my colleague at Seattle Pacific University, made significant contributions to the chapter on Continuity and Legal Issues.

Special thanks to Leo Blodgett, a career educator now retired, who hired me as a beginning teacher and later encouraged me to become a principal and superintendent. He set my course for which I am especially grateful. Mr. Jaye Compton of Sue's Secretarial Center in Lacey, Washington, prepared the manuscript and was always professional and timely in his assistance. Thanks also to Tina Barland, an outstanding copyeditor, and to Richard Adin whose attention to detail is deeply appreciated. Finally, I was able to learn from both my son, Mark, and daughter, Angela, who both are teachers. I thank them for entering this profession which creates all the others.

PREFACE

Many human resource functions that had previously belonged to the central office are now the responsibility of principals. The principal's role is changing, but how that role is orchestrated within the context of site-based management is also changing. This text is a guide to the understanding of those changes and provides both the principal-in-training and the experienced principal with a resource to some of the best practices to use in this ever-changing and increasingly demanding role.

A few examples will give some perspective: Principals are taking on more of an active and decision-making role in interviewing and the selection of prospective teachers. Previously, the staff at the central office was the major player in recruiting, announcing the vacancy, and developing the selection criteria, with the principal getting involved at the end of the process to interview the final three to five candidates and make his or her selection/recommendation. A more common current practice is to involve the principal from the very beginning of the hiring process.

Induction of staff is another area which was previously the responsibility of the central office and now is the responsibility of the principal and staff. Selecting quality staff members is a major task, but assisting them to become effective teachers is now a major duty of today's principal.

The field of personnel and human resources administration is changing rapidly. Consider the major Supreme Court rulings on affirmative action and you soon come to the conclusion that the principal needs to be cognizant of the changing legal landscape. This text is aimed at assisting both the principal-in-training and the experienced principal in these areas. It is meant to be used as a guide to some exemplary practices and as a future reference.

TABLE OF CONTENTS

1

INTRODUCING HUMAN RESOURCES ADMINISTRATION

REASONS FOR STUDYING HUMAN RESOURCES ADMINISTRATION

- In any school over 80% of the budget is spent on the human resources function. This includes the salary, benefits, and training costs of the certificated, classified, and administrative personnel in the school. As such, it is clear that principals must have a comprehensive understanding of the human resources function if they are to be accountable for their school.

- When people fail at their job it is not always because of their lack of technical expertise, but more often because of their poor interpersonal relations.

- You cannot use yesterday's skills for today's job and expect to be in business tomorrow. The principal's knowledge, skills, and abilities must be current in order for the school to be effective.

- The whole is greater than the sum of its parts. It is critical that the principal have an understanding of the interrelated parts of the human resources system.

Schools are, after all, a people business.

INTRODUCTION

This chapter, Introducing Human Resources Administration, provides an overview for the book. It briefly discusses the major topics and provides an overall framework for the more detailed chapters that follow. The principal should think of the spiral curriculum in which the topics are first introduced, then explained in detail. This book discusses these topics from the perspective of the school principal and the school. Central office human resources specialists and superintendents will also benefit from this book because it will give them an understanding of the emerging role of principals in human resources administration so they can provide guidance to them.

The chapter topics are:

- School-Based Leadership
- Planning
- Recruitment
- Selection
- Orientation and Induction
- Supervision and Evaluation
- Assisting the Marginal Teacher
- Staff Development
- Collective Bargaining
- Continuity and Legal Issues
- Technology and Human Resources
- A Glance into the Future of Human Resources

Figure 1.1 graphically gives the reader a template for this chapter as well as for the remainder of the book. But first some sample definitions of Human Resources Administration.

DEFINITIONS OF HUMAN RESOURCES ADMINISTRATION

It is the balance between the school's need to accomplish its mission and the individual's need to achieve and to perform useful, satisfying work.

It is an attitude that people are paramountly important in any organization, especially schools.

FIGURE 1.1. AN EFFECTIVE EDUCATIONAL HUMAN RESOURCES MANAGEMENT SYSTEM

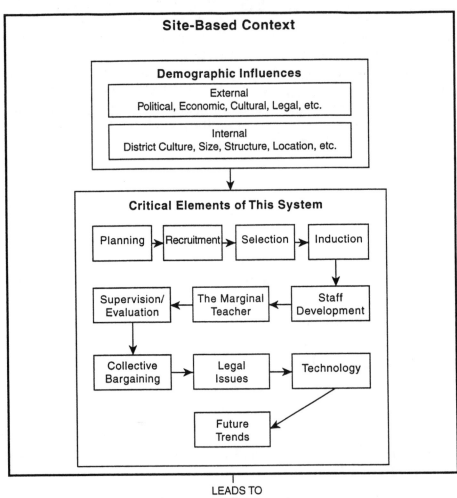

Site-Based Context

Demographic Influences

External
Political, Economic, Cultural, Legal, etc.

Internal
District Culture, Size, Structure, Location, etc.

Critical Elements of This System

Planning → Recruitment → Selection → Induction

Supervision/Evaluation ← The Marginal Teacher ← Staff Development

Collective Bargaining → Legal Issues → Technology

Future Trends

LEADS TO

Human Resources Effectiveness

LEADS TO

Student Learning

It focuses on everything that influences the effectiveness or ineffectiveness of school personnel.

It is doing *what is best for teachers*. Principals should adopt this definition much like teachers believe that they should do *what's best for students*. Most, if not all, of the time, doing what's best for students is, for principals, doing what's best for teachers.

It is concern for people—all people and their needs.

THE MAJOR CRITICAL ELEMENTS OF HUMAN RESOURCES ADMINISTRATION

SCHOOL-BASED LEADERSHIP

One of the major changes in education is the movement toward school-based leadership (SBL). Many of the management functions which were previously centralized for control and standardization are now being decentralized to the building level where they become the responsibility of the principal and/or the school-based council made up of the principal, teachers, parents, and students. It is in this context that this section is included in a text on human resources administration. School-based leadership is the framework in which the human resources function is, and increasingly will be, implemented.

Given this context, it is incumbent upon the principal to develop knowledge, skills, attitudes, and ability to be effective in this redefined role. The staff at the district office in small school districts is almost nonexistent (other than the superintendent who already wears too many hats). In larger districts the pressure to cut the administration and overhead has resulted in the cutback and/or elimination of the professional staff and thus, the services of the human resources department.

The principal's ability to provide effective leadership to the human resources function of the school will, in large measure, determine the effectiveness of the teachers, the school, and the students. Whereas in the past, the principal was often called upon to be the instructional leader of the school, now the principal will be called upon to be the leader—of instruction, of human resources, of the plant, and of public relations. The ability to set up the framework for school-based leadership and to provide leadership within that framework is critical. Teachers, parents, students, superintendents, and communities are expecting that the "new" principal will be able to accomplish all this and more. School-based leadership is not a normal topic for a textbook on human resources leadership, but things are changing. Principals must be proactive in developing new abilities within this new context.

PLANNING

This is both a short- and long-term focus on the future. Most schools have long-term planning for the curriculum and textbook adoptions but rarely focus on the needs of the teachers and others who will implement those plans. The failure to plan is to "plan to fail," especially when there is a crisis.

Almost all principals who are providing leadership in their school will fight any movement to reduce the planning time for teachers. Teachers need it and principals safeguard it at almost all costs. Further, principals will also assume that planning is one of their key responsibilities, along with organizing, directing, and supervising. However, few if any principals have a designated time for planning during the school day and almost feel guilty if they are in their office planning for their school and the people in it.

Principals are excellent at daily planning as witnessed by their calendars. However, most of the items on the calendar are activities and few are related to the goals and mission of their school or district. Chapter 2 helps principals to focus on monthly and yearly planning by giving examples and a format to accomplish the goals and mission of the organization. Being busy is not important to the role of the principal—accomplishing goals is.

RECRUITMENT

The recruitment of teachers is a critical element of the human resources function, because no matter how sophisticated your selection process is, if you don't have the right people in the applicant pool, it is impossible to select them. Many school districts and schools boast about the number of applicants for a position. However, the emphasis should not be on quantity, but rather on the quality of applicants who meet the preestablished criteria.

Most recruitment is done through college and university placement offices, professional associations, or regional school districts which notify teachers of the vacancy in a school district. Brochures are also an asset to the recruiting process. One of the major, usually untapped, sources for the recruiting of teachers is the current staff. These individuals often may know of teachers who possess characteristics which would match the community, district, and school culture. There should be a systematic effort to seek referrals from the staff.

In addition, districts that are attempting to diversify the teaching force will have to use special efforts to reach special groups of applicants. College or job fairs are also sources of potential applicants. Most often the recruitment element is neglected while selection gets most of the attention. Good recruiting increases the possibility of good selection, whereas poor recruiting methods almost always lead to poor selection.

SELECTION

The selection process generally has three main components: paper screening, personal interviewing, and reference checking.

It is helpful to draw the parallel between the requisitioning of a capital purchase and teacher selection: for example, a $100 student desk and the selection of a $1 million-plus teacher (over a 30-year career). The principal will very tightly specify what is wanted: seven-ply top with medium brown plastic laminate, chrome legs, book rack under the seat, solid thermo-set plastic back ¾" thick, all metal joints welded by 1" welds, 17" high seat, etc. This process is usual for the requisition and purchase order process. Now, contrast that with the usual personnel requirements: we need a high school mathematics teacher, or a fourth grade teacher. Clearly it is incumbent on principals to be very specific about the qualities of the teachers they wish to hire. As they review the completed files of teachers they need to make accurate judgments about applicants and make a match between the applicant and the opening.

A KEY IDEA

Do not use teachers, students, parents, or community members on the selection team unless you train them in the selection/confidentiality process.

The *completed files* need to be reviewed according to the criteria of the certificated personnel requisition by either the principal or the principal and selection team. A strong word of caution here: The files that are being reviewed are confidential, and when there are many people reviewing them there is a chance that the confidentiality might be violated. Therefore, do not use teachers, students, parents, or community members on the selection team *unless* they are trained in the selection/confidentiality process. Not doing so violates the writer of the letters of reference—usually other principals.

One usual part of the complete file is an *application*. This usually consists of three or four pages to be completed by the applicant. Applicants who want to put their "best foot forward" will type their application responses. However, the skill of using a typewriter in the age of the computer is weak; the application form blanks are never long enough for long-charactered school districts (Steilacoom Historical School District No. 1) or names (Dr. Marilyn R. Johnson-Bender) and there are no two application forms alike. These factors can be very discouraging to the applicant who is applying for many positions in different districts. Some suggestions:

- Use a computer disk for the application and when the applicant requests an application send the proper disk.
- Develop a region-wide application to be used by many districts.
- Use only the applicant's letter of application, professional résumé, copy of license to teach, and placement file to select interviewees. All other information (disclosure forms, transcripts, application forms) is needed only for the candidate who has been selected for recommendation to the superintendent and the school board.

The *interview* is the most time-consuming part of the process. The interview consists of getting more information from the candidate for responses to preestablished questions. The major error in this segment of the selection process is that there is no agreement on what constitutes a good response to the questions. The parallel here is that after a teacher makes out a test for students, an answer key must be developed. The same must be done for the interview questions. The "look-fors" must be identified in advance or major discrepancies may surface later in the process.

It is most helpful to the principal if the selection committee does not rank-order the candidates but instead lists strengths and weaknesses and questions that should be investigated during the reference checks. If the committee must rank-order the candidates, then have each member do that individually. What may often happen is one dominating selection committee member can unfairly influence the decision. Consider this case: The selection committee ranks the candidates first, second, and third. During the reference checks, the first candidate does not check out clearly and the second candidate decides to take another position. The principal then is left with the third candidate or reopening the position and repeating the process. Suppose the third candidate gets the position. The selection committee now feels that it was not listened to and the principal feels that the decision must be explained to the committee—a possible relationship problem.

The *reference check* is another phase of the process to which care must be given. A key point here is to contact people who are *not* on the list of references. Find professionals who would know the candidate's ability but are not listed on the résumé or the application and call them. If the principal and representatives of the selection committee can visit the school of the applicant, do it. A major decision is about to be made and the decision makers need all the information they can get.

INDUCTION/ORIENTATION

Induction can be considered assistance to your newly hired employees and consists of two main segments for two different types of employees. Figure 1.2 illustrates the emphasis to be considered here.

FIGURE 1.2. INDUCTION/ORIENTATION OF NEW AND EXPERIENCED TEACHERS

		Orientation	Year-Long Induction
T E A C H E R S	New	Emphasis	Emphasis
	Experienced	Emphasis	Secondary Emphasis

Most districts have a short orientation process of one to three days for all teachers new to the district. However, the wise principal would also develop a comprehensive program to assist teachers new to the profession throughout the entire school year. The experienced teacher could also be invited, encouraged, and in some cases directed to attend all induction activities. It is not surprising that many teachers new to the profession do not return after one or two years. In many cases this decision can be traced to the lack of proper induction to the school, district, and community.

Further, attention should be given to transfers to new assignments within the building. Department chairs, grade level coordinators, and cocurricular advisors are also key employees that deserve attention during the induction process. Finally, the employees involved in the induction process should be given an opportunity to evaluate the process and make suggestions for future induction activities, or even leading some of them.

SUPERVISION AND EVALUATION

The process of supervision and evaluation is critically important for both the teacher and principal. It is important for the teachers to receive support or redirection. They deserve support if they are doing well, and redirection if improvements are needed. In both cases this is the task of the principal and it relates directly to teacher effectiveness and student learning.

The principal must develop a trusting relationship with the teachers and have the skills to furnish them with objective data about their teaching. It is helpful for principals to think of an instructional model when they are in the role of teacher/coach to the employee. They should prepare to teach, teach, and reflect on the teaching. That is, they must be *well-planned* to conduct the preobservation conference, the observation, and the postobservation conference. Prior to the postobservation conference, the principal should consider the information gathered during the observation, as well as the curriculum and the learner (teacher), and then determine the *most effective method of sharing* the data with the learner. The principal also will want to *reflect on the effectiveness of the postobservation conference* and continue to refine his or her skills as a supervisor and evaluator.

> ### A KEY IDEA
>
> If the teacher won't do the job, then you have a motivational problem. If the teacher can't do it, then you have a training problem.

This process is important to the principal since failure to evaluate can become very serious, even leading to dismissal of the principal. A teacher would never think of not grading the students, likewise, a principal should also never think of not evaluating the teaching staff.

Supervision is much like formative evaluation while evaluation is similar to summative evaluation. In both cases, teacher growth is the goal.

ASSISTING THE MARGINAL TEACHER

The marginal teacher represents a special case of supervision and evaluation. Fortunately, there are few of these teachers in the system, but there are some, and thus, the principal needs to identify and provide assistance to them. In most cases, these teachers will take more of the principal's time, planning, and energy than all the others combined. This is an example of the Pareto Principle: Twenty percent of the teachers will take 80% of the time.

In many cases, the principal can assist the teacher significantly. In other cases, extra resources and professionals will be needed to assist both the teacher and the principal. It is key that the principal work diligently with the marginal teacher because students' learning is affected. This takes courage on the part of the principal, as well as support from the district.

The marginal teacher may be one who needs the services of an Employee Assistance Program (EAP). The principal must be skilled in recognizing these problems and in making appropriate referrals and furnishing support as needed.

STAFF DEVELOPMENT

The old adage "hire the best, train the rest" is no longer appropriate, if it ever was. The growth and development of staff is directly related to the growth and development of students. Teachers are generally well trained at the initial level when they receive their license to teach. However, the principal must continue that growth and training in order that the school's and teachers' goals be realized.

This development process starts with the induction program and continues throughout the teacher's career. The principal is the coach in the development of the teacher as a person and as a professional. If done correctly, the principal will feel a sense of accomplishment, much like a teacher does who sees the students growing, developing, and succeeding.

The development of staff is dynamic and comprehensive. Its objective is to increase student achievement through ongoing staff development. A comprehensive staff development program includes:

♦ Training in curriculum development and implementation

+ Training in instructional strategies
+ Employee Assistance and Wellness Programs
+ Climate improvement
+ Incentives
+ Supervision

COLLECTIVE BARGAINING

The role of the principal in collective bargaining is often a secondary but important one. However, the basic techniques of collaborative bargaining are ones that will serve the principal well during the daily tasks of leadership and management. Communication, listening, working together, and understanding others are all basic skills which the principal needs to develop to be effective.

Further, the principal, who is part of the district's leadership team as well as the leader of the school, is in a vital position to assist both the district and the education association with the collaborative process.

The salary schedule and benefits program are subjects of bargaining and are addressed superficially since those activities are almost entirely the responsibility of the district staff and school board.

CONTINUITY AND LEGAL ISSUES

The principal plays a minor role in this area at the present time. However, with the downsizing of the central office staff, many of these responsibilities could become part of the principal's responsibility. Nevertheless, the exposure to an understanding of basic principles, as well as potential problems, will alert the principal of dangers and when to seek outside assistance.

TECHNOLOGY AND HUMAN RESOURCES LEADERSHIP

This topic will increase in use and value to the principal in the future. It is a vital area of information, communication, and decision making. The wise principal will continue to develop technological skills in order to provide effective and efficient service, as well as modeling, to the staff.

A GLANCE INTO THE FUTURE

Some trends are discussed briefly as to the future of human resources administration. These trends could provide a base for understanding and anticipating the future. They could also provide discussion topics and growth areas for principals.

The previously outlined information provides an introduction and template for the principal to anticipate the areas which will be covered in detail in the forthcoming chapters. Figure 1.3, which begins on the next page, is an example of the human resources responsibilities of the principal in a school-based leadership district.

CONCLUSION

This chapter provided an introduction to the detailed human resources administration topics to be covered in detail in the remaining chapters of this book.

FIGURE 1.3. HUMAN RESOURCES RESPONSIBILITIES FOR PRINCIPALS IN SCHOOL-BASED DISTRICTS

The principal shall, within district policies, the superintendent's guidelines, and the management team's decisions and agreements, administer and direct all activities of the personnel assigned to his/her school.

Duties and Responsibilities

- Direct and supervise all personnel assigned to the school.

- Maintain only a working personnel file for all employees of the school except for the principal.

- Determine staffing needs in cooperation with the various department chairs and direct the staff selection process.

- Cooperate with others to develop a program of recruitment of classified, professional, and para-professional personnel large enough to provide an uninterrupted flow of qualified new employees and replacements.

- Be actively involved in recruiting activies.

- Participate in state and national recruitment fairs.

- Supervise job descriptions and writing of job postings, obtain job applications, and screen applicant files and conduct interviews.

- Conduct all reference checking of new employees.

- Recommend employment of classified, professional, and para-professional personnel to the superintendent.

- Develop a professional growth program for all staff assigned to your school.

- Develop both long- and short-range plans for the personnel needs of your school.

- Work cooperatively with others to maintain a pool of substitutes to provide for the needs of the school and district. Evaluate the work of substitutes.

- Act as compliance office for employment and assignment of all personnel.

- Evaluate and supervise all employees of the school according to the district-approved forms and procedures.

- Conduct a comprehensive induction program at your school and grade level.

- Actively participate in a training program for evaluators.

- Monitor and support the student teaching programs in your school.

- Monitor and support the administrative internship programs in your school.

- Be actively involved in the preparation of staffing reports and other personnel-related information for district and state records.

- Support the district goals regarding diversity.

- Support the district Employee Assistance Program.

- Support the district Wellness Program.

- Perform such other related duties assigned by the superintendent.

These functions and responsibilities have been discussed and agreed to this _____ day of _____, 19___.

Signed: _____
                                                      Principal

Signed: _____
                                                   Superintendent

2

STRATEGIC HUMAN RESOURCES PLANNING

REASONS FOR STUDYING HUMAN RESOURCES PLANNING

- Planning is one of the most critical management functions.
- Planning leads to organization and the development of effective work plans.
- Planning is a prerequisite to the achievement of goals.
- Planning is an important part of good time management.

> *We need to be concerned about the future, for that is where we will spend the rest of our lives.*

INTRODUCTION

The purpose of this chapter is to provide for school administrators, *particularly building principals,* an overview of what *strategic human resources planning* is at the building level. This is followed by strategic human resources planning within the context of districtwide comprehensive strategic planning, and then by the process of collaborative planning at the building level. Schematics are presented depicting the role and duties of a building level human resources administrator (principal) both within the context of the school district and at the building level.

WHAT IS STRATEGIC PLANNING AND WHY DO WE DO IT?

> *Planning is...attending to the goals we ought to be thinking about and never do, the facts we do not like to face, and the questions we lack the courage to ask.*
>
> Bruce Perryman

What is strategic planning? Strategic planning arose within the business community in the 1970s as a technique for helping managers make decisions which maximize organizational objectives. Pfeiffer, Goodstein, and Nolan (1986) defined strategic planning as

> the process by which an organization *envisions its future* and develops the necessary procedures and operations to achieve that future. This vision of the future state of the organization provides both the direction in which the organization should move and the energy to begin that move.

When an organization has *"envisioned its future"* it has begun the process of strategic planning. These are key words: strategic plans are about "seeing" the future and finding a *vision* of what an organization might become in this future.

Why do we do strategic planning? L.E. Scarr, former superintendent of the Lake Washington School District (WA), introduced a planning document by writing about *why* it is that we plan:

> It is a rare individual, a rare organization, which is capable of altering its behavior or managing itself successfully without a well-defined plan.

Educators today understand how Daniel felt among the lions. Armed with tattered spears of an antiquated authority, we field questions from parents about the value of education programs and even the idea of public education itself. We try to answer concerns about rising costs and decreasing test scores. We scramble to meet the needs of children from single-parent families, from families of non-English speaking refugees, of handicapped children and parents with diverse interests and needs.

New pressures and demands require new skills. New roles must be carved for school staff. New processes to include the community and business in educational planning must be developed. New attitudes about ideas like involvement, authority, and expertise must be developed among the entire educational community.

Change seldom happens by accident. It must be carefully planned, orchestrated, measured, and revised. It must be nurtured, encouraged, and watched closely to make sure the results benefit children. It must be tailored to fit individual school districts, communities, and students.

The model for district master planning...is a practical process for bringing staff, parents, students and community along a path of *planned* change and improvement.

WHAT IS STRATEGIC HUMAN RESOURCES PLANNING?

Strategic human resources planning is an organized process of enabling an organization to achieve its mission by the effective anticipation of human resources needs. The plans developed by this process must be directly related to, and congruent with, the organization-wide strategic plan.

The Strategic Planning Model (Figure 2.1) illustrates the process of human resources planning. It is important to scan both the external (society) and internal (district and school) environment as an initial part of the planning activity. There are several reasons for this:

♦ Schools are a subset of society and as such are reflective and dependent upon it.

♦ An examination of past trends allows us to understand the present and anticipate the future.

FIGURE 2.1. STRATEGIC PLANNING MODEL

Environmental Scanning

| External Scanning | Internal Scanning |

Strategic & Operational Planning

Strategic Plan

| Develop Mission | Develop Strategic Objectives | Conduct Gap Analysis | Develop Strategies |

Operational Plans

School Operational Plans

School 1	School 2	School (n)
* Budgeting	* Budgeting	
* **Personnel**	* Personnel	
* Pupil Services	* Pupil Services	

System Operational Plans

| Pupil Personnel Services | Human Resources | Finance & Business Affairs | Area (n) |

Feedback

Feedback

Implementation

♦ Schools have been called upon by society to solve many of its problems. A thorough understanding of such problems provides an opportunity for taking appropriate action with regard to program and personnel development.

 Schools and the school staff are part of this culture. An understanding of the culture helps us understand and meet staff needs.

If schools are to be ready to meet the challenges of the twenty-first century with appropriate programs and personnel, then the principals must be aware of the national and local demographic trends as the first step in environmental scanning of strategic human resources planning process.

A KEY IDEA

Demographics, both national and local, need to be studied in order to effectively plan for the future.

EXTERNAL SCANNING

NATIONAL DEMOGRAPHIC TRENDS

Environmental scanning is a process of analyzing local, state, and national data and trends for influence and impact on schools, students, programs, and educational personnel. The detail presented here is offered as a template for the principal to understand and use the environmental scanning step in the total planning process.

Students in the twenty-first century will be much different than the students of the past. Because of the demographic changes in contemporary society, today's student will be much more likely to:

♦ have more handicaps

♦ have more special needs

♦ represent more cultures

♦ have English language deficiencies, yet have efficiencies in another language

◆ have more choices for education, for example, home school, private education, charter schools.

POPULATION PROJECTIONS

The Census Bureau predicts that the states of California, Texas, and Florida will account for more than one-half of the U.S. population growth that will occur before the turn of the century. California will remain the most populous state, Texas will move into second place, and New York will descend to third. Arizona will be the fastest growing state. There will be general movement to the south and west. Many people will leave large cities to reside in the suburbs. Between 1991–1993 enrollment increased most dramatically in these states: New Jersey, New York, Pennsylvania, Florida, Georgia, Louisiana, North Carolina, Tennessee, and Texas (increased 104,000 students).

SPECIAL EDUCATION/HANDICAPPED ENROLLMENT

During the 1990–1991 school year, 9.9% of all children in public school received special education services. Most of those students (4.9%) needed◆ help for specific learning disabilities, while 2.4% had speech or language impairments, and 1.2% were mentally retarded. The remainder had serious emotional disturbances, hearing or orthopedic impairments, or multiple disabilities. Massachusetts serves the largest percentage of children with disabilities (15.7). Of the other states, 25 had special education populations of 10% or more. The state of Washington now spends $213 million a year to meet a federal requirement to completely pay for services to the disabled. The number of disabled grew from 66,223 in 1984 to 107,434 in 1995. Money is distributed according to the average needs of a disabled child and does not address the children with high degrees of need.

VIOLENCE

Communities across the United States—large and smal—lare struggling under the dramatic increases of violence. The impact of the heightened crime rate has been felt in the schools. District staffs are forced to handle fights, deal with gang activity, and confiscate weapons in schools as never before. Many districts have implemented strong safety measures to ensure the safety and security of their students. A poll funded by the Joyce Foundation and conducted by Louis Harris of LH Research for the Harvard School of Public Health reported these results about children 10–19 years of age:

- 15% said they had carried a handgun within 30 days of the survey
- 4% said they had taken a handgun to school at least once during the past year
- 9% said they had shot a gun at someone else
- 11% said they had been shot at by someone else in the past year
- 22% said they would feel "safer" having a handgun if they were going to be in a physical fight
- 39% said they know someone who has either been injured or killed by gunfire
- 59% said they could get a handgun if they wanted one

Parents are looking to the schools to guarantee the safety of their children. The schools have an increasingly tough responsibility. Funding that might have gone toward school programs now must be used to keep the students safe.

AT-RISK STUDENTS

Students at risk of school failure are becoming more clearly identified. With school failure comes the inevitable economical and social failure, posing a major concern to educators. Having one or more of the at-risk indicators (Figure 2.2) becomes nearly universal by eleventh grade (86%). Educators have been identifying the problems and have developed programs aimed at prevention and/or early intervention in the lives of our youth. It would be wise to intensify the efforts not only for the health of our children and schools, but also for the prosperity of our country's economic health.

ETHNIC DIVERSITY

It is important for those involved in education to know that the ethnic make-up of the United States is changing. Migration, fertility patterns, and immigration are changing the ethnic makeup of our country's youth today. "Geographical, racial, economic, and cultural diversity in the student body means a diversity of parent attitudes toward children, child rearing, and school responsibility" (Moore, 1994). In the next decade, 90% of the immigrants will settle in U.S. metropolitan areas—specifically, cities such as New York, Los Angeles, and Chicago.

FIGURE 2.2. INDICATORS OF HIGH RISK OF DROPPING OUT OF SCHOOL

School	Personal	Family
• Lack of basic skills • Performance consistently below potential • Poor grades or failure in subjects • Record of non-promotions • Low standard test scores • Irregular attendance and frequent tardiness • Pattern of disruptive or aggressive behavior • Poor study and work habits • Lack of academic motivation • Little or no participation in extra-curricular activities	• Alcohol or drug abuse • Physical health problems • Mental health problems • Poor self-concept • Married or pregnant • Poor social skills • Friends not school-oriented • Lack of realistic goals • Lack of supervision	• Low educational level of parents • Family pattern of dropping out • Negative parental attitudes or low educational aspirations • Broken home • Frequent family moves • Unstable home environment (severe conflicts between parents or between parent and child, family violence, alcoholic parent) • Parent unable to find employment • Low economic status

White students are already in the minority in the state of California. Non-whites comprise 51.3% of California's school-age population—31.4% Hispanic, 8.9% black, and 11% Asian and other nonwhite groups. Even when people of all ages are included, whites only make up 58% of California's population. Previously thought of as minorities, these students are already in the majority in the District of Columbia, Hawaii, Mississippi, New Mexico, and Texas.

Public schools, especially, will have to meet the needs of increasing culturally diverse students. Once, America was a microcosm of European nationalities. Today, America is a microcosm of the world. People of color are comprising a larger proportion of the student population in many districts across the nation. By the year 2000, 21% of American children will be ethnic minorities—primarily black or Asian-American. If the white Hispanic population under age 18 is added to black and Asian populations, the minority youth population will be 34% by the year 2000. By the year 2010, as many as 38% of Americans under the age of 18 will belong to minority groups. In seven states and the District of Columbia, more than half of the children will be nonwhite. In the overall population, the rate of growth among whites is not keeping pace with that of other ethnic groups.

SCHOOL CHOICE

Student enrollment in the public schools of this country is primarily influenced by changes in birth rate, migration patterns, and social/economic conditions. This population can also be affected by the presence of local private schools and, to a lesser degree, by the number of families choosing to home school their children. A good rule of thumb is that approximately 10% of the student population in most areas or communities will attend private schools. The Department of Education's National Center for Educational Statistics predicts there will be about 6 million additional students enrolled in private schools by 2003.

The number of students attending private schools is increasing due to several factors:

- the removal of traditional religious influence from the public schools
- the parents' desire for a "family-like" atmosphere
- private schools being responsive to parents and students
- the ability of private schools to control the type of student populations
- parents perceive them as "safer" schools
- baby boomers are turning to religion
- students can attend specialized schools
- communities are experiencing a growth in fundamentalism and localism

The home school movement continues to grow across the country as parents exercise their right to accept the responsibility to teach their own children. Parents choose to home school for a variety of reasons, but at the core is their desire to control what their children are learning. National support for the movement has increased. Home school families often work in cooperation with their local public schools to supplement areas of their child's curriculum and to also provide for them an opportunity to be involved in sports and other extracurricular activities. The home school movement will no doubt continue to grow, and greater cooperation between home and school will be necessary.

School choice (vouchers) also continues to gain popularity nationally, although it has suffered some setbacks. With the number of people dissatisfied with the effectiveness of the public schools, school choice may become inevitable. The concept of charter schools has also gained attention and will provide a growing option for the education of students.

LOCATING LOCAL DEMOGRAPHIC DATA

Many principals are unaware of the vast amount of demographic data available to them. Often those who propose changes for the educational systems of the future only take into account the implication of the total number of students without looking at the compositions of the total. For example, when we consider that by the year 2000 the majority of the population in some states will be made up of minorities, it becomes clear that it is not to everyone's best interest to ignore the ethnic changes in the population. Failing to consider the specific changes that are occurring can result in educational programs that are not pertinent to the students; many students may underachieve, become disruptive, or drop out of school. No matter what the curriculum content, if students have difficulty understanding the material because of cultural and language barriers, content becomes irrelevant.

Computerized statistical packages have a place in assisting in short-range projections of five years or less. Other sources of demographic data include census data, county planning departments, building permits, district surveys, health departments, commercial surveys and projections, utility companies, and a community's Chamber of Commerce.

IMPLICATIONS FOR HUMAN RESOURCES PLANNING

The previously mentioned concerns have many implications for schools and school districts. To meet the needs of this new student profile, school staffs must offer services that correspond to student needs. Schools must plan to develop:

- early childhood education programs
- day care centers in schools
- parenting education

- health clinics in schools
- dropout prevention programs
- improved preparation of students for the transition to the work world
- a broader base of offerings instead of a more limited curriculum

Changing demographics will have implications for school staffing. Teachers in the future will have to be prepared to face:

- more special-needs children in the mainstream
- larger classes
- the need to be more of a social worker than a subject matter specialist
- more home/school responsibilities
- greater skills as career and guidance counselors
- students with a wider range of needs and problems, and must be capable of instructing, motivating, and controlling a group with more diverse needs

Following is a brief checklist for a principal's external and internal environment check:

Strategic Personnel Planning Checklist
*Clarify the **external** context (opportunities and threats)*

- community input on what students need to know and be able to do
- culture, demographics
  - racial/ethnic community composition
  - age distribution
  - socioeconomic status
  - politics
- legal arena
- technology
- relationships with teacher training institutions
- competition with private schools, other districts, and programs, e.g., Running Start

♦ **scan and communicate the trend in terms of threats and opportunities**

Strategic Personnel Planning Checklist
*Clarify the **internal** context (strengths and weaknesses)*

♦ history
♦ board policies
♦ capacity to implement anything
♦ organizational culture and climate
♦ financial human, facility resources
♦ employee dress, greetings, body language, ceremonies, gossip, jokes
♦ how decisions are made
♦ real versus formal leadership
♦ how individuals and organization controls information; how system communicates; how people communicate
♦ **scan and communicate the trends in terms of strengths and weaknesses**

STRATEGIC PLANNING

Diligent environmental scanning efforts lay the groundwork for the general strategic plan, from which the strategic human resources plan will arise. Strategic plans follow organizational *mission statements,* but before discussing mission statements, consider how mission statements come to be. Mission statements often arise out of *dreams and visions.* Dreams and visions are hard to describe; they are often based on demographic and environmental scanning work, but take place in the heart of educators who begin to get a mental picture of what they want their school to look like.

Mission statements apply more precise and more measurable language to dreams and visions. Many, many hours of collaborative planning by administrators and staff are required to produce a mission statement. But they are hours well spent because mission statements are an essential part of strategic planning.

Ground rules for the development of mission statements:

♦ A mission statement must be stated in specific and definitive terms. It must be the motivational focus that encourages all points of view and still maintains a coherent organization moving toward common aims.

♦ Any mission statement should include the following three primary elements

  • "Schools are for kids"

  • "Schools belong to the people"

  • "Schools are people developers"

♦ To receive commitment to a mission, people in an organization need to go through four steps:

  • awareness that the mission exists

  • written communication to all in the organization of what the mission is

  • planned and intermittent reinforcement of the intended mission

  • power to perpetuate that mission

♦ The mission statement must be developed by a team effort if there is going to be commitment to that statement. A sample mission statement follows:

SAMPLE MISSION STATEMENT

Our mission is to develop the intellectual, vocational, physical, creative, cultural, and social capabilities of students. Our plenary commitment is to develop young people and to build positive relationships with them. We recognize that a quality staff is the key to providing quality education. We are dedicated to the development of professional skills and the full human potential of all staff members.

A KEY IDEA

The mission of every school is the growth and development of students through the growth and development of staff.

Out of the mission statement should come strategic objectives which are clear and measurable. Webb et al. recommend a "gap analysis," which is another way of saying that we should understand the difference between where we are today and where we want to be concerning each strategic objective. From these objectives and a sense of where we are *now,* strategies are developed that lead to a reasonable realization of the mission statement. Following is a principal's checklist regarding things to think about during the strategic planning process:

Strategic Personnel Planning Checklist
Strategic and Operational Planning

Commit to quality service, continuous development; seek optimum professional staff mix

Strategic Plan

◆ Develop **Mission**
  • accommodate environmental dynamics
  • clarify function of school system
  • clarify who it will serve
  • clarify how it will go about its business
◆ Develop **Strategic Objectives**
  • establish critical success indicators that clients understand and value
  • connect indicators and objectives to resources (time, energy, $)
◆ Conduct **Gap Analysis**
  • compare desired outcomes to current status
◆ Develop **Strategies**
  • clarify how strategic objectives will be achieved

OPERATIONAL PLANNING

The critical aspects of operational planning are depicted in the darkly shaded section of the strategic planning model (Figure 2.1). This is planning at the building level, where the principal is most involved. **The operational** plans at the school level are to be consistent with the strategic plan developed at the district level, as the graphic demonstrates, but also each school should do its own strategic planning process, its own environmental scanning, and its own strategic planning, with mission statement, strategic objectives and strategies to realize these objectives. Note the two-way arrow between the school operational planning box and the environmental scanning box at the top of the chart. It denotes that the process is bilateral. Personnel planning, highlighted in bold in Figure 2.1, is to be done with general district and building strategic plans in mind and in cooperation with the human resources department at the district office. Following are some suggestions concerning building level operational planning that principals should keep in mind:

Strategic Personnel Planning Checklist
Operational Plans

Integrate School Operational Plans and human resources operational plan.

- ♦ Create professional staff mix to accommodate needs of school.
- ♦ Make data-based decisions; involve people or sources of relevant information in decision making.
- ♦ Create short term plan (12-month calendar).
- ♦ Create long term plan (60-month calendar).
- ♦ Plan personnel staffing needs and goals before budget; budget can reflect needs.
- ♦ Attach specific assignments and responsibilities to all activities.

STRATEGIC HUMAN RESOURCES PLANNING CHECKLIST

SURGE *AND* FLOW OR SURGE *VERSUS* FLOW

In nonsystematic and nonstrategic personnel planning the calendar and actions duplicate a volunteer fire department fighting a fire: no prevention, all time and activities are spent fighting fires. In this model of personnel *un*management, vacancies occur, the most convenient applicant is quickly interviewed and hired to fill the spot, handed a grade book and chalk, wished well and not seen again until the law mandates an evaluation, or the applicant drops off the grade book and unused chalk at the office with a notice of resignation. The vacancy occurs, the most convenient applicant is quickly interviewed and hired to fill the spot, handed a grade book...and the process repeats itself like fires occur in the community.

In systematic and strategic personnel planning, there is room for the surge times of the year and there is room forcibly made for an ongoing flow of planning, implementing, and evaluating with feedback as shown in Figure 2.3. Proactive planning means that before the first moment of recruitment, all the prerequisite steps of environmental scanning and strategic planning must be in place. Feedback from previous exit interviews should be incorporated into both recruiting and selection plans and strategies. Then operational plans for recruitment can occur. Part of the recruitment effort is to package the strategic plan and environment in a brochure or other handout that can be sent to prospective applicants so that they can self-appraise their compatibility with the school and the district. Also, the recruiting administrator should have a very clear sense of what kind of person she or he is seeking. Proactive clarification will avoid the waste of energies and resources on applicants out of synchronization with what the administrator is seeking. Since travel and advertising logistics are involved in the recruiting efforts, planning in advance will assure travel and purchased advertising in a most cost-productive manner. But one should not conclude that recruitment should be relegated to a particular time of the year; it can and should occur all the time. Conferences, college homecomings, weekend ski trips, summer vacations, any time there is a gathering of people who might be interested is a recruiting opportunity. To be sure, the best thing for recruiting is to have a very good school that sells itself.

During the recruitment phase, the selection criteria and process, the nature of supervision, staff development opportunities, and evaluation procedures and criteria should be thought out and available as information to the prospective candidate. More thoughtful candidates are going to inquire about such matters and the principal had better have the answers.

Thus, planning should be seen as a constant necessary *flow* of energy—the *important* aspect of personnel systems. Recruitment, selection, staff development, evaluation, and exiting processes should be seen as *surge* imes and are appropriately *urgent*. Flow *and* surge. Presented below is a broad checklist of things to remember when implementing a strategic human resources plan:

FIGURE 2.3. PERSONNEL SYSTEM OVERVIEW

Strategic Personnel Planning Checklist
Implementation

♦ Capture product and process data that become feedback for the entire plan

♦ Forecast personnel needs and student enrollments

♦ Recruit

♦ Select in

♦ Assign

   • Supervise and develop staff

   • Evaluate staff

   • Compensate staff

   • Induct staff

♦ For staff selecting out, conduct exit interview and provide feedback to the selection and assignment process.

Figure 2.4, beginning on page 37, is a sample planning document that a principal can use to accomplish the school and district goals. This document is used by the principal in coordination with the daily and weekly planning calendar.

CONCLUSION

The effective principal with increased responsibilities in the same amount of time needs to plan well. The human resources responsibilities of the principal in a site-based leadership school are enormous in both number and significance. The principal needs to understand and anticipate the internal and external demographic changes, understand the strategic planning model, and be able to implement the plans effectively to realize the mission and goals of the school and district. One of the main planning responsibilities of the principal is the recruitment of staff, which is the focus of the next chapter.

REFERENCES

Duckworth, A., and R. Kranyik (1984). What business are we in? *The School Administrator*, August.

Harrison, R. (1983). Strategies for a new age. *Human Resources Management*, 22, 217–223.

Hart, T.E., and L.S. Lumsden (1990). Demographic analysis. *OSSC Bulletin*, 34 (4), December.

Moore, A.J. (1994). Meeting the challenges of the principalship in a complex society. *NASSP Bulletin*, 78 (558).

Nkomo, S.M. (1980). Stage three in personnel administration: Strategic human resources management. *Personnel*, 57 (4).

Pfeiffer, J.W., L.D. Goodstein, and T.M. Nolan (1986). *Applied strategic planning: A how to do it guide*. San Diego, CA: University Associates.

Scarr, L.E. (1984). *Rx for effective schools*. Lake Washington School District, WA.

Webb, L.D., et al. (1987). *Personnel administration in education*. Columbus, OH: Merrill Publishing Company.

FIGURE 2.4. STRATEGIC AND OPERATIONAL PLANNING: MONTHLY CALENDAR

Month: **August**

My Objectives/Activities:

Objective/Activity	Accomplished	Carry to Next Month
√ New teacher/mentor selection with Education Association		
√ Orientation of new Certificated/Classified staff.		
√ Orientation of experienced staff.		
√ Present list of substitutes to Sup't./School Board for approval.		
√ Welcome letter to continuing and new subs.		
√ Present list of volunteer coaches to Sup't./School Board for approval.		
√ Plan teachers' aides schedules.		
√ Schedule preobservation conferences for teachers.		
√ Welcome letter to staff.		
√ Finalize staffing needs.		
√ Conduct last round of interviews, selection of staff for last-minute vacancies.		
√ Introduce and Celebrate new employees.		
√		
√		
√		

Notes/Feedback for next year planning:

Comments about the Big Picture:

Month: **September**

My Objectives/Activities:

Objective/Activity	Accomplished	Carry to Next Month
√ Check first aid certification of staff.		
√ Collect and compare enrollment data.		
√ REMINDER: set timeline for "at risk" teachers' evaluations.		
√ Coordinate mentor participants.		
√ Plan committees.		
√ Finalize teachers' aides schedules.		
√ Finalize schedule of preobservation conferences for teachers.		
√ Promote staff attendance of October Professional organization conferences.		
√ Introduce and Celebrate new employees.		
√ Welcome letter to new and continuing substitute teachers.		
√ Visit all new teachers' classrooms (informal).		
√ Visit all new employees at work site (informal).		
√		
√		
√		

Notes/Feedback for next year planning:

Comments about the Big Picture:

Month: **October**

My Objectives/Activities:

Objective/Activity	Accomplished	Carry to Next Month
√ Conduct enrollment and class size counts.		
√ Develop staff profile.		
√ Introduce and Celebrate new employees.		
√ Attend October Professional Conferences.		
√ Have staff members report on Professional Conferences.		
√ Report on Summer Staff Development Activities.		
√		
√		
√		
√		
√		
√		
√		

Notes/Feedback for next year planning:

Comments about the Big Picture:

Month: **November**

My Objectives/Activities:

Objective/Activity	Accomplished	Carry to Next Month
√ Notify local media of staff highlights or news.		
√ Provisional employees evaluated by 90th calendar day.		
√ Schedule spring staffing conference with Personnel Department.		
√ Introduce and Celebrate new employees.		
√		
√		
√		

Notes/Feedback for next year planning:

Comments about the Big Picture:

Month: **December**

My Objectives/Activities:

<u>Objective/Activity</u>	<u>Accomplished</u>	<u>Carry to Next Month</u>
√ First observations completed for all Provisional employees.		
√ Plan for evaluation of Classified staff.		
√ Orientation of experienced staff.		
√ Possible probation? Need 3 observations and evaluation.		
√ Present list of volunteer coaches to Sup't./School Board for approval.		
√ Introduce and Celebrate new employees.		
√		
√		
√		

Notes/Feedback for next year planning:

Comments about the Big Picture:

Month: **January**

My Objectives/Activities:

Objective/Activity	Accomplished	Carry to Next Month
√ Begin staff projections.		
√ January 15 — Probation Conference Deadline; make recommendations to Superintendent.		
√ January 25 — notify probationary teachers.		
√ Work with site council on March Inservice and general staff development options for next year.		
√ Introduce and Celebrate new employees.		
√		
√		
√		

Notes/Feedback for next year planning:

Comments about the Big Picture:

Month: **February**

My Objectives/Activities:

Objective/Activity	Accomplished	Carry to Next Month
√ Review nature of probationary period and procedures with staff on probation.		
√ Gather staffing information, including leaves being taken and duration.		
√ Update staffing projections with Personnel Services.		
√ Start building master schedule with class size and staffing expectations.		
√ Introduce and Celebrate new employees.		
√		
√		
√		

Notes/Feedback for next year planning:

Comments about the Big Picture:

Month: **March**

My Objectives/Activities:

Objective/Activity	Accomplished	Carry to Next Month
√ Attend recruiting fairs off campus.		
√ March 15: Applications for leaves and sabbaticals due.		
√ Internal transfers requested and assignments settled.		
√ Administrative intern applications due.		
√ Introduce and Celebrate new employees.		
√		
√		
√		

Notes/Feedback for next year planning:

Comments about the Big Picture:

Month: **April**

My Objectives/Activities:

Objective/Activity	Accomplished	Carry to Next Month
√ April 1: Contracts issued.		
√ April 15: All resignations, retirements, terminations shall be in writing and submitted to Personnel Office.		
√ April 15: All department head positions and job openings for the next school year posted.		
√ April 24: Contracts returned.		
√ District meetings to determine staffing needs and priorities among buildings.		
√ Recruiting continues at college career fairs.		
√ Meeting with teachers to establish career goals.		
√ Administrative observation due.		
√ PTSA gives annual awards for Teaching Excellence.		
√ Introduce and Celebrate new employees.		
√		
√		
√		

Notes/Feedback for next year planning:

Comments about the Big Picture:

Month: **May**

My Objectives/Activities:

Objective/Activity	Accomplished	Carry to Next Month
√ May 1: Probationary period ends for teachers on probation. Consult with Personnel, Superintendent, and lawyer regarding recommendations/findings.		
√ Department chairpersons chosen. Names forwarded to Personnel.		
√ By May 15: notify teachers on probation of the results of probation.		
√ By May 15: complete teacher evaluations and teacher conferences.		
√ Continue working with Personnel Department on staffing for next year.		
√ Known vacancies posted for voluntary transfers (curricular and extra-curricular).		
√ Celebrate retiring employees.		
√ Introduce and Celebrate new employees.		
√		
√		
√		

Notes/Feedback for next year planning:

Comments about the Big Picture:

Month: **June**

My Objectives/Activities:

Objective/Activity	Accomplished	Carry to Next Month
√ By June 5: Provide all Certificated staff with written documentation of final evaluation.		
√ By June 12: Deliver completed evaluation documentation for continuing and provisional employees to Personnel.		
√ Coordinate Exit Conference and Interview for employees with Personnel Department.		
√ Continue working with Personnel regarding staffing.		
√ Finalize contract for next year.		
√		
√		
√		

Notes/Feedback for next year planning:

Comments about the Big Picture:

Month: **July**

My Objectives/Activities:

Objective/Activity	Accomplished	Carry to Next Month
√ Continue interviewing and hiring teachers as needed.		
√		
√		
√		

Notes/Feedback for next year planning:

Comments about the Big Picture:

3

RECRUITMENT

REASONS FOR STUDYING PERSONNEL RECRUITMENT

- Many personnel systems focus on the selection process; however, if you do not have the right people in the applicant pool it is difficult to select them.
- Visiting colleges and universities increases district visibility and personal relationships with the faculty and placement officials.
- Recruiting at Career Fairs also increases district visibility and you can gain ideas from other districts.
- Your current teachers are often an excellent source for leads on prospective applicants. You need to tap that source in an organized fashion.
- Recruiting is a good reason for the district to develop a brochure clarifying the district mission and its selection criteria for new teachers.

Recruitment is not so much about the numbers of applicants as it is about the number of quality applicants who match the criteria.

INTRODUCTION

There is no question that the number one influence on the quality of schools and the instruction they provide is the quality of excellence found within their instructional staff: TEACHERS! It is the caliber of the personnel in a district that makes it mediocre or effective. It is not the rules, policies, procedures, or curriculum programs that bear the burden, but rather those who teach the students. Thus, it follows that significant effort should be spent in seeking the very best match for each and every position opening in the schools, from Kindergarten to Honors English, from Music to Science, and from elementary to middle to high school. Anyone can fill a position, for where there is an opening, there will be many candidates to fill it. The focus of this chapter is not on "filling" an open position, but rather on the recruiting phase which, if done well, will lead to the selection of an outstanding staff member.

Figure 3.1 denotes the elements of key personnel functions. It is helpful to refer to this figure to develop an understanding of the role recruitment plays in the total system.

WHY RECRUIT?

The question isn't whether you can fill a teaching position or how to fill it, but rather to do it well. There are three compelling rules for effective recruitment of school personnel:

1. Recruit Widely—Good instructional programs rely on having the best staff

Schools should seek out only highly qualified personnel to fill positions in order to maintain quality organizations. This is often not the case with educational institutions. Rather, schools and administrators seek only to fill positions, holding the notion that "a good teacher can teach anywhere" and thus, look for generic qualities like "a fourth grade, or social studies" teacher. These are generic and mediocre at best. Administrators must change their frame of reference and processes to seek out the perfect match for each and every individual job opening. Whether it be to balance out a program, bring in "new blood" and ideas, bring on a veteran to provide stability, or whatever the criteria, it must be done in order to improve the quality of the instructional programs. Teaching will only be as good as the person doing the teaching!

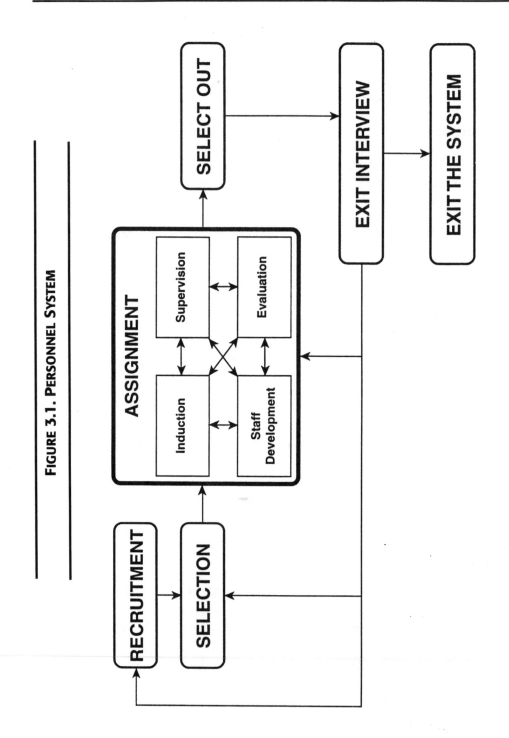

FIGURE 3.1. PERSONNEL SYSTEM

2. Recruit Efficiently—Filling positions costs money and failing to do it well costs even more

Every time a position is filled it costs a district substantial money. Funds are allocated on time invested in arriving at desired needs and writing of job description, posting, advertising, form processing, and on interviewing, induction, and training. The average cost in many places for this process can be in the range of five figures. Keeping this in mind, schools and districts would be wise to do it well the first time. A wrong selection not only costs monetarily, but also costs in lost effectiveness for staff and students.

3. Recruit Legally—Fairness is the right thing to do

It is important that applicants are treated equally, honestly, fairly, and with caring. A system and procedure should be developed and followed in order to stay out of trouble legally and ethically. Further, administrators should be careful to consider district-adopted affirmative action guidelines as well as the Americans with Disabilities Act when recruiting. In addition, state and private colleges, professional associations, and current employees are often excellent sources for applicants. The principal and others must be careful not to allow personal biases to adversely affect the recruitment process.

BEFORE YOU RECRUIT

Prior to recruiting, time should be taken to seek feedback from the departing teacher through the *exit interview* process. This process generally reveals both positive and negative comments. Both are helpful as feedback to the human resources system. If the feedback is positive, then administrators can use that information to plan future activities. If it is negative, now is the time to make modifications, if possible.

Nevertheless, the exit interview is a necessary tool to help in planning for recruiting. The experienced employee has an idea of the system's strong and weak points. Saville and Hill (1989) suggest a formal, oral interview scheduled within the last 4 weeks of employment should include:

♦ reason for separation
♦ positive aspects of the job
♦ employees' feelings about their supervision

- adequacy of salary, benefits, and working conditions
- employee complaints or suggestions
- possible existence of unresolved problems
- separation formalities/information

Of course, there are some problems with administering such interviews, such as persuading the employee to tell the truth about reasons for leaving or changing positions. In a paper submitted to a regional conference of businessmen, these research suggestions were compiled as considerations to minimize problems for the interviewer:

- prepare carefully for the interview
- put the employee at ease
- seek information
- use tact
- be honest
- conclude the interview
- complete the exit interview report (Schmidt, 1984)

During the exit interview, administrators need to express "thank you and best wishes" if that is suitable, especially to an employee retiring or moving to another district. The employee also can benefit, by being viewed as an expert who can contribute to effective management, and whose contribution will be significant in helping the school or district further its goals.

In most cases, it is best if the human resources department conducts the exit interview and develops a report of all such interviews to the superintendent, board of directors and principals. If trust between the principal and the departing teacher is high, then the teacher could request that the principal also be involved in the interview to aid the communication process. The goals of the exit interview are to:

- assist the employee with the transition
- provide feedback for the school and district
- turn the departing teacher into an ambassador for the school district

Figure 3.2 is an example of an exit interview survey.

FIGURE 3.2. SAMPLE EMPLOYEE EXIT INTERVIEW

The purpose of this survey is to give you an opportunity to provide feedback regarding your employment experience here. In your specific area of expertise, please make suggestions about what the district can do to make improvements and to make the _____ School District a better place to work.

PLEASE NOTE: If you have been covered by a district medical/dental plan, you may be eligible for COBRA benefits. If you have not received a notice about COBRA, please contact the Payroll Department (555-XXXX) immediately.

NAME _____

EMPLOYMENT LOCATION _____

JOB TITLE _____

DATE LAST WORKED _____
                                              (month, day, year)

REASON FOR LEAVING (please circle):

    1. Other position/new business   5. Going back to school

    2. Retirement   6. Medical

    3. Moving from area   7. Cost of living

    4. Dissatisfaction with job   8. Other _____
                                                                                  (specify)

Please indicate a rating for the areas listed below by circling a number on the scale of **4 (highest) to 1 (lowest):**

A.   Were you satisfied with your job location?

    4   3   2   1

B.   Were you satisfied with your work environment?

    4   3   2   1

C.   Were you satisfied with your opportunity for growth?

    4   3   2   1

D.   Were you satisfied with consistency of supervision when performing job duties?

    4   3   2   1

E.   Were performance expectations clearly defined?

    4   3   2   1

F.   What suggestions do you have for improving your teaching position?

    _____

G.   What suggestions do you have for improving the school?

    _____

H.   What suggestions do you have for improving the district?

    _____

I.   What suggestions do you have for improving the recruitment and selection process?

    _____

J.   How can the school or district help you?

    _____

CERTIFICATED PERSONNEL REQUISITION

Having identified needs and acquired recommendations from the exit interview process, that information can be used to complete the Personnel Requisition (see Figure 3.3). This requisition is a descriptive outline format which should be available to district principals. Its purpose is to let staff and other administrators know what type of employee is being sought. Further, such a format better assures getting the right person into the "pool" to select a candidate. It is from this requisition that the Position Description (Figure 3.4) will be developed. The requisition also provides the characteristics and criteria to select the top four or five candidates for interviews. With the idea that the right people can "make a difference," a district's planning for the best personnel will fit with its mission and purpose rather than focusing on rules and policies.

In the "Special Requirements" section of the requisition form (Figure 3.3), certain considerations must be included:

- conditions which might have immediate impact on the position such as pending state or local funding
- inclusion of curriculum requirements
- special teamwork expectations
- staff development as chosen by district/building in previous planning year, and so on

It is important and commonplace for a school to fill out purchase requisitions of desks, chairs, and other capital outlay in detail to make certain it gets what it wants. The same is true for human resources, only more so since they cannot be sent back as easily.

POSITION ANNOUNCEMENT

If an exit interview has been conducted of the teacher exiting the position, the information should be used as part of the new job description and vacancy announcement. Likewise, the basic needs of the district, its demographic makeup, the particular school and its students will all be factors in designing the unique match of candidate to the position.

Within the framework of the Personnel Requisition, the additional specifics would be listed by the principal. It seems obvious then that the district

(Text continues on page 61.)

FIGURE 3.3. SAMPLE CERTIFICATED PERSONNEL REQUISITION

1. **Position Title:**
   Elementary _____
   Secondary _____
2. **Experience Requirements:**
   Teaching _____
   Other related experience _____
3. **Educational Requirements:**
   Degree _____
         Major _____
         Minor _____
         Specialities _____
   Rank in class (Academics):   Average _____; Superior _____
   Special Courses: _____
4. **Personal Requirements:** (i.e., self-confidence, stability, adaptability, empathy, humor, organization, creativity, firm discipline, etc.) Rank in order of importance:
   a._____   d._____
   b._____   e._____
   c._____   f._____
5. **Position Requirements:**
   Is this position likely to change? _____
   If so, how?
   a._____
   b._____
   What special things is this person expected to do?
         Classroom expectation: _____

         Extra duty assignments: _____

         Daily Schedule and class load:
         a. _____ _____   e._____ _____
         b. _____ _____   f._____ _____
         c. _____ _____   g._____ _____
         d. _____ _____   h._____ _____
   What special programs will this person have to teach?
   _____
6. **Special Requirements:**
   _____

FIGURE 3.4. POSITION ANNOUNCEMENT—ENGLISH DEPARTMENT

POSITION TITLE: Ninth Grade Language Arts Teacher

DIVISION TITLE: Instruction

SCHOOL: Junior High

TITLE OF IMMEDIATE SUPERVISOR: Principal

GENERAL DUTIES:

- Develop and maintain a classroom learning environment that places students' needs in a primary position.

- Develop and maintain a classroom management policy that is friendly, fair, firm, and consistent.

- Present a role model that sets the example for the development of good citizenship by the students.

- Perform your "fair share" of co-curricular and other duties beyond regular classroom activities as determined by the principal. Fair share equates to approximately four evenings/nights per year.

- Provide for the care of school property and see that pupils use equipment and utilities properly.

- Maintain cordial and cooperative working relationships with colleagues and participate in the business and activities of the faculty.

- Recommend to the department head suitable programs, courses of study and materials that meet the needs of ninth grade Language Arts students.

- Perform other duties as may be assigned.

SPECIFIC DUTIES:

- Follow policies and procedures as set forth in the Teachers' Handbook.

- Develop short-term instructional objectives consistent with the district's and school's long-range educational goals. These objectives should identify the end results or standards of performance expected.

- Plan and implement an instructional program to assist all students to progress toward the accomplishment of established goals and objectives.

- Cooperate with and participate in the planning and evaluation of the school program.

- Direct and evaluate the learning experiences of the pupils and maintain adequate and careful records as required by the principal, superintendent, and state.

- Participate in such staff meetings and inservice training programs as are scheduled for teachers in our building and/or district.

- Make adequate and regular reports to parents as required by district policy.

- Participate in the formulation of the annual budget by submitting budget requests for supplies and equipment on schedule.

- Maintain close and continued communications with parents when dealing with student problems.

QUALIFICATIONS:

Required:

- B/A in Education - major in English/Language Arts
- Appropriate state professional education certification.
- If not current regular employee - an I-9 form to provide proof of employment eligibility.
- Persuant to state law, as amended, a disclosure form, criminal conviction history record, and submit to be fingerprinted.
- Candidate must have the ability to maintain and continue a tradition of excellence in English educational techniques.
- Candidate must be able to work positively with diverse students and staff.

Desired:

- Skills, competencies, and knowledge of the English language as it relates to junior high/adolescent learning styles.
- Candidate should enjoy adolescent students, be a positive and active role model as well as have a good sense of humor.
- Should be flexible.
- Should have ability to organize ideas, time, and materials to accomplish goals.
- Should be enthusiastic.
- Should possess ability to express ideas clearly.
- Should have ability to learn new ideas and skills.
- Should have ability and willingness to develop favorable relationships with students. Should possess current knowledge of approaches to teaching.
- Should have willingness to model behavior deemed appropriate by the district and community.

This position description has been discussed in full and agreed to this _____ day of _____ by (administrator) _____ _____, and (new hire) _____ _____.

mission statement or outcomes of it should be part of the Position Announcement format, as well as an analysis of the position based on the previous exit interview. The Sumner School District of Sumner, WA, announces its position vacancies with the introductory question, "Is this the position for you?" It then states four specific descriptors necessary for teachers who become a part of their instructional team. They are: "We're looking for teachers who—"

◆ believe in setting high expectations for themselves and their students

◆ possess a core of professional knowledge and skills that enable them to be effective with all students

◆ have knowledge and skills specific to the developmental stages and social and emotional needs of students

◆ can demonstrate depth and breadth of knowledge in the content areas, as well as skill to facilitate students becoming active learners.

Figure 3.5 is an example of a Position Announcement for an elementary learning support teacher. Such a descriptions would be sent as an announcement to regional placement or personnel offices as well as posted in the district's central office and other personnel areas. Remember, this is but one step in the recruitment process.

ADVERTISING THE POSITION

When advertising a teaching position information on the school district, the school, and the position are all essential. All three must be supplied to ensure a match. The position to be filled is not the only item being advertised, but rather all three. You as the principal are looking for a person to fulfill not only your criteria, but also you want to be sure that your position is a match for the candidate. This means that you want the candidate to be well-informed, rather than "in the dark" about key elements of the position. You want to present potential employees with factual (all sides, not just the "glowing") information on which they can base their decision. You want to avoid the scenario of you having found the perfect person for the job, but come to find out that he or she was misled and is unhappy about every other aspects of working for you (i.e., not liking the community, district, staff, school location, weather, and so on). This can be detrimental and expensive for all parties involved.

FIGURE 3.5. POSITION ANNOUNCEMENT—ELEMENTARY LEARNING SUPPORT TEACHER

The School District seeks outstanding professionals who are committed to helping young people achieve success, enjoy working in a collaborative environment, look for opportunities to expand their capabilities, and view education as a partnership of students, staff, parents, and community.

MAJOR RESPONSIBILITIES

Work with one or more of the following types of categorical programs: Chapter I, LAP, Special Education.

Plan and provide in-classroom, small group, and/or individual specialized instruction for elementary-aged (K-6) students considered "at risk" or with special needs (mild handicaps).

Develop student goals and objectives based on I.E.P. and recommendations from multidisciplinary and/or school improvement team.

Work cooperatively with building staff to implement an integrated and inclusive educational program.

Provide a positive learning climate which promotes appropriate behavior and achievement.

Utilize various intervention techniques to modify social/emotional behaviors of some students.

Implement a record keeping system to monitor and evaluate student performance.

Effectively communicate with students, parents, support staff, building personnel, and outside agencies.

Supervise instructional functions and supervisory duties of educational assistant(s).

Attend to the physical needs of students such as toileting, feeding, positioning, as needed.

Work Year	—	180 days (teachers new to District will have a 181-day obligation)
Salary	—	Determined by placement on teachers' salary schedule
Benefits	—	Our benefits package includes health insurance coverage, retirement plan, and other benefits

QUALIFICATIONS REQUIRED

Valid Washington State Teaching Certificate with the following endorsements: Special Education (K-12) and Elementary Education (K-8).

Previous training and/or experience related to students considered "at risk" or mildly handicapped.

Previous experience as a regular elementary classroom teacher, desirable.

Previous experience as a self-contained special education teacher, desirable.

Skill in diagnosing student learning needs and knowledge of test procedures.

Skill in developing and implementing instructional strategies based on strengths and deficits of individual students.

Skill in managing student behaviors in a positive manner.

Ability to organize and coordinate schedules for instructional sessions.

Ability to work cooperatively and productively with other staff members.

Experience in use of computers (Macintosh, Touch Window, etc.) for computer-assisted learning program.

Ability to lift students who weigh up to 70 pounds from floor to chair height.

APPLICATION INFORMATION

Submit a completed *District Application* (application packets available from the Human Resources Division).

Current District employees, in order to be considered for this position, must submit the letter of application and include authorization for the hiring committee to review their personnel file or submit an official application form.

Applications or letters of interest must be received by the closing date.

Questions? Call: Human Resources at _____.

Job Sharing:
The School District will accept applications from individuals wishing to share a certificated position.

Extracurricular Student Activities:
The School District seeks teachers with the ability and willingness to advise, supervise, and/or coach student activities.

UPON HIRE

If you are hired, you will need to complete an Employment Eligibility Form and present documentation to Human Resources for review and verification to comply with the Federal Immigration Reform and Control Act.

It is important for a school and district to put some thought (and, yes, money) into an attractive portrayal of what the schools and surrounding community have to offer a candidate. Through this process, the administrator will find not just outstanding teachers for the positions, but also community members who are happy in all areas of their lives.

SOURCES OF RECRUITMENT

As stated previously, recruiting potential employees is definitely a sound human resources practice. There are many places to consider when seeking candidates:

- ◆ **Lateral transfers or internal recruiting of current staff members**

  This is a very viable avenue for finding a match for your opening. You may well have someone *within the building* who not only has the right qualifications, but also is looking for a move. This person may be stuck in an inappropriate match, or may just be looking for a change. Schools need to look to promoting from within, like many businesses do. It sends the message that "you are important and valuable" and you aren't "stuck" in the same spot forever. Lateral transfers should only be done once you have made an appraisal of current staffing and the certified personnel requisition. It may be that even though someone is qualified, you may need to go outside for reasons like equity, diversity, balance, and so on. Lateral moves *within the district* are also a good option. This works in cases where the person is not in a conducive environment, but you can offer it, or where personality conflicts may need to be defused, or just a change is needed, and the person meets your predetermined criteria. The spring rite of internal transfers of incompetent teachers, or as some call it "the dance of the lemons," must be avoided.

- ◆ **External recruiting**

  - • **Referrals from current staff members**

    Don't overlook the rich resource you have in your current people. They may know of an outstanding candidate that you wouldn't otherwise reach. Caution is warranted to avoid hiring within a "friendship" circle. If you have carefully followed all previous steps, then this is avoided.

- **Placement offices of colleges and universities**

  This can often be done through reputable acquaintances who can steer you in the direction of their "brightest." It is advisable to actually set up interviewing times at or near the colleges in order to narrow down the selection field. This is often done by the district office personnel as well as by principals.

- **Placement services of professional organizations**

  Probably not a conventional avenue to follow in school districts, but an opportunity may arise in which you can utilize organizations outside the school sector to fill a vacancy.

- **Recruiting letters**

  These can be written to professional colleagues. Often you may find colleagues who have met staffing requirements, but who have a reputation for getting the "best." They may well have a candidate they would hire in a minute, but can't because there is no available position. Or, they may know of someone who would be perfect for your position, but not for their own. Use the people you know, they are valuable resources!

- **Newspaper advertising—locally and statewide**

  Don't feel you have to limit your search within your city or to your neighboring college. Expand your search to reach out and find the quality people you are seeking. Remember that you are not looking to fill a position, but rather to find the best person available.

- **Advertising in professional education journals and newsletters**

  This type of search will take you to a national audience. You may find the perfect teacher who is looking to relocate.

- **Services of "search" consultants**

  Most districts cannot afford such a service for teaching positions, but in certain instances, to fill a particularly specialized position, this may be a good option.

SUCCESSFUL RECRUITING PLAN

Inclusive of the above elements, but not exclusive to them, is the following plan which is designed to enhance the recruitment process:

- The district administration and school board need to make a public statement through written policies, district goals, and budget about the commitment of the district to recruiting. If your district will not do so, this doesn't mean that you as principal cannot do so on your level.

- The recruiting program must be a year-round program. It should also be ongoing in that you can have your connections in continuous touch, and your "feelers" out, so that when your opening comes you have an action plan. The time to begin the search is not when the opening is posted. Administrators need to be alert to coming changes, know the staff, and look early to ensure the best selection of candidates.

- Recruiters need to be carefully selected and trained (especially if you go outside the administrator realm).

- Recruiters must sell the community as well as the school and the district.

- The district's intent to hire the best needs to be publicized with staff, community, and potential candidates. This alone may attract the quality personnel you are seeking.

RECRUITING

The success or failure of a recruiting program rests primarily with the individuals who do the recruiting. Personnel decisions will be influenced by the evaluations of the applicants submitted by the recruiter. Candidates see the school system through the presentation of the recruiters. Should the impression be unfavorable, the chances of the candidate accepting employment are slim. Therefore, the selection and training of recruiters is extremely important.

- **Selecting Recruiters**
    - Recruiters need to be very knowledgeable about the district and the community

- Recruiters must be from the various grade levels and areas: for example, K-3, 4-8, 9-12, special education
- Principals who go through personnel training should be selected to recruit
- District teachers, after training, may also be part of the recruiting team
- When an administrator is attending a conference, seminar, and so on, the administrator should contact a college and/or university in that area for possible arrangements for interviewing potential applicants

♦ **Recruiting Sources:**
  - Other school districts, in state and out of state
  - Colleges and universities in state and out of state
  - Publications such as *Reading Teacher Journal*, and so on
  - Job Fairs

♦ **Recruiters Need to:**
  - Know what questions are legal; generally the law requires that information requested from an applicant focus on job-related considerations
  - Be familiar with and be prepared to explain postinterview procedures and hiring timelines during the interview
  - When possible, hold campus group interview seminars in order to influence a large group of teachers-in-training
  - Feel comfortable interviewing for all levels of positions
  - Be able to discuss salary schedules, extracurricular, insurance plans, tax-sheltered annuities, leave regulations, and so on
  - Be aware of type of positions currently available within the district
  - Be aware of the special endorsement requirements
  - Be aware of qualifications requirements
  - Be able to tell the applicants what they should do next

♦ **Aggressive Recruiting Strategies:**

• There is a difference between interviewing and recruiting. Interviewing is what takes place after applicants sign up to be considered for the position. Recruiting is what a school district does to ensure that quality applicants sign up to interview. Special effort usually generates special results. Some special efforts include:

> inviting career/placement center personnel to visit your district

> inviting major educational professors to visit the district to learn about curriculum and facilities

> sending district representatives to college campuses to meet and talk to career/placement staff about district goals, accomplishments, needs, and benefits

> sending preorientational material to individuals and colleges

> making a request to present programs to student educational groups on college campuses

> developing a videotape about the school district so that it may be shown when recruiting

> hosting a reception for applicants and faculty the night before a job fair or scheduled interview day

♦ **If an applicant is found who is too good to pass up and needs immediate consideration, the Human Resources Office should have special procedures to follow.**

CONCLUSION

This chapter on recruitment emphasized these points:

♦ Recruitment is essential to the selection of teachers and, as such, should be well-planned.

♦ The exit interview is at the end of the employment cycle but is the place to start when considering recruitment.

♦ The certificated staff requisition is a very useful tool and should be used. The old adage, "if you don't know what you are looking for, you won't know it when you find it," applies here.

- All certificated teachers come initially from the colleges and universities, thus it will pay dividends to visit the campus and maintain a professional relationship with the placement officials.
- The district's current teachers are a source of leads for new teachers.
- A position description should be developed, discussed, and signed by the teacher and the principal. Teachers need to know what they are responsible for.
- The principal must learn from the human resources department personnel and principals from other districts, new and creative approaches to the recruiting process.

The next chapter, "Selection," continues the process started in recruiting.

REFERENCES

Anfusa, D. (1993). Recruitment by the numbers. *Personnel Journal*. December, 71–74.

Fielder, D.J. (1993). Wanted: minority teachers. *The Executive Educator*, 15 (5), 33–34.

Jensen, M. C. (1986). *Recruiting and selecting the most capable teachers*. Eugene: Oregon School Study Council, University of Oregon.

Osborne, J. E. (1992). Job descriptions do more than describe duties. *Supervisory Management*. February, 8.

Saville, A., and J. Hill (1989). *The exit interview: A generic model*. Non-classroom Material. ERIC Document Reproduction Service No. Ed. 310–523.

Schmidt, W.V. (1984). The exit interview as monitor for change: A review of the literature. Paper presented at the annual conference of the American Business Communication Association. San Antonio, TX.

Witty, E.P. (1990). *Teacher recruitment and retention*. West Haven, CT: NEA Professional Library.

4

SELECTION

REASONS FOR STUDYING PERSONNEL SELECTION

- The single most important decision you make for students is to hire a teacher.
- The selection process has legal implications that must be understood and followed.
- It is important to have a process that is fair to all—candidates, students, staff, and principal.
- If you don't think the teachers in your school are more important than the curriculum, think of this: What would you rather have: the 10 best basketball plays or the 10 best basketball players?

What is needed in schools are persons who are tender of heart and extraordinarily sensitive to the needs of students. Such persons are not ordinary in society. Perhaps it is time we consider extraordinary means of selecting them.

Phillip Schlechty

INTRODUCTION

As demographic and curriculum changes influence the direction of the education system, selection of the best teacher candidates becomes more and more specific, and in turn, more critical, since it is the teacher who is responding to the demographic needs of children and the curricular changes of the school and district. The match of candidate to position must be decided by individuals who understand both the specific needs of the position as well as the characteristics, education, and experience of the chosen applicant.

The instructional need of the individual classroom is necessarily bound by the district goals, curriculum choices, and individual building administrators and their current staff. Responding to a district population's social, physical, and educational needs is a continuous evaluation process—not a final decision. So, then, recruiting and selecting the best teachers possible will have great impact on the effectiveness of the education system. It is clear that selection is both a marvelous opportunity and a time of great risk, if done without care in the decision-making process.

As shown in Figure 4.1, the selection process might best start with a statement of a district's central focus, such as Wenatchee (WA) School District's

---

FIGURE 4.1. WENATCHEE SCHOOL DISTRICT–STAFF SELECTION PROCESS

Goals of the Wenatchee School District

We believe that the most important component of any organization is its people. With this in mind, we recognize the importance of selecting excellent employees. All people in the district, regardless of role, are part of the future of the young people they seek to serve.

Goals of Staff Selection/Staff Development Services

It is the purpose of the Personnel Office in the Wenatchee School District to search out, select, and maintain outstanding employees to lead, educate, and provide supportive services to the students of the district. All of the efforts of personnel services are ultimately directed toward this task.

The Selection Process

This handbook describes the selection process used in the Wenatchee School District. The selection process for hiring personnel will have several ingredients in common for each employee, but there are three separate and distinct processes. One process focuses upon the selection of teachers and other non-administrative certificated staff members. A second category focuses upon certificated administrators at the school site and the administrative services center level. The third category focuses upon the non-certificated/classified staff selection....

"most important component of any organization is its people." It further noted that the specific goal of the Staff Selection Service is to "search out, select, and maintain outstanding employees to lead, educate, and provide supportive services to the students of the district." Through such statements, presented in a brochure for distribution to interested applicants during the recruitment and selection process, applicants would have a heightened awareness of Wenatchee's vision of employing an excellent staff.

In addition, some school districts involve the staff members with the development of generic characteristics of effective staff members. The list of characteristics enables the school and district to be clear about what they are seeking in a teacher and conversely, for the teacher to know the high standards and expectations. Such a list is the Bellevue (WA) School District's Characteristics of Effective Certificated Staff (Figure 4.2).

THE APPLICATION PROCESS

In reality, teacher selection is a rather complex process rather than an event, and selection decisions are made at several stages within the process. The two main stages are: (1) the screening of the applicants' papers to select applicants to be interviewed; and (2) the interview and subsequent selection of the candidate who best matches the criteria set forth in the personnel requisition. This section deals with the application and initial screening stages.

When developing your application forms, ask only for information that you need and will use in your screening process. Most information falls into one of the following categories: personal data, education and/or professional preparation, experience, and references. In addition to factual information, application forms can also devise methods of extracting applicant's attitudes, options, and values. Many districts do this through a writing sample, or the answering of predetermined questions. This format can help provide additional information to help you decide who should be interviewed.

A KEY IDEA

The application form should ask only for information which will assist in the screening of applicants.

FIGURE 4.2. BELLEVUE SCHOOL DISTRICT—CHARACTERISTICS OF EFFECTIVE CERTIFICATED STAFF

1. Flexibility
   - is willing to learn new concepts or ways of doing things
   - adapts to changing conditions in the learning environment
   - adapts to professional changes
   - cooperates with students and adults
   - uses democratic approach to teaching and decision-making
   - incorporates new technology into job performance
   - deals effectively with ambiguity

2. Commitment to Accomplishment
   - possesses sense of mission
   - desires and exerts efforts to attain particular goals
   - organizes ideas, time, materials, and space to accomplish goals
   - demonstrates regular attendance and punctuality
   - demonstrates ability to prioritize and be thorough on important tasks
   - has evidence of past and current success
   - is self-motivated

3. Enthusiasm
   - has overall optimism and zeal for what he/she is doing
   - encourages and promotes willingness of others to be involved in task
   - fosters interpersonal relations with others

4. Communication Skills
   - demonstrates clarity of expression
   - listens with understanding
   - uses non-defensive communication skills
   - comprehends and follows oral and written directions
   - is sensitive to nuances of language
   - maintains confidentiality when appropriate

5. Conceptual and Technical Skills
   - demonstrates commitment to lifelong learning
   - adapts to function effectively in the local setting
   - learns new concepts and skills as the job changes
   - uses new ideas and skills to solve job-related problems
   - is willing to develop curriculum
   - applies knowledge of effective classroom management and behavior management skills

6. Professional Orientation
   - has high interest in students
   - is willing to work out problems so that all involved are satisfied
   - has working knowledge of current approaches to teaching
   - has working knowledge of learning and child development
   - possesses breadth of background and applies it for the benefit of the school district
   - has ability and willingness to work with others in a team
   - is constructive in relationships with others
   - demonstrates awareness of community needs
   - is willing to share concerns and raise questions openly

7. Modeling Appropriate Behavior
   - models appropriate behavior
   - demonstrates global perspective
   - maintains a sense of humor
   - demonstrates confidence in own abilities
   - has positive models/mentors
   - demonstrates higher level thinking skills
   - uses a variety of problem-solving techniques

8. Relating to Students/Staff
   - has ability and willingness to develop favorable relationships with students and staff
   - likes students and staff
   - exhibits listening, patience, caring, empathy
   - responds to students/staff needs
   - is open and desires to have a positive relationship with students/staff
   - has high expectations of students/staff
   - believes every student can learn
   - accepts responsibility to motivate students/staff
   - instills confidence in the abilities of student/staff

9. Relating to Parents and Community
   - exhibits listening, patience, caring, and empathy
   - involves parents in classroom; recognizes parents as valuable contributors to the learning process
   - is willing to work in a partnership with community, parents, and business
   - values and is willing to use parents in the decision-making process when appropriate
   - is willing to involve self and students in community when appropriate

Items typically requested from candidates as part of the screening process include:

- a placement file usually requested by the applicant from the college career planning and placement office or letters of recommendation and references
- a letter of interest in the position
- a professional résumé

In addition, most school districts require:

- a completed application form
- copies of transcripts

The key point here is to request only those items which pertain to this position and will be used in the screening process. The preference of a few districts is not to use an application form for professional positions like teaching but to use the letter of application, placement file, and professional résumé to provide a completed file. This provides ample information on which to screen for an interview and does not duplicate information. Transcripts generally are only required of the successful candidate. This is a very "user friendly" approach. Prior to paper screening of applicants, each packet should be received by a designated central-office staff member who checks for completeness, dates each one, and places in the appropriate file for the screening team. This step provides integrity to the process and will establish a method of monitoring the progress of filling positions. Figure 4.3 is a sample application form.

Some school districts also require that an applicant give professional reference forms directly to supervisors which are then returned to the district.

In addition, other districts also request Affirmative Action information, which is collected, summarized, and reported to the Board of Directors as part of an Affirmative Action Plan.

SCREENING

After the closing date or opened-until-filled (OUF), three weeks minimum, the completed applications need to be reviewed and screened according to predetermined criteria. During this stage of the process it is important to make fine distinctions between excellent and good candidates, and between that which you are searching for, and that which you are not!

(Text continues on page 81.)

FIGURE 4.3. PROFESSIONAL EMPLOYMENT APPLICATION

PUBLIC SCHOOLS PERSONNEL COOPERATIVE

601 McPhee Road S. W.
Olympia, Washington 98502
Phone: (360) 753-2855   Fax (360) 664-2057
Job Line: (360)664-2058

PROFESSIONAL EMPLOYMENT APPLICATION

QUALITY PERSONNEL = QUALITY STUDENTS

Name: Last	First	Middle	Home Phone	Work Phone

Street Address:	Social Security No.

City:	State	Zip	Message Phone:

I Am Interested In The Following Districts:

___ Centralia   ___ Olympia   ___ Tumwater   ___ Yelm   ___ Chehalis   ___ North Thurston
___ Griffin   ___ Oakville   ___ Tenino   ___ Toledo ___ Onalaska   ___ ESD #113

Check Position(s) Desired:

__ Teacher   __ Librarian   __ Special Education Teacher   __ School Psychologist

__ Substitute Teacher   __ Counselor   __ Speech Language Pathologist   __ Occupational Therapist

__ Administrator   __ Nurse   __ Physical Therapist   __ Social Worker

__ Multi-age (elementary)   __ Coach   __ Other _____

Please list in order your choices by subject or grade. Secondary, please check middle or high school or no preference.

_____ _____ _____   __ Middle School __ High School __ No Preference

When will you be available for employment? _____ Present Position _____

Certification:

Type (Initial, Continuing, etc.)	Endorsements	Number	Issued	Expires

Hiring Process: When job openings occur, applications will be screened by the hiring school district according to the job description submitted by that district. Copies of selected applicants papers will be provided to the district for **their** consideration. Interviewing and hiring will be determined by the district. The district will contact the applicant directly for interviews.

Federal and/or state criminal history fingerprinting/background checks will be required of candidates who will or may have unsupervised access to children or persons with developmental disabilities. Any offer of employment is conditional and subject to the acceptable outcome of a criminal history background check.

EQUAL OPPORTUNITY EMPLOYERS

Educational Training:

Name of School, College or Occupational Education	Location	No. of Years	Major

Graduate Work

Educational Employment Experience: (Includes teaching, substitute teaching, counseling, and other contractual services.) Please include student teaching if you have no cert. experience.

Dates: From - To	Name of School or College	Location	Number of years

Other Employment Experience: Include work experience and military service.

Dates: From - To	Location	Name of Company or Branch of Service	Number of years

References: Give three references. Include (most recent) supervisors under whom you have worked, who have first-hand knowledge of your character and professional skills.

Name	Address

Minor	Did you graduate? (yes/no)	Under Graduate College GPA	Bachelor's Degree or Certification	Master's Degree	Total Credit Hours Beyond Bachelor's Degree	
					Quarter Hours	Semester Hours

Subjects/Grade Levels Taught or Positions Held (*Full Time Positions)	Activities Handled	Reason for Leaving	Name and Present Phone Number of Supervisor

Type of Work (Mark with * Full Time positions)	Reason for Leaving	Name and Address of Employer

Phone Number(s) Home and Work	Official Position

1. Please re-examine your **full name** as recorded on page one of this application. Have you used any other name in your educational preparation or employment experience? If so, please specify.

_____
                    Last   First   Middle

2. Are you eligible/authorized to work full time in the United States? This does not include practical training. (If hired, you will be required to provide proof of U. S. Citizenship or alien identification documents entitling you to work.)   ____ **Yes**   ____ **No**

3. **Extracurricular Activities** you would be interested in supervising: (**Circle** if your experience includes head coaching/lead experience.)

____ Band	____ Drill Team	____ Baseball	____ Tennis	____ Soccer
____ Chorus	____ Cheerleaders	____ Basketball	____ Track	____ Softball
____ Orchestra	____ Annual	____ Football	____ Swimming	____ Volleyball
____ Debate	____ Newspaper	____ Golf	____ Wrestling	____ Diving
____ Drama	____ Photography	____ Gymnastics	____ Intramural	____ Cross Country
____ Other	____ Other	____ Other	____ Other	____ Other

4. If you have completed **Special Training** in any of the following areas, specify the training and the number of **contact** (the number of hours spent in class) class hours.

Instructional Improvement   **Curriculum**   **Training in Specialized Student Needs**

Instructional Improvement		Curriculum		Training in Specialized Student Needs	
ITIP		Computer Training		Students with Special Needs	
Quality Schools		Child Abuse/Personal Safety		Gifted	
Cooperative Learning		Math Problem-Solving		Remedial	
Mastery Learning		Sex Equity Awareness		Drug/Alcohol Problems	
Outcome Based Ed		Multicultural Awareness			

The districts served by the Public Schools personnel Cooperative prohibit discrimination on the basis of race, creed, color, national origin, age, sex, marital status or the presence of a disability (Title VII of the Civil Rights Act of 1964 and RCW 59.60). These districts are equal opportunity employers and support the spirit, policies and practices of affirmative action.

I certify that the information given by me to Personnel Cooperative member districts is true and complete to the best of my knowledge. I understand that if I am employed, the discovery that I gave false or misleading information on this form or in the course of an interview may lead to disciplinary action, up to and including termination from employment.

Signature _____   **Date** _____

Paper screening of applicants is the reviewing of all required forms and materials submitted by the applicant. The criteria used in examining the application file needs to match the need assessment and personnel requisition done earlier in the process. Below are suggested general criteria for narrowing the field for interview purposes:

- **Incomplete or late applications and files** are good indicators of a candidate's competency, organization, and effectiveness and should send up a "red flag." In most cases, this means an automatic rejection. In other cases, it may clearly be a clerical mistake, and a highly qualified educator may be overlooked. This is something that will have to be determined at the individual site.

- **Written statements of philosophy or a portfolio** should contain ideas, beliefs, and values related to education and the applicant. They should be supported with evidence, not just the applicant's self-serving statements. These materials provide information about the applicant's ability to organize thoughts, think, communicate, and use correct English.

- **Questions specific to the position, district, or philosophy** can also assist in the screening process. These do essentially the same as a statement of philosophy but can make even finer distinctions because questions can be narrowed and directed to address a specific position or target of interest.

- **Review transcripts if requested** that give attention to the overall GPA and to grades in the academic major. Look in depth at the areas or courses that relate to the personnel requisition.

- **Check for academic awards** given at the university level. Those with honors have demonstrated exceptional ability, and when considered with other factors, these applicants can serve as models for students, and will tend to be adaptive to the many shifts in teaching.

- **Make direct contact with the candidate's personal and professional references.** You should not only contact those people listed, but also make an effort to contact at least one reputable person not listed who will give you an honest evaluation of that individual. This is a key point. You must inquire from professionals other than those listed on the reference forms or applications. Having a conversation with such persons enables you to probe areas of strength and areas of needed growth. Remember to ask open-ended questions, and always ask this question near the end of reference checking, "You know this applicant better than I do, what should I ask about this applicant that I haven't?" Reference checking can be done at this stage, or it can be used after the applicant field has been narrowed and interviewed. It will be looked at in depth in a subsequent section. Pay attention to who is listed as a reference and who wrote letters. Ministers, friends, and coworkers should carry less weight than supervisors and principals.

Practitioners generally put less value on the recommendations of college supervisors but they can provide valuable information. While the college supervisor may not know the person's work in great detail, he or she has watched the applicant in the college class as well as during student teaching and can also rate one candidate against many others at the same stage of development. The supervisor usually has responsibility for 10–15 teachers per year. This perspective should be important to the principal.

♦ **Look at whether the file is "open" or "closed."** If open (nonconfidential), most writers will tend not to be as candid, and a closed (confidential) file can prove to be more accurate. This is not always true, as there is really no such thing as a "closed" file since access often can be obtained through devious ways.

A KEY IDEA

Principals should write recommendations as if they will be seen and read by the teacher even though the file is marked confidential.

♦ **Look for gaps in credentials, employment, references, time, or paper.** You need to have specific criteria by which you will evaluate each application. You can do this by using a screening or application checklist and rating system. This will allow you to keep a record of why a candidate met or did not meet the criteria. One caution is to be sure that all of your criteria in your search are legal and nondiscriminatory. Legalities related to screening are discussed in more detail in the legal chapter.

The following are instructions and a scale for rating the applicant's file:

Application Rating Instructions

- Rate applicants one at a time.
- Read the application form or résumé to get a clear understanding of the applicant's work history, training, and education. Consider the organizational setting, the length of time employed, and role in the organization.
- Consider all of the evidence provided in the letter of application to substantiate that the applicant can do the job. Focus as much as possible on the content; the format, presentation, and so on, should carry less value unless the rating criteria specifically calls for it.
- Do not give credit for claims to have done the work ("I have done this for 10 years") unless there is other information in the applicant's materials to substantiate the claims.
- Avoid giving too much consideration to credentials for credentials' sake; rather, consider how the credentials relate to the applicant's ability to perform the work.
- Avoid giving consideration to other things you may personally know about the applicant. Rate the information and evidence provided by the applicant.
- Using the rating scale and the specific criteria listed under each element, rate the applicant in each of the major elements based on work experience and training, and the specific examples provided.
- Add up the major element ratings, and put the total at the bottom of the rating sheet. The total of the major element ratings will be the applicant's rating.
- Typically, applicants who receive below a two-average rating on major elements would be considered "below passing."

Applicants who receive a three-average or better rating could be considered for an interview, since they have been identified as being acceptable or better applicants. However, you may want to interview only "above acceptable" or "superior" applicants, depending on the total number of applications received.

Application Rating Scale

♦ **UNACCEPTABLE.** The applicant presents *no* evidence that he or she has done this aspect of the work in the past, or would not be able to perform this aspect of the work if hired.

♦ **MARGINAL.** The applicant has some understanding or familiarity with this aspect of the work, but would require *significant* guidance, training, or help to perform at an acceptable level.

♦ **ACCEPTABLE.** The applicant provides evidence from prior employment and/or training that he or she could perform this aspect of the work at an acceptable level, given normal orientation and training for the position.

♦ **ABOVE ACCEPTABLE.** The applicant provides evidence from prior employment and/or training that he or she could perform this aspect of the work at a proficient level and would require little or no guidance.

♦ **SUPERIOR.** The applicant provides evidence from prior employment and/or training that he or she could perform this aspect of the work at a *highly proficient* level. The applicant could train or instruct others in this aspect of the work.

Figure 4.4 is an example of the form used to rate and summarize the information from the applicant's file.

When the files have been evaluated, the principal completes the Certificated Hiring Checklist (Figure 4.5). Completing this form can assist the administrator in organizing this stage and the interviewing stage of the selection process.

(Text continues on page 88.)

FIGURE 4.4. FILE REVIEW SCREENING–CERTIFICATED APPLICANTS

Instructions from screener: Summary File Review Rating:

____ Request additional information or   ____ 1 Outstanding (5%)
       references (see comments)
                                               ____ 2 Good (10%)
____ Arrange a screening interview
                                               ____ 3 Acceptable (25%)
____ Other
                                               ____ 4 Marginal (50%)

                                               ____ 5 Unacceptable (below 50%)

Comments: _____

_____

_____

Signed: _____   Date: _____

FILE REVIEW SCREENING GUIDE

Professional Recommendations - Teaching Observed (letters) 1 2 3 4 5
    - superlatives   - humor   - work ethic
    - attitude   - enthusiasm/   - flexibility
    - skills   rapport   - caring

Recommendations- Professors/Personal 1 2 3 4 5
    - superlatives   - humor   - work ethic
    - attitude   - enthusiasm/   - flexibility
    - skills   rapport   - caring

Professional - Other.. 1 2 3 4 5
    - grade point   - neatness/accuracy
    - file completeness   - course work/related experience

Personal Contact... 1 2 3 4 5

OTHER   _____

_____

_____

FIGURE 4.5. CERTIFICATED HIRING CHECKLIST

Please complete this form, sign, and return with the applicant's file.

Position: _____ Location: _____

Position Closing Date: _____ Administrator: _____

**Check
Completed**   **Activity**
____   Screen applications, using District File Review Screening Sheets. Review supporting
            papers in personnel files of any in-district applicants. Indicate applicants selected for
            interview. If any in-district applicant is not to be interviewed, note the specific
            requirements he/she fails to meet.

____   Appoint interview team. Notify Personnel of team members. Orient team to hiring
            procedures/process.

            Members: _____   _____
                     _____   _____
                     _____   _____

____   Schedule interviews or contact Human Resources to do so. If scheduling from the
            building, please inform Personnel of the schedule in order to assist in answering
            public inquiries.

            Date: _____ Time: _____   Location: _____

            Candidates: _____   _____
                       _____   _____
                       _____   _____

            Use sample provided by Human Resources or design interview questions/rating sheet
            related to criteria listed on the job announcement and from other factors determined to
            be related to predicted job performance. Use Interview Rating Sheet to accurately
            document responses and objectively rate each candidate.

____   Conduct interviews, asking each candidate the same questions. Each interview team
            member completes a rating sheet for each candidate. Complete Candidate Rating
            Form for each candidate.

____   Rate and identify top candidate(s) from interviews using the Candidate Rating Form.

____   Conduct employment reference checks (2 minimum, 3 recommended) and include
            notations as part of formal documentation. Use Telephone Reference Form.

___   Contact Personnel regarding the following:

         Recommended Candidate: _____

         Requested Start Date: _____

         Recommended Contract: _____ or Long-Term Substitute _____

___   Deliver interview/recommendation materials to the Human Resources Department:

          ___   Applications
          ___   Interview questions/rating sheets with notes
          ___   Reference check notations
          ___   Certified Hiring Checklist

         Principal's Signature: _____

RETURN TO PERSONNEL

PERSONNEL DEPARTMENT:

___   Confirm receipt of required materials.

___   Confirm candidate recommended; review related issues.
         (Certification, Affirmative Action, district employee, overlap time, etc.)

___   Authorize contact with successful candidate.

___   Notify candidates who were interviewed but not selected for the position.

___   Process paperwork for payroll.

Screening Team

If done well, the recruiting and application screening stages should provide excellent candidates who match school and district needs. It is also critical to have qualified, trained people to do the screening. If you do not have competent personnel doing the screening, you may miss out on excellent candidates who would have been a match for the position. Typically, paper screenings are done by the personnel department and selected district administrators based on predetermined characteristics as defined by your team. However, as a principal you should be on the screening team so that you have a hands-on look and can use your best judgment rather than relying solely on others to compare applicants against the criteria. The compilation of a screening summary report for each candidate to be considered, including specific reasons for elimination, is recommended.

Principals should consider use of either of these two methods of selecting those to be interviewed and subsequent steps to be followed.

Method 1

- ♦ Completed Application
- ♦ Reviewed by the Principal
- ♦ Applicants Selected by the Principal for Interview
- ♦ Train the Interviewers
- ♦ Selection Team Interview
- ♦ Recommendation to Principal
- ♦ Principal Interviews
- ♦ Principal Does Reference Checks/Site Visits
- ♦ Principal Recommends to Superintendent/Human Resources to Hire
- ♦ School Board Offers Contract

Method 2

- ♦ Completed Application
- ♦ Review by the Principal and Selection Team
- ♦ Applicants Selected Cooperatively by the Principal and the Selection Team
- ♦ Train the Interviewers

♦ Selection Team and the Principal Interview
♦ Recommendation to the Principal
♦ Principal/Selection Committee Does Reference Checks/Site Visits
♦ Principal Recommends to Superintendent/Human Resources to Hire
♦ School Board Offers Contract

SELECTION OF INTERVIEWEES AND NOTIFICATION OF NONSELECTED APPLICANTS

The applicant pool now is in two groups: those who have been selected for interviews and those who have not. The principal typically notifies the district human resources department to notify both groups. As school-based management becomes more of a reality, it will increasingly become the principal's role to notify the applicants. Typically, the nonselected applicants are notified by letter at this stage since there is usually such a large quantity. Candidates to be interviewed are notified by phone and scheduled for an interview.

PREPARING FOR THE INTERVIEW

The importance of the interview is paramount. The administrator should be well prepared for this stage of selection since it involves a commitment of time and resources. Several aspects will be looked at:

INTERVIEW TEAM

It is not enough to simply select the best people to conduct the interview; they also need to be trained in interviewing. Let's look first at the format and selection of the team:

Selection

It is recommended to select five to nine people on the interview team. How you choose to format the interview is of personal choice. You may choose to:

♦ Do team interviews (including the Principal)
♦ Interview with Principal alone followed by the team interview

♦ Group interview the candidates and then individual interview: this is a concept where candidates come together and are given a task to perform while the team watches them interact and their roles and behaviors observed. Then, each candidate is interviewed individually by the team.

When choosing those to be on the interview team, they must, above all else, agree to use whatever criteria and guidelines are chosen. You should also strive to get as heterogeneous a group as possible in terms of age, gender, status, and attitudes. If you get a group that is simply made up of clones of you, then there is no way to reach the best possible hiring decision. Beyond that, the suggested makeup of your team might include any of the following:

♦ One administrator of the building Principal's choice

♦ The team leader/department or grade level chair in the area of the vacancy

♦ Two members of the department or grade

♦ One other teacher (other grade level or subject area) and maybe one specialist

♦ One or two parents

♦ One or two students

♦ Secretary, or classified staff where applicable

♦ Alternates for each category in case of absences

TRAINING OF TEAM

Once you have selected your interview team, they must be trained for the interview. Keep in mind that you will need to adapt these suggestions to whatever interview model you choose to use. Following are elements of training:

♦ **Understanding the purpose of interviewing.** Each interviewer needs to have a clear understanding of the objectives: the selection of the best qualified candidate for the position, determining appropriate experience, training and personality for the given position, narrowing down to who is most able to perform effectively within the job description and environment, and to choosing a match for the demographics, culture, and needs of your students, staff, and community. The group should refer regularly to the Personnel Requisition Form used to initiate the selection process.

♦ **Applicant information file.** Interviewers should have knowledge about the individual's background in terms of information from the district application form, the résumé, and other pertinent data. Most often, the practice is to give the confidential placement file to the team. However, it is recommended that the letters of reference, placement file, and phone references should be seen and handled only by the building administrator in the interest of confidentiality for all involved. The ultimate responsibility for hiring the best person for the job is the principal's.

♦ **Knowledge of the job.** Interviewers need to know the predetermined criteria for applicant selection in terms of the job requisition and description, and in terms of how applicants were screened. Everyone must be clear as to what is being sought from the candidates.

♦ **Rules of the district for interviewing.** Each district may have established rules for the interview that it has found to be effective. Such rules could include: statements and questions not to ask according to district rules as well as the law, what information can and cannot be referred to, whether to ask additional questions besides those assigned, what role the interviewer should play, and so on.

♦ **Personal attributes and skills interviewing.** Individual interview team members should:

- treat candidates with fairness and respect
- have awareness/avoid stereotypes and biases
- learn to pay attention to body language and visual clues
- have the ability to make fine distinctions and perceive accurately
- have the ability to record accurate records after the interview (not rating, but strengths and weaknesses)
- be willing and committed to using criteria as established
- have the ability to give the candidate every chance to be successful

- maintain eye contact
- become familiar with interview questions and structure
- know what to expect as an appropriate answer to a question and how to delve further
- know how to paraphrase an applicant's answers
- stay focused
- make the candidate feel welcome and at ease

Cautions for the interviewer to be alert to:

- making judgments too early
- putting too much merit on unfavorable information versus favorable information
- being influenced by comparisons between one candidate and another
- using your "version" of the criteria to judge
- imposing personal biases (e.g., looks like old boss, hair color, etc.) that may turn you off

It cannot be assumed that interviewers know and understand the above items. They must be taught extensively to arrive at the best decision through shared vision and expectations.

INTERVIEWER TRAINING WORKSHOP

- ◆ The Interviewer Training Workshop will include:
  - How to screen applicants' résumés and cover letters
  - How to confirm information from the résumé and cover letter
  - How to maintain eye contact and flow during the interview
  - How to become familiar with the oral and written structure of the interview questions
  - How to know what to expect as an appropriate or inappropriate answer and how to respond with additional questions
  - How to paraphrase an applicant's answers
  - How to note body language and visual cues

- How to STAY FOCUSED!

♦ The Interviewer Training Workshop is typically 3 hours long. It is best to use the room for the training in which the interviews will actually take place.

A KEY IDEA

Have one person sit unobtrusively to the side of the interview team with a laptop computer and record the questions and the responses of the candidate. In the break between candidates, the recorder can print the responses from a portable printer and make copies for the entire group. This frees the team to concentrate on the nonverbal cues and maintain eye contact with the candidate.

THE INTERVIEW

Now that the interview team has been selected and trained, preparation for the interview itself takes place. In the process of preparation there are six steps to include:

A KEY IDEA

Have a host or hostess meet the candidate, describe the process, give printed information (salary benefits, education association contract, brochure about the district programs, etc.), and be cordial to the candidate. Important impressions are made at this juncture.

♦ **Planning the interview (format, questions, roles)**

In this stage, the team determines who will design questions (individuals, team, or principal). The questions should be focused and should be based on agreed upon criteria. Each question should meet the following criteria:

- be open-ended

- have a clear purpose tied to criteria
- be tied to job requirements
- be focused and clear
- be repeatable
- have a meaningful place in the entire interview sequence

The interview schedule should be developed with these questions in mind:

- What is the best time to conduct the interview?
- How long will the interview last?
- How will the room be set up?
- Who will introduce and welcome each candidate?
- What is the order of questions?
- Who will ask what questions?
- What will be happening while individuals are answering questions?

These details need to be mapped out in advance for the interview process to run smoothly.

The last thing that needs to be planned is the "rating" criteria. This may not mean a literal rating process — although it might — but rather, what you are looking for and what format you will use in recording and comparing that information. You may use a number system, or a statement format in which to write thoughts about each candidate's strengths, weaknesses, and other information.

♦ **Giving information**

You are not only trying to find a match for your school but also a match for the candidate. An unhappy employee who was not well-informed prior to hiring about the job, school, district, and community tends not to be effective. Time needs to be spent planning what specific information to give the candidate about responsibilities, salary, benefits, the culture and the community, how the district and school operate, with whom he or she will work, and so on. How and when this is to be done needs to be determined.

◆ **Getting information**

Strategies and methods for eliciting desired information are to be determined. Questions need to be designed that will solicit specific information being sought based on the interviewee's response. Information will also be acquired from the reference checks to be done by the principal.

◆ **Personal impact**

The candidate is expected to impress the team! Keep in mind that you are also selling your school, district, and community to the candidate as well. An excellent prospect may well have many options for employment and you want to "hook" him or her. To do so, you need to create a positive and memorable impact. Plan your timeline and procedures for notification, and what you can do to leave a positive impression on each candidate so that he or she will want to return to your district even if not hired.

◆ **Responding to the applicant**

Anticipate questions that the applicant may ask, and plan answers and determine who will answer them. Usually, the principal is more prepared to answer these questions.

◆ **Processing the information**

After the interview is complete, you need a way to compile the information on the candidates and a way to compare and reach a decision. Will all have an equal vote in the process, does the principal want it limited to the best two candidates, what format will be used in discussing each, how will it be sifted out, and how will the best candidate be determined?

The interview questions are important sources of information. Figures 4.6 and 4.7 (beginning on page 99) are samples of interview questions and appropriate responses.

INTERVIEW PROTOCOL AND FORMAT

The following is the suggested general format for the actual interview, which is designed to be a positive and productive process.

(Text continues on page 102.)

FIGURE 4.6. CERTIFICATED INTERVIEW

Candidate name _____   Date _____

Interviewer _____   Rate
                                                                    low -----> high

1.   Please review your educational background and preparation as   1 2 3 4
     it relates to this position.

     -Appropriate courses, education
     -Continuing education
     -MA
     -Professional reading

2.   Do you want students to like you? (If yes, why is that?)   1 2 3 4

     -Yes, for the right reasons
     -Sees "liking" as beneficial to student learning
     -Emphasizes relationship-building qualities

3.   With all the adverse publicity about education today, why did you   1 2 3 4
     want to become a teacher? What do you wish to accomplish?

     -Wants to do something for students; seeing their growth
     -Satisfaction in helping others
     -Contribution to society
     -Always wanted to be a teacher
     -Experience with students confirmed their interest

4.   Some teachers are better than others; what do you think makes   1 2 3 4
     the difference?

     -Focus on relationships
     -Specific reference to and description of an instructional model
     -Understands planning--goals, objectives, outcomes
     -Applies new ideas and skills
     -Pacing, instructional level, diagnosis and assessment

5.   What do you see to be your strongest areas, and share an example   1 2 3 4
     that explains why.

     -Relationships   -Organization
     -Ability to diagnose own strengths -Goal-oriented
     -Describes how they developed
     -Able to describe specifics

| | Rate |
| | low -----> high |

6. How do you provide for individual differences in students?   1 2 3 4

    -Assessment: tools, methods; interest survey
    -Accounts for learning styles
    -Has management strategies

7. As a teacher you are required to interact with administrators,   1 2 3 4
    other staff, parents, etc. Please describe how you work with a
    variety of individuals and describe a situation you were involved
    in which was difficult and sensitive. How did you handle it?

    -Perspective as a team member as well as an individual
    -Courtesy, professionalism
    -Look for support for solution from others

8. Describe your classroom management style and discuss discipline   1 2 3 4
    strategies you would use with students at this level.

    -Specific strategies
    -Positive reinforcement
    -Preventive methods
    -Communication strategies

9. How have you grown professionally recently, and what areas would you   1 2 3 4
    like to develop in yourself? How was this/will this be accomplished?

    -Able to diagnose own needs
    -Professional plan for self
    -Actions taken to implement the plan

10. Can teachers be too empathetic--can they put themselves too much into   1 2 3 4
    another person's shoes?

    -Understands empathy as different from sympathy

11. What do you enjoy most about teaching?   1 2 3 4

    -Student growth

12. A student told another teacher that your class was boring. What would   1 2 3 4
    you do?

    -Seeks more information based on a concern for student needs

		Rate low -----> high

13. A student is constantly out of his/her seat, bothers others constantly,   1 2 3 4
    and has difficulty staying on task. What are some possible causes,
    and possible remedies?

    -Content too difficult
    -Medical causes
    -.I've had a student like that, and....
    -Age-appropriate reasons, strategies

14. Tell me what you do to cause students to be successful.   1 2 3 4

    -Listening
    -Helping students
    -Teaching strategies
    -Identifying needs and interests
    -Positive attitude
    -Building positive relations

15. How do you know when you are doing a good job of listening?   1 2 3 4

    -Looks to person speaking for clues
    -Person continues to share
    -Person comes back another time
    -When the person speaking is helped

16. Follow up questions, if any?   1 2 3 4
    _____
    _____

17. Please seek the following information:
    _____
    _____
    _____

Summary

    Strengths:
    _____
    _____
    _____
    _____

    Weaknesses:
    _____
    _____
    _____
    _____

TOTAL POINTS: _____

FIGURE 4.7. INTERVIEW QUESTIONS

The goal of the interview process is to identify leading candidates for employment who are: (1) **best qualified** to produce the results sought in this position, (2) **best equipped** by experience, training, and temperament to perform effectively in this type of job environment, and (3) **most able to perform effectively** the priority actions required in this position. The following are a sample of questions that could be used to evaluate a prospective applicant's teaching abilities. All questions will relate to the Certificated Personnel Requisition and are used to define the skills of teaching as well as evaluate performance.

1. Please review your background and tell us how your educational experiences have prepared you for the teaching profession.
    — appropriate educational background: course work, subject area classes
    — plans for continuing education
    — Master's Degree
    — extensive study with age level / subject matter
    — professional activities

2. Why did you want to become a teacher and what do you wish to accomplish?
    — purpose for being a teacher
    — desire to help students learn; commitment *to each* student
    — positive statements / feelings about teaching profession
    — seeing students grow and develop
    — satisfaction in helping others
    — contribute to society
    — willingness to grow and be the best

3. What experiences have you had that have prepared you to teach middle school students?
    — student teaching
    — substitute teaching / long-term assignments
    — prior contractual experiences
    — volunteer work outside of school day
    — extra-curricular experiences
    — civic experiences
    — positive experiences with students

4. What instructional skills should an effective teacher demonstrate and what methods should be used to implement these skills?
    — knowledge and use of instructional techniques
    — references to specific instructional models
    — plans and implements effective lesson plans
    — understands goals and objectives
    — implements new skills and ideas
    — uses a variety of learning styles and methods in presenting lessons

— ability to assess students' needs and prescribe programs to meet those needs
— plans and paces appropriate lessons

5. What is your strongest asset that you will bring to the teaching profession and please share and explain an example of that strength?
— self-awareness assessment
— ability to diagnose personal strengths
— ability to describe

6. What area would you like to develop in yourself and what strategies do you have for improving your own performance?
— ability to diagnose own needs
— plan for professional growth
— plans to implement growth
— commitment to education as a profession

7. How and with whom do you see yourself interacting in this teaching assignment? Give an example of how you have worked with individuals and describe how you handled a situation that was difficult or sensitive.
— ability to work both as an individual *and* as part of a **team**
— understands complexity and makeup of team members
— ability to work within a consensus model of decision making
— respectful, sensitive, and understanding of others
— development of interactive strategies
— professional

8. How would you prepare your classroom and yourself prior to the first day of school?
— ability to present ideas into logical statements
— prepared and positive toward assignment
— demonstrated ability to sequence activities
— thoroughness of specific plan described
— demonstrated ambition, involvement, high energy level
— initiative
— ability to pace self in activities
— successful in implementing plans

9. Describe your classroom management style and discuss discipline strategies you would use for middle school students.
— establishment of clear parameters; teach the rules
— understands that positive reinforcement and high expectations are vital to student success
— importance of student individual needs; consistency, fairness
— appropriate, positive, preventive approach

— caring, sincere concern for others
— well-formulated plan
— provides clear, positive feedback
— assisting toward self-discipline
— development of courtesy, self-control, respect, responsibility

We have one more question to ask you and then we will be happy to answer any questions that you may have.

10. What are some ways in which you would enhance our Block Program (Social Studies, Language Arts, and Reading) to make it challenging, interesting, a meaningful learning experience, and popular?
> — demonstrates a depth and breadth of knowledge of theory and content
> — extent and quality of basic preparation
> — evidence of planning and good organization
> — variety of instructional techniques
> — effectively supports curriculum design
> — knowledge of current and new educational developments
> — continues professional preparation and growth

11. At this time, do you have any questions? Should any questions arise after you leave here today, please feel free to contact me, at any time, and I will try to answer your questions.

Following the completion of the interview process a designated interviewer should thank the candidate for coming, and should give the candidate guidelines as to the procedures that will follow. A timeline for notification should be given and a personal contact should be made to the candidate, whether or not he or she is hired.

At this time the interviewing team needs to have an in-depth discussion about the candidate to determine some of the following:

- Overall communication skills
- Evaluation of written materials
- Organization of thoughts
- Clear, on target, thoughtful, appropriate responses to questions
- Enthusiastic, intuitive, caring, knowledgeable, alive, a learner, a risk taker, a team player
- Ability to understand questions without clarification
- Concise in expression

Was the team able to identify a leading candidate who is **best qualified, best equipped, and able to perform effectively** as a teacher in your school? Do reference checks match the decisions of the interviewing team?

ALL KIDS DESERVE THE BEST TEACHERS IN THE WORLD!!

♦ Greeting by host and giving of information.

- Start by making the candidate comfortable: always offer water/coffee; some quick small talk; and introductions. Supply name cards for all members of the team and role (parent, principal, student, 3rd grade teacher, secretary, etc.) as well as for the candidate.

- Statement to set the tone: "I want to tell you how pleased we are to have you as a candidate. Of 60 applicants, you are one of six chosen to be interviewed."

- Tell the candidate about the position: grade level, school, strengths and weaknesses of situation, teamwork at that location: "We're looking for someone to mold into that team and make Franklin Elementary more effective."

- Tell about yourself, the PTO, whatever is specific to the building.

- NOW: "We're going to ask you some questions, then you can ask us some."

- "Could you tell us about yourself, your experience, education, family, interest areas, so we have a common place to launch into our questions?"

- Ask candidate to tell about a particular lesson he or she has taught in the last few years (months) where he or she really enjoyed the process. You are listening for details, connections, kids' learning. (Use of Personnel Requisition can guide you.)

- "If I were to come into your room sometime during the year, tell me what I'd see; what the students would be doing, what your role would be, what the room would look like."

- STRENGTHS: "If I were to call your principal or someone who knows your work, what would they tell me about you AND your work at...?" (Record mentally, as interviewee doesn't know if you've called or not.)

- WEAKNESSES: "I have one more question. Then I'll give you an opportunity to ask some of us....What is it you are working on as a teacher, so that if I hired you, I could help you with that?" This gives you as administrator a beginning place for later reference checks or assistance that you need to provide.

- CLOSE: Candidate asks questions; then you express your thanks to him or her, state when you'll be doing your reference checks, and the day when you will be calling finalists. Also: "If you have questions in the meantime, please call me at...." Reaffirm by telling candidate that all of the candidates COULD fill the position, that you are simply looking for the BEST MATCH. Candidates can now leave with a positive feeling about themselves and the district.

A SPECIAL CASE—APPLICANTS WITH DISABILITIES

The Americans with Disabilities Act (ADA) was signed into law on July 10, 1990. It affects every employer with 15 or more employees as of July 26, 1994.

The intent of the ADA is to prevent discrimination against qualified people with disabilities. The law requires that employers no longer screen out disabled individuals solely on the basis of their disability. School districts may no longer conduct preemployment inquiries into the nature of the applicant's disability, but can inquire about the candidate's ability to complete job tasks that are part of the job description. School districts generally make sure that the physical facilities are handicap-accessible but should also provide current, accurate, and relevant job descriptions.

The interview process must also be handled appropriately:

- make the interview accessible
- do not automatically assume that the applicant needs assistance, but be ready to provide it
- ask all questions in a professional and straightforward manner

During the interview process, questions should not be asked about:

- the nature of the disability
- the severity of the disability
- the condition causing the disability
- any prognosis or expectation regarding the disability

- whether the applicant will need special treatment or special leave because of the disability

---

A KEY IDEA

- Provide the applicant with the job description and ask if there is any reason why he or she cannot perform the essential functions of the job.
- Further, provide the previous employer or student teacher supervisor with the job description and ask the above question.

REFERENCE CHECKS

When making reference calls, listen for specific areas the previous principal might mention which are critical, such as discipline/management. Asking a question such as "Since you know Miss J. better than I, what question should I ask that I haven't asked?" This part encompasses part of "Getting Information"—the reading between the lines, or listening for what is *not* said.

In some cases, a district has prepared job-related questions as part of its "Verifying References" step. At this point it is common for a district to use a telephone reference check form. Such a form is shown here as Background Reference Check (Figure 4.8). Another excellent suggestion for checking references is to visit the candidate's current place of employment.

POSITION DESCRIPTION

An effective instrument for the principal's use is the Position Description. It is similar to the Position Announcement, but serves as a communication piece between the principal and the teacher at time of hiring and induction. It can be discussed between the two individuals, and further defines the required and desired qualifications and duties of the position. When the two parties complete discussion about this description, both will sign and date the form to make a collaborative agreement. Figure 4.9 is a sample of a position description.

FIGURE 4.8. BACKGROUND REFERENCE CHECK

This review is to be completed and submitted to the Human Resources Office prior to recommending an applicant for hire.

Applicant: _____Checked by: _____   Date: _____

Name of Agency: _____

Name of Reference & Position: _____

Procedure:
      1.   Identify yourself by name and position
      2.   Indicate you are considering hiring this applicant and that all information given will be confidential.
      3.   Indicate N/A if question does not apply.
      4.   Complete the following by verifying it:

1.   Verify dates of employment from application and/or résumé. _____

_____

2.   How did you know this applicant and did you evaluate him/her? _____

_____

3.   Why did applicant leave employment with your organization? _____

_____

4.   Do you know of any health conditions that would interfere with job performance or attendance?

    _____ No   _____ Yes (if yes, indicate reasons.)

_____

5.   What is this person's greatest strength? _____

_____

6.   What is this person's greatest weakness? _____

_____

7.   Would you rehire this person? _____ If no, why?

_____

BACKGROUND REFERENCE CHECK

8.   Are you aware of any circumstances or activities where this applicant has been involved in substance abuse, addictions, or sexual misconduct?

_____ No   _____ Yes

If yes, give details. _____

9.   How would you rate this applicant on a ten-point scale (1 = low 10 = high) in the following areas? Indicate number given after each area.

9.1   Effort to improve   _____

9.2   Degree of adaptability/flexibility   _____

9.3   Level of cooperation with others   _____

9.4   Instructional abilities   _____

9.5   Strengths of teacher   _____

9.6   Staff relationships   _____

Additional Questions and Answers

10.   Question: _____

      Answer: _____

11.   Question: _____

      Answer: _____

FIGURE 4.9. POSITION DESCRIPTION

---

1. Position Title: Primary Teacher

2. Division Title: Multi-Age Program

3. Department or School: Elementary School

4. Title of Immediate Supervisor: Principal

5. General Duties:
- Teach primary students in a contained, non-graded classroom setting, planning instruction that meets individual needs, interests, and abilities of students
- Cooperatively plan with the multi-age teacher team

6. Specific Duties:
- Teach language arts, math, science, social studies, health, art, and P.E. per district-adopted curriculum
- Assist in the teaching of music, computers, and library skills
- Create a safe learning environment by establishing clear learning and behavioral expectations
- Keep appropriate records on students' progress
- Evaluate students' academic and social growth
- Communicate students' progress with parents through report cards and conferences, or at times when the rate of learning/behavior changes significantly
- Attend and participate in staff meetings
- Participate in staff development sessions for personal/professional growth
- Work with multi-age staff on learning themes, curriculum spirals, and discipline model for the school
- Keep the principal informed

7. Qualifications:
- Current State Teaching Certificate with an elementary endorsement (Required)
- Training in Developmentally appropriate Science and Health Curriculum (Desired)
- Training in Math-Their-Way (Desired)
- Experience in integrating the curriculum (Desired)
- Experience in dealing with multiple ages, developmental stages, and abilities in a contained classroom setting (Desired)

8.   **Discussed and agreed to this** _____ **day of** _____

        Between _____ **&** _____

IMPROVING THE PROCESS

It is important to seek feedback from those interviewed in order to improve the interview process. This feedback should be sought from all interviewed candidates. Figure 4.10 is an example of such a form.

RECOMMENDATION

Once the committee has determined a candidate for selection, the district personnel office takes responsibility to review the committee's work. This review is the formal checking of legal and other information, including:

♦ credentials such as training and recommendations

♦ letters of application

♦ responses to topics on supplementary application

♦ responses to interview questions

♦ contact with previous supervisors

The chosen candidate often must have a final interview with the principal or district personnel officer. This final interview is intended to verify that the candidate meets all the district requirements for employment. If this interview confirms the earlier finding of the interview team, then the candidate is recommended to the superintendent and/or board for hire.

Supporting documentation in behalf of the candidate along with the screening evaluation, interview evaluation, and telephone reference check reports go on file for future reference. Upon candidate acceptance of the offer, the personnel officer reviews the written recommendation and supporting information from the interviewers and informs the candidate that he or she will

♦ be recommended for the position

♦ receive a general statement about the type of contract that will be issued (Letter of Intent)

♦ be expected to verify in writing his or her willingness to accept a contract if offered

♦ be expected to present documents, as per P.L. 99-603, which establish eligibility to work, and attest, in writing, his or her eligibility to work.

FIGURE 4.10. CANDIDATE'S EVALUATION OF INTERVIEW TEAM

As we continually strive to refine our selection process, we are interested in feedback from you, the candidate, who are obviously a key participant in the process. We do not ask for your name to protect your right to confidentiality. Please complete your rating following the directions noted below. You may leave this form with the building secretary or send it directly to the School District, Attention: Human Resources Department.

Position: _____   Location: _____

Directions: Please rate your interview team on a scale from 1-6,6 representing the most positive rating. Place the numeric rating in the blank line.

_____   Were you appropriately introduced to the interview team?

_____   Was the size of the interview team appropriate?

_____   Was the interview conducted in a professional but congenial manner?

_____   Were all questions job-related?

_____   Through both questions and answers, did you feel well informed about the position and its expectations?

_____   Were you provided ample opportunity to ask questions?

_____   Did the team adequately respond to your questions?

_____   Did the team explain the timeline(s) for selection and future notification to you?

_____   Your overall assessment of your interview.

_____   Your overall assessment and rating of the team.

Other Comments: _____

_____

Thank you for completing this evaluation and for your interest in the School District.

The personnel office then proceeds with securing official statements from previous employers, evaluating transcripts for salary schedule placement, issuing the appropriate contract, and taking care of the business issues of payroll information and teaching certificate registration. Usually the new teacher's principal or district office will also proceed with issuing standard handbooks and other policy information, performance standards and expectations, and responsibilities.

CONCLUSION

Teacher selection is such a complex process and an important administrative task. In selecting the most capable professionals for teaching positions, interviewers must be wise appraisers of candidates and astute forecasters of future teacher performance. Selection and staffing is only one part of the human resources continuum. It is about matching people as well as their career needs and capabilities with the positions and career paths that a particular district has available. It is just the beginning of what should be a productive relationship for both the new staff member and the district. Yes, we want TOP-NOTCH teachers, but it takes TOP-NOTCH selection processes to get them. It is a growth process, where the teams are trained for interviewing, questions are meaningful and attuned to the "match" desired, and the resulting assignment is evaluated for staff development and analysis. Thus, the Human Resources Staffing Function Cycle, as illustrated in Figure 4.11, never stops!

REFERENCES

Al-Tubaiy, K. (1993). Five steps to better hiring, *The Executive Educator,* 15 (8), 21–22.

Bateman, C.F. (1986). Want superstar teachers? Scout for talent and recruit like crazy. *American School Board Journal,* 173 (6), 27.

Buffie, E.G. (1989). *The principal and leadership.* Bloomington, IN: Phi Delta Kappa.

Coastal Human Resources (1996). *Legal and effective interviewing.* Virginia Beach, VA: Coastal Video Communication Corp.

Collier, B.H. (1987). Don't let employees slip away unnoticed: Learn from them. *Executive Educator,* 9 (5), 17–19.

DeLandsheere, G. (1980). Teacher selection. *Prospects: Quarterly Review of Education,* 10 (3), 318–324.

FIGURE 4.11. HUMAN RESOURCES STAFFING FUNCTION CYCLE

Fear, R. A. (1984). *The evaluation interview,* 3rd ed. New York: McGraw-Hill.

Goldstein, W. (1986*). Recruiting superior teachers: The interview process.* Bloomington, IN: Phi Delta Kappa.

Greathouse, C.L. (1992). 10 Common hiring mistakes. *Industry Week,* January 20, 22–24.

Herman, S.J. (1993). *Hiring right: A practical guide.* Thousand Oaks, CA: Sage Publishing.

Niece, R. (1983). The interview and personnel selection: Is the process valid and reliable? *Clearing House,* 56, 234.

Paulk, L. J. (1984). Employee exit interviews. *Spectrum,* 2 (1), 7–13.

Saville, A., and J. Hill (1989). *The exit interview: A generic model.* Non-Classroom Material. (ERIC Document Reproduction Service No. ED 310-523.)

5

ORIENTATION AND INDUCTION

REASONS FOR STUDYING ORIENTATION AND INDUCTION

- After recruitment and selection, induction is the next major human resources activity geared to enable the teacher to be a success.
- Induction is often not well done in schools, or not done at all.
- Time proactively invested during the induction period will pay off handsomely during the career of the teacher.
- High expectations for teachers are very important. The induction period is the time to communicate those expectations.

> *An effective induction program is the mortar that cements pre-service training to professional development.*

INTRODUCTION

The recruitment and selection process is time-consuming and expensive. After reading through hundreds of applications, sitting through interviews, calling to check references, recommending a candidate for the position, and the principal and selection committee have obtained the employee of their choice, what should the principal do to ensure the success and retention of this new staff member?

The ideal induction program assists in the successful assimilation and development of the beginning teacher, the veteran teacher newly hired into the district, the teacher transferred from other buildings within the same district, and the teacher transferred into different grade or content areas within the same building. Induction is the process designed to acquaint the newly employed teacher with the community, the school district, the school, the program and their colleagues.

Most school districts provide an *orientation program* designed to inform new employees about payroll, health and insurance plans, rules and regulations, and locations of district buildings. These orientation programs also introduce district administrative staff and give an overview of the community. *Induction programs*, on the other hand, are designed to include the information given during orientation as well as provide collegial connections; instructional support; and acculturalization to the community, school, and classroom throughout at least the first year as a new employee.

Research shows that in the United States a gradual systematic induction of new teachers is the exception. This is a problem because the teaching profession is one of the few in which beginners are expected to fulfill the same responsibilities as veterans (Reinhartz, 1989). Consider what the research literature has to say about new teachers:

♦ Almost 15% leave teaching after 1 year.

♦ Between 40 and 50% leave after fewer than 7 years.

♦ As a group, the most academically talented teachers are the least likely to stay in the profession.

♦ Younger teachers, when compared to more experienced teachers, report more emotional exhaustion and a greater degree of depersonalization. (Tonneson and Patterson, 1992)

New teachers often enter the teaching profession possessing three characteristics: they are often *unfocused workers,* meaning that they are unable to think of appropriate ways to improve their teaching; they are *highly* motivated and coachable; and they tend to be *idealistic,* with their expectations often exceeding what they can reasonably achieve. These characteristics point to the need and possibilities for teacher induction programs (Young et al., 1993). Additionally, first-year teachers share common problems. According to Kevin Ryan (1986), there are six common problems facing the beginning teacher:

+ **Shock of the familiar:** Teachers have to meet many unexpected demands now that they are "on the other side of the desk." These demands include paperwork, a need for information by the administration, communication with parents and colleagues, managing several activities and students at one time, lesson plans, and lesson implementation. An additional demand is created by the difference between being a student-teacher and the teacher in charge of everything from instruction and discipline to assessment, organization, and room decorations.

+ **Students:** Teachers usually enter the profession because they are concerned for children and want to be an effective force in the lives of young people. However, new teachers are unfamiliar and discouraged by the reality of students' attitudes and behaviors that are incongruent with the teachers' personal experiences and views of school culture. Teachers are also confused and discouraged by the social distance that students want in the student-teacher relationship. Students do not want another buddy; they want an effective teacher. This role confusion may cause discipline problems in the classroom. Student discipline for new teachers is sometimes a problem because they must learn to be comfortable with their new authority, plus learn to deal with students respectfully. Beginning teachers also need to learn how to deal with misbehavior quickly and effectively.

+ **Parents:** Teachers usually aren't taught how to deal with parents. They often expect to find the "June and Ward Cleaver" support from the 1950s, but instead they find conflict due to parents' concerns about their competency, or the "my child can do no wrong" attitude. Also of concern to beginning teachers is the stability of the home life of students. New teachers may have a difficult time relating to the feelings and pressures of the parents, interpreting shortness of time or money as neglect.

- **Administrators:** Beginning teachers may have ambivalent feelings about the principal. On one hand, they feel indebted to the principal for their job; on the other hand, they feel anxious because of the authority the principal has over them. It takes time to build trust.

- **Fellow teachers:** Beginning teachers often feel isolated because of jealousy or pettiness stemming from rumored or feared talents and energy of beginning teachers. Neglect and social differences stemming from already developed social groups is another source of isolation.

- **Instruction:** Beginning teachers are expected to know what to teach and when to teach it. However, district-provided resources are often lacking and because of generic preservice preparation, they may lack the specific skills to develop effective lessons, presentation, and assessment materials for their assignment.

Several of these same problems, such as obtaining resources, authority conflict, collegial relations, and parent/student relationships, also affect veteran teachers in transition.

Awareness of these problems is the first step in developing a solution that can be pursued by the individual teacher, the training institutions, and the school district. This chapter will focus on the following components for an effective induction program:

- Purpose
- Implications
- District Orientation Programs
- School Orientation Programs
- Role of the Principal
- Mentorships
- Models and Frameworks of Induction Programs

PURPOSES OF INDUCTION PROGRAMS

The single most important thing you can do in administration is to hire good teachers; the second most important thing is to find ways to keep them (Tomlin, 1993). The main purpose of a teacher induction program is to acculturate the new employee into a specific school district and/or teaching position. School districts usually begin this process by formally welcoming the new employee and providing information about the district. Information regarding demographics, payroll, district rules and policies, and the introduction of district administrators are key elements to the orientation session. It may also include visits to district school buildings, a tour of the community, and visits with their principals and department or grade-level chair. Figures 5.1 and 5.2 list objectives of induction programs.

The induction process should be ongoing and is planned based on district educational goals and expectations. It encourages experienced staff to mentor new teachers in the areas of building processes and procedures, curriculum implementation, and collegial networking. The principal's role is to help develop professional skills in the form of knowledge, attitudes and values necessary for the new employee to become an effective teacher within the school district and the specific building.

IMPLICATIONS

School districts, teachers, and students will all benefit from a well-developed induction program specific to the needs of the community, the district, and the teacher. The program will also help weed out ineffective teachers and teaching practices while developing a context-specific vision of effective teaching practices for promising teachers.

An induction program fosters professional growth of the individual through staff development and collegial relationships. To meet the goal of professional growth for teaching staff, the district must have in place good instructional supervision procedures complete with formative and summative evaluation systems. Also, mentoring and networking, both contrived through district assignment and naturally occurring, will provide good teaching models and strategies for the employee, resulting in professional growth.

Positive outcomes and/or implications include:

♦ Organized mentorships improve communication and facilitate the acculturation into the school community.

♦ Teachers who feel that they belong, that they are learning and improving, and who feel good about themselves and their teaching will be more successful.

♦ Teacher performance will be improved.

♦ Retention rate of promising beginning teachers will increase.

FIGURE 5.1. OBJECTIVES COMMON TO ALL INDUCTION PROGRAMS

1. To make teachers feel welcome and secure
2. To enable teachers to become members of the faculty team
3. To offer all newly hired and transfer teachers instructional support and collegial connections
4. To assist teachers to adjust to the work environment
5. To provide information and orientation about:
    - the community
    - the school district
    - the school
    - the faculty and staff
    - the students
    - the educational program
6. To facilitate the opening of the school year
7. To assist teachers in having a sucessful year -- personally and professionally

FIGURE 5.2. OBJECTIVE FOR HELPING THE FIRST-YEAR TEACHER

1. To explain the school and community culture
2. To aid in gathering materials and equipment
3. To provide a mentor to support and assist
4. To carefully arrange class size and students for success

- Mandated state requirements for orientation, mentorships, and continuing education for certification will be satisfied.
- Trusting relationships will develop between staff and administrators.
- Teachers will be involved in associations and community organizations.
- People skills will improve.
- Open communication will improve as new teachers are able to speak openly (negatively or positively), without fear of reprisal, at cohort group meeting or with mentor/team groups.

IMPLEMENTATION

There are several ways to implement an effective induction program. Provided here is an exemplary framework. It is only a framework, so adjustments may be made to "fit" the dynamics of individual district and school goals, expectations, and the demographics of the community. Specific models of successful induction programs are included within the framework, with emphasis on mentoring, district orientation responsibilities, and building and administrative responsibilities.

FRAMEWORK

The staff developer and principal, charged with orientation and induction responsibilities, will encounter groups of anxious beginning teachers each year. How well they orchestrate those activities may determine the length and quality of an individual's professional career, and will also contribute to the level of competence of the district staff.

For beginning school teachers, many questions remain unanswered as they prepare to assume their new professional responsibilities. No matter how thorough the training, how broad the preservice experience, or how successful the student teaching, they approach their first teaching assignment with considerable doubt, concern, and anxiety.

Programs offered by school districts to teachers in the orientation or induction phase of their careers can meet both the needs of the new professionals and the needs of the districts. Based upon findings of research, current practices, and common sense, the following multiphase induction model is presented to assist school districts and staff developers in establishing a program that will achieve positive results. This teacher induction model (see Figure 5.3) has five phases: Definition, Development, Orientation, Operation, and Evaluation.

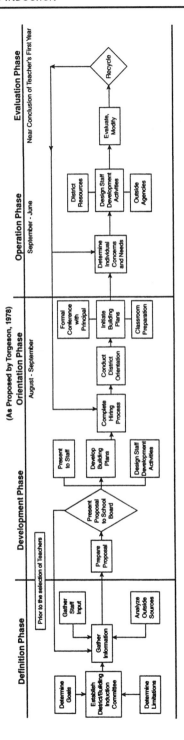

FIGURE 5.3. MODEL TEACHER INDUCTION PROGRAM

(As Proposed by Torgeson, 1978)

DEFINITION PHASE

The first step in developing an effective teacher induction program for a school district is the establishment of a Teacher District Committee. The committee should include a central office administrator such as the director of staff development, an elementary principal, a secondary principal, experienced teachers, and teachers who are completing their first year. A member of the community may be included or, at least, should be available for consultation about appropriate community events and activities.

The committee's first task is to determine the goals for the induction program (see Figure 5.4). Suggested goals include: enhancement of teacher competence, reduction of teacher attrition, improvement of students' instruction, and increased organizational strength for the school.

The committee should also give consideration to the limitations that will influence the committee's proposal. First, budget allocations will indicate funding restrictions. Justify your induction program in terms of the dollars spent as an investment, rather than an expenditure, in the teachers and for the district. Secondly, the committee should note the amount of time projected for involvement by administrators and beginning teachers. In addition, the district's negotiated contract with the local teachers' association

FIGURE 5.4. MODEL TEACHER INDUCTION PROGRAM

should be consulted so that the proposal is in compliance with agreed-upon practices and procedures. And, inevitably, the committee should reflect on various personal philosophies concerning a planned program for induction.

Once the goals of a district induction program have been established, the committee should begin gathering information about similar programs. Even teachers with many years of experience vividly remember their days as beginning teachers and will have suggestions. In nearly every district some induction activities occur each year. The committee needs to be aware of effective past programs. It is appropriate to survey the district's staff about their perspectives concerning their "first year" experiences. A list of questions for the staff might include:

- ◆ What information is necessary for a new teacher prior to the beginning of the school year?
- ◆ What information should be included during the year?
- ◆ How should the information be delivered to the teacher (e.g., small group, large group, handbook, etc.)?
- ◆ Who would be best to give the information (e.g., central office, principal, mentor teacher, the teacher's association, etc.)?

Torgeson (1987), in a study of induction in the State of Washington, found that while induction activities occur, some are rated as more effective than others. Figure 5.5, on the next page, displays the activities and their respective ratings which should be considered as the Induction Committee develops its proposal.

In addition to the district staff, sources outside the district need to be investigated. Other school districts should be contacted in order to identify their current induction practices. An inquiry sent to the state office of education can determine the availability of state-sponsored programs and/or special funds for beginning teacher programs. Also, the regional educational service district should be contacted about the availability of regional programs. A review of current and professional journals and educational research can ascertain suggested strategies.

Having gathered information from both inside and outside the school district, the committee is ready to begin the process of analyzing the data in light of the previously determined needs and limitations in preparation for designing a teacher induction program. The proposed induction program consists of these phases.

FIGURE 5.5. EFFECTIVENESS OF INDUCTION ACTIVITIES AS
RATED BY BEGINNING TEACHERS IN PUGET SOUND (WA)
SCHOOL DISTRICTS

INDUCTION ACTIVITY	Percentage of Responses			
	VE	E	SE	NE
Early notification of building and grade assignment	66	24	10	0
Additional time provided to prepare	73	21	6	0
Mentor teacher selected to assist	58	33	7	1
Opportunities to observe experienced teachers	46	25	21	7
Inservice offered throughout the school year	30	58	12	0
Principal observation and feedback	19	61	12	7
Teachers' Association played a role	10	28	42	19
College maintained relationship to support	24	36	19	21
District-wide orientation for new teachers	27	40	24	9
Individual conference with the principal	33	57	7	3
Teacher Handbook was issued	12	43	34	10
Reduced class load was assigned	24	22	27	25

VE = Very Effective   E = Effective   SE = Somewhat Effective   NE = Not Effective

DEVELOPMENT PHASE

Following this analysis, the committee may begin formulating the induction program for the school district. As the program is being designed, attention is given to coordination with other district programs and/or activities, e.g., the existing staff development program.

The final written proposal includes the goals and objectives of the induction program, an outline of possible activities, and a method of evaluation. With the approval of the superintendent, the proposal is ready to be submited to the school board.

The written proposal should be presented to the school board for approval and/or adoption as a district program. Such a presentation will increase the school board members' awareness of the critical nature of the teachers' first year and demonstrate the need for the district's commitment to support the teachers as they begin their careers.

Once accepted, the induction program is then presented to administrators and staff. They have an opportunity to discuss their roles in the plan and brainstorm strategies to be used. Because, in practice, principals assume the majority of the responsibility for the ongoing induction program, they should develop a formal plan for the coming year (Badertscher, 1978). There are advantages to having principals work together in order to draw from a wider span of experiences and ideas in the development of such a plan. They may also draw from the activities suggested in the adopted program.

The formal plan designed by the principals should be structured to cover the needs of the beginning teachers and the goals of the district. For example, the principals can prioritize areas to be covered during the conference between beginning teacher and their principal. A variety of approaches to disseminate information about areas of concern should be considered to conserve time and avoid overwhelming the beginner. And most importantly, the principal should schedule a specific time for the conference to occur. The length of the conference should be adequate to allow both parties to express themselves.

The district's staff development department may begin developing a year-long program for professional growth. Other groups, such as the local teachers' association, the parent-teacher organization, and the Chamber of Commerce, may participate in the planning. This program may include in-service sessions focusing on district adoption curriculum and/or workshops on the district's instructional model. The staff development department may also wish to request colleges and universities in the area to conduct courses which may be needed by the beginning teacher, for example, classroom management. Another agency with which to coordinate plans would be the regional educational agencies.

ORIENTATION PHASE

DISTRICT ORIENTATION PROGRAMS

This step of the orientation phase (Figure 5.6), which is the initial part of the comprehensive program, usually begins with a districtwide session and should take the form of an extended contract for beginning teachers, as they are generally required to report to work before other teachers, often from one to four days. If so, they should be compensated for the additional days.

The actual implementation begins as the hiring process is completed. As the decision to hire a specific individual is made, the Director of Personnel telephones the candidate and welcomes the individual to the district. Written confirmation of selection follows promptly. As soon as possible the

FIGURE 5.6. MODEL TEACHER INDUCTION PROGRAM

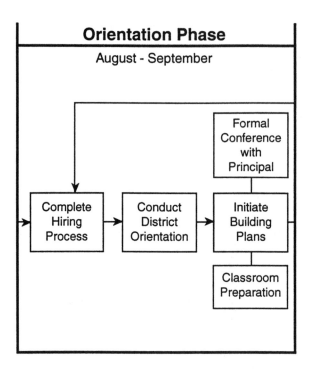

newly hired teacher is notified of the specific grade level and building as-signment. Once those assignments have been determined, the principal tele-phones the new teacher and invites the teacher to visit the building and makes curriculum guides available.

The school district has an opportunity to make a favorable first impres-sion on the new employee during the orientation session scheduled before the beginning of the new school year. The district orientation is imple-mented and designed by the personnel department and the staff develop-ment department. The district orientation program serves as a formal wel-coming of all new staff members, and provides necessary information regarding the district, community, and schools. Suggested components in-clude: introduction of chief administrators, explanation of necessary busi-ness office procedures, a tour or overview of the community, and the statement of district philosophy, vision, and mission. Shelton et al. (1992) offer a six-session orientation plan consisting of:

- **Making contact.** This session gives the new teacher an opportunity to meet the people the teacher will be working with. "Key people" should be introduced, with a description of how each will assist in the transition of the new employee.
- **In school and around town.** This session gives new employees a sightseeing tour of the community and school district building
- **Part of the big picture.** This is the organizational session. An overview of the district's vision, philosophy, goals, and objectives will provide the new employee with a better idea of how his or her efforts will contribute to the school district's mission.
- **Student matters.** During this session topics should include classroom management, positive reinforcement strategies, classroom rules and expectations, grading, corporal punishment or the absence thereof, alternative education programs, and suspension and expulsion.
- **Teacher dos and don'ts.** Review teacher illness procedures for reporting, bad weather days, school closures, and day-to-day procedures.
- **Tools and techniques.** Clarify curriculum expectations, the process for ordering materials, and introduce mentor partnerships.

As an overall component of the teacher induction program, the school district can take the following steps to making the transition easier and more rewarding for new teachers:

- Develop policies that stress the importance of induction programs and that require their implementation.
- Work with local universities to offer classes and programs new teachers can take for college credit. In-service credits are available, as well as college course credit. A booklet with a listing of all courses available is provided to each district employee before the closing of the school year, and employees are encouraged to participate in this staff development and professional growth.
- Reimburse new teachers' tuition for courses designed to help them.

- Provide training for mentor teachers.
- Introduce new teachers to school board members and invite them to attend board meetings.
- Provide an in-depth orientation to the district that begins during the summer, before the hectic opening of school. Include facility and school tours, discussion about the organization, and introductions to key administrators.
- Hire substitute teachers to fill in so new teachers can observe the classes of exemplary teachers.
- **Interview new teachers at the end of the first year to find out whether and where they need additional help** (Tonneson and Patterson, 1992).

Although a beginning teacher induction program may exist in a school district, two groups of beginners may slip through the cracks of even the most structured programs. These groups include teachers employed after the start of the school year and itinerant staff such as speech therapists or music teachers. Because the first of the two groups misses the orientation activities conducted before school and the second group of teachers is not assigned to a specific building, their induction needs may be overlooked. Special efforts should be made to assist these teachers.

Acknowledging the importance of the district-wide orientation session and the conference(s) with the principal, the time for the new teacher to prepare the classroom and plan for instruction must be protected. Torgeson (1987) stated that this task is uppermost in the mind of beginning teachers.

PRINCIPAL'S ROLE IN THE INDUCTION PROGRAM

In addition to the orientation session, this would be an appropriate time for the principal to confer with the new employee. Time should be made available to hold several shorter conferences rather than one or two longer ones. It would be appropriate at this time for the principal to introduce the staff handbook.

The orientation process now becomes more personalized as the new employees are introduced to those with whom they will be working directly. The same components should apply at the building level as in the district orientation process.

The second segment of the orientation phase occurs upon the return of the experienced staff. During these days before school begins, the tempo of the preparation for the opening of school accelerates. The new teacher, like the veteran, needs to put the finishing touches on the classroom and then direct attention to planning for instruction.

A KEY IDEA

Besides orientation of the beginning teacher by the principal and teachers, provide for some time for the school secretary and custodian to meet with the new teachers.

It is during this time that the principal conducts the first staff meeting and reviews the staff handbook containing schedules, building policies, discipline procedures, and so on. The principal should see to it that the beginning teacher is introduced to "key" staff members and parents (Applegate, Flora, & Lasley, 1980). If it was not done earlier, the principal should make certain the new employee knows the location of teaching supplies and curriculum materials and how to requisition them.

As the opening of school approaches, the principal should confer with the beginning teachers about remaining questions, about supplies, and about final plans for the opening of school. This is the time for the principal to express confidence in and support for the new teacher. If ever a pep talk was needed, this is the time.

The principal assumes many roles in the beginning teacher's first-year experience. The role of the principal is vital to the success of the new teacher. Research indicates that inadequate support by administration contributes significantly to teacher attrition. As a principal you play a vital role in the retention of educators.

The first role of the principal is that of master teacher. The principal can ease the process of acculturation by holding regular sessions specifically designed to assist the new employee. These sessions may be held monthly, or weekly, but should be designed to target areas of concern to the beginning/new teacher. As a master teacher, the principal should provide recent information from journals and research, but also refer to experiences others have had during the induction period. Offer the new teacher tools for enhancing instructional techniques. Tools you may suggest to the new teacher include a voice-activated tape recorder or a video recorder. This will allow the teacher an opportunity for informal evaluation. Allan S. Vann (1991) suggested the following topics for orientation/induction meetings. This process may take several months, but helps alleviate the high dropout rate of beginning teachers.

Classroom Management	Classroom rules
	Effective techniques
	Assertive discipline
	Planning for early finishers
Instructional Techniques	Instructional guidelines
	Effective questioning
	Pause/wait time
Home-School Communication	Monthly newsletter
	Phone calls/notes/conferences
Conferencing	Meet the Teacher night
	Parent-teacher conferences
	Positive attitude
Grading and Testing	Frequent assessment
	Comments and reactions
	Checking assignments
Homework	District guidelines
Motivation	Techniques
Time Management	Time guidelines for subjects
	Overplanning vs. underplanning
	Gifted/average/handicapped time needs
Confidentiality	Avoiding gossip
	Maintaining confidentiality
Special Students	Contact with special education teachers
	Pullout assignments
	Referral process
Curriculum Priorities in Reading and Writing	Grade-level objectives
	Journals/silent reading
	Teaching of reading process
Unit/Lesson Planning	Techniques
	Unit plan model
	Sequential development
Curriculum Activity File	Sharing creative ideas
Professionalism	Professional associations
	Professional journals
	Activity beyond classroom

The principal must also serve as an evaluator of the beginning teacher. During the orientation phase, provide the beginning teacher with information that clarifies expectations in the classroom and how these will be evaluated. Establish an observation time with the teacher within the first month of school. Explain how the evaluation process will be implemented using the following cycle:

- Preobservation Conference
- Observation
- Data Analysis and Strategies
- Postobservation Conference
- Postconference Analysis

For this cycle to be effective, it is critical that the principal establish trusting relationships and furnish the teacher with objective data. Observations and evaluations should be timely and effective, providing the teacher with meaningful and applicable feedback for improvement.

Further, the principal needs to be a "guardian angel" for the new staff member. It is the principal's responsibility to limit the new teacher's cocurricular activities, committee involvement, teaching responsibilities, and student load. There will be plenty of time in the future to get involved.

An effective principal will invest time and commitment to the beginning teacher. If you consider this investment as one which affects the lives of hundreds of children each year, it is definitely worthwhile.

A KEY IDEA

Limit the role of the new teacher in extracurricular activities so that the focus can be on becoming successful in the classroom.

MENTOR PROGRAMS

Early in the orientation phase, a mentor teacher should be identified for the beginning teacher. The most important qualities for effective mentors are good communication skills, outstanding classroom skills, respect of their peers, and desire to participate (Loucks, 1993). Mentors are a source of support and advice to the new employee. Mentors serve as coaches, observing and providing feedback, while demonstrating effective techniques and strategies. Studies found that mentoring programs improve teaching, raise teachers' self-confidence, and increase teacher retention (Ladestro, 1991). Preparation of the mentor teacher is vital to the success of the mentorship, and should be addressed as a priority of the induction program.

> **A KEY IDEA**
>
> Select one of the best teacher mentors from your staff, pre-
> ferrably not the same grade or subject as the mentee. The
> new teacher will have plenty of opportunity to obtain assis-
> tance from teachers in the same grade or subject.

It is important that the district provide training for the mentor prior to the assumption of the new responsibility and continue that training throughout the mentoring process. Training of mentor teachers in relation to teacher induction programs should include school district philosophy, needs, and priorities; district policies and operating procedures; working with the adult learner; stages of teacher development; concerns and needs of beginning teachers; clinical supervision, classroom observation, and conferencing skills; teacher reflection, and fostering self-esteem and self-reliance in the novice teacher.

The mentor needs more than pedagogical skills; he or she must be able to communicate with the newcomer openly and supportively. Ideally, the mentor should be someone who enjoys the chance to learn from the helping relationship and who considers working with a newly trained teacher an opportunity to enhance his or her own skills. The mentor teacher is likely to influence more than the new teacher's instructional skills; the mentor can have a powerful impact upon the values and norms of the new teacher (Fagan and Walter, 1982).

Developmental relationships such as between a mentor teacher and protégé can be powerful stimuli for change and learning. Research indicates that mentors as well as beginning teachers find that the program enhances their classroom abilities, increases their enthusiasm for teaching, and that they experience positive results involving their teaching, professional growth, and impact on the profession. Teacher retention, collegial relationships, important decision making, development of visions, active learning, support of new professionals, promotion and maintenance of professional standards and emotional support are evidence of the impact a mentor program can have as part of the overall induction program.

With the grim reality of budget cuts, it is evident that school personnel must pursue other means of support for the survival of mentorship programs. Other alternatives to funding mentor programs include utilizing retired teachers to serve as mentors, principal coverage of teacher's classroom to allow the teacher to observe other teachers, and the Collaborative Induction Model, a zero-based budget program undertaken by the state of Texas. However it is funded, the importance of maintaining a mentor program is vital to the success and retention of the beginning teacher.

OPERATION PHASE

During the first month of school, the principal should monitor the performance of the beginning teacher carefully by visiting the teacher's classroom and initiating regular discussions with the new teacher. By the end of the month, both parties should begin to identify areas of interest and/or concern which may be addressed in an individually designed program for professional growth (see Figure 5.7).

FIGURE 5.7. MODEL TEACHER INDUCTION PROGRAM

With the teacher's needs identified, appropriate staff development activities may be selected. The principal may have already generated a list of possibilities he or she considered during the development phase of the building level induction program. Resources both within and outside the school district need to be considered.

Within the district, the principal and beginning teacher may select from available curriculum and instruction inservices. Observation of experienced teachers may be scheduled as well as a day or two of released time during which the beginner could do long-range planning. The principal should be committed to observations of classroom performance with prompt feedback. New teachers are not best left alone to learn (Ryan, 1979). Classroom visits and conferences support the beginner's instructional goals and prevent the teacher from repeating costly errors. The frequency of the visits, however, should be determined by the individual needs of the beginning teacher.

Sources independent of the school district may once again be used. For example, the local teachers' association may be encouraged to conduct sessions that explain the negotiated agreement and the goals of the organization. College and university bulletins may reveal worthwhile classes that are available locally. It may not be too early for the new teacher to inquire about advanced educational degrees or, at least, about requirements for permanent certification. The regional educational service districts that also conduct workshops and inservice sessions should be consulted. Lastly, community agencies may offer activities that provide information about the community as well as recreational benefits.

Once the list of appropriate activities has been selected, attention should be given to scheduling them in a balanced manner throughout the school year. By individualizing the selection, and jointly determining the schedule, the principal and beginning teacher have developed a long-range program of induction.

Throughout the implementation of this plan, the principal needs to closely monitor the progress being made by the beginning teacher. The principal should caution the new teacher to limit the building and district committee assignments during this busy first year and help the new teacher to say "no" when that response is in the best interest of the teacher and the instructional program.

EVALUATION PHASE

The final phase of the induction program is the evaluation phase (see Figure 5.8). This phase is important to provide data upon which to base

FIGURE 5.8. MODEL TEACHER INDUCTION PROGRAM

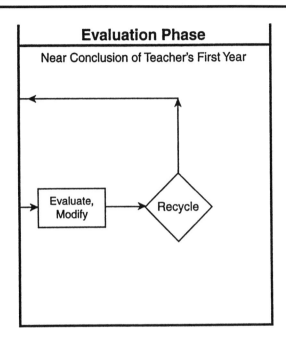

improvements to the program. The plan is then ready for recycling for the in-coming group of teachers.

Before the end of the school year, both the district and the building induc-tion programs need to be evaluated. On the district level, all beginning teachers need to be surveyed regarding their impressions of the compo-nents of the induction program. A New Teacher Questionnaire (Figure 5.9) is provided to serve as a model for receiving information. The comments and suggestions from this questionnaire should be used along with data from administrators to make needed improvements in the program.

At the building level, the principal and the beginning teacher need to evaluate the growth achieved and discuss future plans. Together they may decide there is less need for a formalized plan during the second year and may identify only a limited number of activities. Or there may be apparent needs which still need addressing through such a plan. In that case, a new in-dividualized plan may be developed. Figure 5.10 is the outline of a plan de-signed to help principals seek information from the new teacher regarding the induction program.

FIGURE 5.9. SAMPLE NEW TEACHER QUESTIONNAIRE

The purpose of this survey is to help us determine whether we've provided the needed support and orientation for you to assume successfully your new role as a professional teacher in our school or district.

Your candid thoughts and comments are welcome. Please do not sign this form. Thank you.

1. After you were hired, but before you moved to the district, your contact with school personnel made you feel:
    ___ very welcome   ___ somewhat welcome
    ___ somewhat unwelcome   ___ not welcome

2. How helpful were district personnel with your move?
    ___ very helpful   ___ somewhat helpful   ___ not helpful at all

3. What was your initial impression of the district's overall attitude to teaching and learning?
    ___ very professional   ___ somewhat professional
    ___ somewhat unprofessional   ___ very unprofessional

4. What is your current impression of the district's overall attitude to teaching and learning?
    ___ very professional   ___ somewhat professional
    ___ somewhat unprofessional   ___very unprofessional

5. Has the district lived up to your expectations?
    ___ very much so   ___ somewhat   ___not really   ___ not at all

6. Please describe what we did best to help you move to and join our school district from the moment you were hired until school started.
    _____
    _____

7. Please describe what we should have done better to help you move to and join our school district from the moment you were hired until school started.
    _____
    _____

8. Please describe in general terms how well we have done in supporting your first two months of teaching in the district.
    _____
    _____

9. Other comments: _____
    _____
    _____

Thank you very much for your response.

FIGURE 5.10. INDUCTION EVALUATION PLAN

Three Surveys

1. **Survey Of Impressions**
   Given during the second week of school to all new classified and certified staff
   > What did we do to assist your transition to our district?
   > What else could we have done to make your transition easier?
   > What are your impressions of our district's commitment to education?

2. **Survey of the Induction and Orientation Program**
   Given following the last training session to all classified and certified participants in the Induction and Orientation Program
   > Was the program offered at an appropriate time?
   > Did the environment make you feel comfortable?
   > Was the agenda put together in logical order?
   > Which event(s) were the most useful?
   > Which event(s) did you consider a waste of time?
   > Which topic(s) should be added next year?

3. **Survey of Mentor Program**
   Given in May to all classified and certified staff participants in the mentor program
   > How did you use your release time?
   > In what area(s) did you make observable progress?
   > Which training session(s) did you find the most useful?
   > Which topic(s) should be included next year?

RECOMMENDATIONS

The following activities are recommended for an effective induction program:

♦ Give teachers ample paid time to work in their classroom prior to the beginning of the school year—minimum of two days.

♦ Select, train, and compensate mentor teachers.

♦ Notify beginning teachers of grade and building assignment early. For teachers hired in spring or early summer, notification should occur no later than August 1.

♦ Provide the equivalent of five days of release time opportunities for the beginning teacher to observe other teachers, participate in joint planning, collaborate with mentor teacher, and participate in building and district level inservice aimed at assisting the teacher.

♦ Induction activities should be scheduled throughout the first year. The activities scheduled at the beginning of the year are necessary but not sufficient.

♦ Observe the beginning teacher early in the school year. This allows the principal to assist before the problems become great.

♦ Invite the local teachers' association and colleges to assist in the planning and implementation of induction activities. Look for ways to reduce the workload of the beginning teacher. For example, limit committee assignments. However, be cautious. Beginning teachers want to be considered as full participating members of the school team.

In the personnel selection process, teachers are reminded that they have only one opportunity to make a good first impression. Likewise, in inducting new teachers the district has only one such opportunity. A carefully designed induction program will not only create that kind of impression but also launch a productive, positive, and professional career teacher. The beginning teacher will be alert to even the minor courtesies. Figure 5.11 lists

FIGURE 5.11. SOME PRACTICAL IDEAS TO CONSIDER —LITTLE THINGS MEAN A LOT

Central Office	Principal
•Lunch/Banquet sponsored by Chamber of Commerce or local service club •Subscription to local newspaper •Housing information •Welcome by community leader •Extended contract •Introduction at board meeting •Presentation at board meeting •Presentation by business and/or personnel office •Personalized memo pads and/or business cards •Frame for diploma/certificate •Activities sponsored by Teachers' Association	•Tour of school neighborhood •Name tags for all staff during first week •Get acquainted potluck dinner with the new teachers as invited guests •Visit new teachers' classroom within two weeks •Schedule meeting for new teachers with secretary to discuss office procedures •Bulletin board with pictures and names of all staff title "Staffed for Excellence" •Send teachers' editions and curriculum guides during summer •Provide complimentary membership in PTA

some practical ideas for both the principal and the central office staff to consider to make an impact.

A Comprehensive Year-Long Calendar of Induction Activities

The induction program costs money but it should be considered an investment in both the teacher and the instructional program. The following is a list of some possible activities for the year-long induction program.

August

- Mentor teams selected
- Mentor teams meet for introductory activities and program overview
- Mentor teams discuss school procedures
- Staff retreat (2 days)
  - New staff introductions
  - Get acquainted activities
  - Review of building goals
  - Committees and calendar
  - Staff development goals and activities
  - Social time for staff
- Staff meeting at end of first day of school to discuss needs and celebrations
- Mentor meets informally with mentee to discuss first day

September

- Mentor seminar
  - Process for mentor training
  - Peer coaching
  - Observation/feedback techniques
  - Classroom management/organization/discipline

    Assignment: Mentor/mentee observe each other at least twice and engage in feedback discussions regarding management/organization/discipline

- Informal mentor/mentee meetings as needed
- Informal observations of mentee by building principal
- Mentor/mentee open house planning
- Principal/mentor program feedback meeting
- Principal/mentee program feedback meeting

October

- Mentor seminar
  - Classroom management/organization/discipline review and feedback
  - Curriculum and lesson planning (daily and long-range)
    Assignment: Mentee to observe a variety of methods for daily and long-range planning from at least three other staff members in addition to mentor
- Informal mentor/mentee meetings as needed
- Informal observations of mentee by building principal
- Principal/mentor program feedback meeting
- Principal/mentee program feedback meeting

November

- Mentor seminar
  - Daily and long-range curriculum planning review and feedback
  - Student evaluation
    Assignment: Mentee to observe a variety of assessment and record-keeping strategies from at least three other staff members in addition to mentor
- Mentor/mentee report card planning and procedures
- Mentor/mentee parent conference planning and procedures
- Goal setting and planning for formal observation by building principal
- Preobservation conferences with building principal
- Formal observations of mentee by building principal
- Postobservation conferences with building principal

- ◆ Informal mentor/mentee meetings as needed
- ◆ Staff Development Inservice (all staff)
  - Authentic assessment
  - Performance-based criteria
  - State guidelines
  - District guidelines
  - SLIG grant decisions
  - Blending of learning objectives and exit outcomes

December

- ◆ Mentor seminar
  - Student evaluation review and feedback
  - Parent communication and involvement

    Assignment: Mentee to meet and discuss parent involvement and communication strategies with at least three other staff members in addition to the mentor
- ◆ Informal Mentor/mentee meetings as needed
- ◆ Informal observations of mentee by building principal and mentor
- ◆ Mentor/mentee meet to discuss management and discipline progress

January

- ◆ Mentor seminar
  - Parent communication and involvement review and feedback
  - Building a professional network of support

    Assignment: Mentee to observe teachers of same grade level or subject area in same building or other district sites. Mentee given release time to observe. Mentor/mentee meet to discuss observations and share ideas for building professional network
- ◆ Mentee makes contacts with others not observed to add to network

- Informal mentor/mentee meetings as needed
- Informal observations of mentee by building principal and mentor
- Mentor/mentee discuss semester grading procedures
- Mentor/mentee discuss daily and long-range curriculum planning progress
- Principal/mentor program feedback meeting
- Principal/mentee program feedback meeting
- Mentee builds network with classified staff and other administrators in the district
- Mentee attends regional workshop or other professional growth inservice to expand knowledge and network

February

- Mentor seminar
  - Building a network of support review and feedback
  - Goal setting and planning for improvement

    Assignment: Mentor/mentee set goals for improvement. Mentor/mentee to plan changes. Mentee to implement changes. Mentor to observe mentee again. Mentor to provide feedback to mentee to self-reflect.
- Informal mentor/mentee meetings as needed
- Mentor/mentee to discuss student evaluation progress
- Informal observation of mentee by building principal
- Staff Development Inservice (all staff)
  - Student assessment continued
  - Portfolios presentation by outside expert
  - Alternative assessment strategies
  - Pilot program developments discussed
  - Attendance at assessment workshop opportunities discussed

March

- Mentor seminar

- Goal setting and planning for improvement review and feedback
- Meeting the needs of culturally diverse students

    Assignment: Mentee to observe culturally diverse classrooms in district or out of district. Mentor/mentee discuss methods for meeting the diverse needs of all students in class. Mentee brings in outside visitors to bring cultural diversity opportunities to class. Mentee becomes sensitive to diversity issue.

- Informal mentor/mentee meetings as needed
- Informal observations by building principal and mentor
- Mentor/mentee to discuss parent communication and involvement progress
- Principal/mentor program feedback meeting
- Principal/mentee program feedback meeting

April

- Mentor seminar
    - Meeting the needs of culturally diverse students review and feedback
    - Meeting the needs of inclusion students

    Assignment: Mentee to spend time with and observe resource, chapter, behavioral, and functional teachers. Mentee to discuss strategies for meeting needs of inclusion students with both special education and regular education staff members. Mentor/mentee to discuss specific strategies and plans.

- Informal Mentor/mentee meetings as needed
- Mentor/mentee meet to discuss goal setting/improvement progress
- Informal observations by building principal and mentor
- Mentor/mentee meet to plan third quarter report cards and conferences
- Principal/mentor program feedback meeting

♦ Principal/mentee program feedback meeting

May

♦ Mentor seminar
  • Meeting the needs of inclusion students review and feedback
  • Conflict resolution techniques
    Assignment: Mentee to meet with intervention specialist to discuss conflict resolution techniques. Mentee to attend inservice on conflict resolution. Mentor/mentee develop plan for implementing conflict resolution strategies.
♦ Informal mentor/mentee meetings as needed
♦ Mentor/mentee discuss culturally diverse and inclusion progress
♦ Mentor/mentee discuss end-of-year discipline and management
♦ Principal/mentor program feedback meeting
♦ Principal/mentee program feedback meeting
♦ Informal observations by building principal and mentor
♦ Staff Development Inservice (all staff)
  • Assessment continued
  • Planning for changes in assessment for next year
  • Analyze improvements made this year
  • Committees for continued progress formed
  • Staff retreat agenda planned

June

♦ Mentor/mentee/principal discuss summative issues for mentor program
♦ Mentor/mentee discuss year-end procedures
♦ Mentor/mentee plan year-end report card and student placement
♦ Mentor/mentee develop plan for ongoing informal support next year

◆ Mentor/mentee celebrate a successful year
◆ Building principal/mentee discuss ongoing educational opportunities for continued growth

July

◆ Mentee rests and starts thinking with excitement about next year

CONCLUSION

Orientation and the induction of the new teacher is a critical component of an effective human resources program. Considerable time and money is often spent in the recruiting and selection phase, whereas, orientation and induction are often not well done or not done at all. The components of an effective induction program include:

◆ orientation
◆ mentorships/cohort groups
◆ timely and frequent formative evaluations
◆ inservice workshops on effective teaching, assessment methods, and classroom management techniques
◆ ongoing staff development
◆ reasonable workload assignments (i.e., manageable preps, a balanced heterogeneous mix of students, gradual inclusion into committee or extracurricular responsibilities, and possibly extra planning time built into the daily schedule)
◆ opportunities to observe other effective teachers
◆ opportunities for team teaching
◆ clear expectations

REFERENCES

Applegate, J.H., V.R. Flora, and T.J. Lasley (1980). New teachers seek support. *Educational Leadership*, 38 (1), 74–76.

Armstrong, C. (1993, Sept.). Do's and don'ts for beginning teachers. *Principal*, 73 (1), 30–31.

Badertscher, J.A. (1978). *Inducting newly placed teachers: Orientation responsibilities of the school administrator.* U.S. Educational Resources Information Center, ERIC Document No. ED 155 805.

Bradley, H.W., and J.F. Eggleston (1978). An induction year experiment. *Educational Research,* 20 (2).

Callari, C.L. (1990, Winter). Beginning teacher induction: The bridge to life-long learning. *Education,* 111, 260–264.

Fagan, M., and G. Walter (1982). Mentoring among teachers. *Journal of Educational Research,* 76 (2), 112–118.

Freshhour, D., and R. Hollman (1990, Sept.). Orienting new teachers for maximum effectiveness. *NASSP Bulletin,* 74 (527), 78–83.

Garten, T., et al. (1993, Sept.). Teacher induction using a shared lesson design model. *NASSP Bulletin,* 77 (554), 76–81.

Goldman, P. (1988, Winter). Introducing the new teacher to the school: Lessons for administrators. *OSSC Report,* 28 (2), 1–7.

Hadaway, N. (1993, Winter). Circumventing the funding issues in induction. *Action in Teacher Education,* 14 (4), 24–29.

Harris, B.H., and B.J. Monk (1992). *Personnel administration in education.* Boston: Allyn and Bacon.

Heck, R. (1988, Nov.-Dec.). Planning and implementing a teacher induction program. *Thrust,* 18 (3), 50–52.

Helping newcomers adjust. (1992, May). *Front Line Supervisor's Bulletin.*

Hofman, J. and H. Feldlaufer (1992, Nov.-Dec.). Involving veteran teachers in a state induction program. *Clearing House,* 66 (2), 101–103.

Huling-Austin, L. (1992, May-June). Research on learning to teach: Implications for teacher induction and mentoring programs. *Journal of Teacher Education,* 43 (3), 173–180.

Huling-Austin, L. (1986, Jan.-Feb.). What can and cannot reasonably be expected from teacher induction programs. *Journal of Teacher Education,* 37 (1), 2–5.

Jensen, M.C. (1987). *How to recruit, induct and retain the very best teachers.* Eugene, OR: ERIC Clearinghouse on Educational Management.

Ladestro, D. (1991, Oct.). Learning from the experienced. *Teacher Magazine,* 3 (2), 20–21.

Lawson, H.A. (1992, May-June). Beyond the new conception of teacher induction. *Journal of Teacher Education,* 43 (3), 163-172.

Loucks, H.E. (1993, Sept.). Teacher induction: A success story. *Principal,* 73 (1), 27–29.

Natale, J. (1993, July). Why teachers leave. *Executive Educator,* 15 (7), 14–18.

Newcombe, E. (1990). *Perspectives on teacher induction.* Philadelphia: Research for Better Schools.

Odell, S., and D. Ferraro (1992, May-June). Teacher mentoring and teacher retention. *Journal of Teacher Education,* 43 (3), 200–204.

Rebore, R.W. (1987). *Personnel administration in education: A management approach,* 2nd ed. Englewood Cliffs, NJ: Prentice-Hall.

Reinhartz, J. (Ed.) (1989). *Teacher induction.* Washington, DC: NEA.

Rosenholtz, S.J. (1989, March). Workplace conditions that affect teacher quality and commitment: Implications for teacher induction programs. *The Elementary School Journal,* 89 (4), 421–439.

Ryan, K., et al. (1979). My teacher education program? Well...first year teachers reflect and react. *Peabody Journal of Education,* 59 (2), 267–271.

Ryan, K. (1986). *The induction of new teachers.* Bloomington, IN: Phi Delta Kappa.

Schempp, P.G., A.C. Sparkes, and T.J. Templin (1993, Fall). The micropolitics of teacher induction. *American Educational Research Journal,* 30 (3), 447–472.

Schaffer, E., S. Stingfield, and D. Wolfe (1992, May-June). An innovative beginning teacher induction program: A two-year analysis of classroom interactions. *Journal of Teacher Education,* 43 (3), 181–192.

Schell, L.M., and P. Burden (1992). *Countdown to the first day of school.* Washington, DC: NEA.

Shelton, M., et al. (1992, Jan). Great beginnings. *Executive Educator,* 14 (1), 27–29.

Tomlin, M. (1993, March). The evolution of new teachers. *Executive Educator,* 15 (2), 39–40.

Tonnsen, S., and S. Patterson (1992, Jan.). Fighting first year jitters. *Executive Educator,* 14 (1), 29–30.

Torgeson, L.M. (1987). *Teacher induction: A study of practices involving beginning elementary teachers in the greater Puget Sound area with a recommended model for implementation.* Ed.D. Dissertation, Seattle University.

Vann, A. (1991, Sept.). A guide to orienting new teachers. *Principal,* 71 (1), 14–16.

Webb, L.D., et al. (1987). *Personnel administration in education: New issues and new needs in human resource management.* New York: Merrill.

Wisley, E.A. (1984). A comparison of the perceptions of beginning elementary teachers and their principals of the forms of assistance for beginning teachers. Ed.D. Dissertation, Oklahoma State University.

Young, T., et. al. (1993, Jan.-Feb.). Helping new teachers: The performance enhancement model. *Clearing House,* 66 (3), 174–176.

6

SUPERVISION AND EVALUATION

REASONS FOR STUDYING SUPERVISION AND EVALUATION

- The supervision of the instructional process is the "quality control" element of student learning.
- The failure of the principal to evaluate is in many instances *prima facie* evidence for the principal's dismissal.
- Teachers need feedback on their performance. If they are doing well they need to be told. If they are not doing well, they need to be told *and helped*!
- Doesn't it make sense that if you are the instructional leader, you need to be very involved with the instructional process?

> *When the process of teacher evaluation is supportive and collegial...the evaluation process will be perceived, by teachers, to be more positive.*
>
> Stiggins and Bridgeford, 1985

INTRODUCTION

Teacher evaluation may be the principal's single most important activity. The evaluation process presents the principal with the opportunity to stimulate growth and improve teacher performance as well as to recognize quality instruction. This chapter is designed to give principals greater understanding of this important process and provide several useful hands-on tools to make the process of evaluation easier to understand and accomplish.

The following quote from "Teacher Evaluation as a Strategy for Improving Instruction" (Weber, 1987) provides a very useful introduction and sets the stage for the presentation of current information and strategies to help the principal perform in a more competent and professional manner.

> The history of teacher evaluation in the public schools of the United States has been marred by a tension between including teachers' input and applying standards from administrative criteria. From the last decade of the nineteenth century, teacher education has been increasingly humanized by including more concerns for the development of teachers' skills.
>
> Before the turn of the century, teacher "inspection" was the evaluation method most frequently practiced. Administrators, who did not need to be trained in teaching or observing, observed teachers for their conformity to district expectations. These expectations could be personal as well as professional. Evaluations might focus on critiques of student behavior for instance, or on a teacher's personality—including out-of-class activities.
>
> The emphasis then shifted to the efficiency of teaching and the "scientific management" of students and school personnel. After this interest in efficiency and economy of effort, however, administrators began to see the need to cooperate with teachers in evaluations. Researchers, too, began to isolate significant teaching behaviors, warranting the belief that good teaching can be developed with adequate attention and effort. By the postWorld War II period, cooperation between supervisors and teachers was an assumption in the research, if not in the majority of schools (Peterson 1982). Through the influence of clinical supervision

approaches, concern for mutual effort and reciprocity are features of nearly all new models of supervision.

On the other hand, as evaluation turned more democratic in theory (if not in the practice of most schools), it has been matched by a growing public pressure for teacher accountability. The result has been numerous programs that combine the historical gains in development-centered evaluations with accountability strategies aimed at ensuring minimum standards and encouraging maximum effort.

In the effort to improve teaching, a great deal of energy has recently been directed at improving teacher evaluations. At the policy-making level, states and school districts have been initiating programs to accelerate schools' procedures for dismissing incompetent teachers or improving competent teachers. For example, in 1985 Kansas began a state-wide, legislatively approved internship program for teachers. Local committees, consisting of administrators and senior teachers (assessed, assisted, and supported) all first-year teachers.

When the teacher evaluation process is carried out effectively and sensitively, the teacher can grow and become more productive. But when the evaluation is conducted ineffectively or insensitively, there are usually troublesome consequences. Teachers can feel insulted or misunderstood; their self-esteem and sense of job security are threatened. Students lose out because their teachers are less effective than they could be. The entire school organization can become tense, and its members can become overly competitive, and distrustful. The entire ambiance can be adversely affected by poorly conducted teacher evaluations.

It is essential, therefore, that the principal develop a thorough understanding of this process and an ability to accomplish it in a competent and professional manner.

The process of teacher evaluation has evolved significantly in the United States in the past century. As Weber noted, in the public schools of the 1800s the process was primarily known as "teacher inspection." As the name implies, it consisted of the administrator periodically observing the teacher to see if the rules were being followed and the established expectations were being met. The observers were the school officials, people who usually were not trained in teaching or supervising.

Predictably, these supervisors scrutinized the teacher's professional and personal behavior in and out of the classroom, as well as values and ideologies. There was generally no sense of reciprocity in which the teacher's viewpoint or professional creativity might have been considered, nor was there any particular effort to enhance the teacher's capacities to do a better job. In such a climate there was little opportunity for professional growth and development, but there was considerable fear, and reluctance to learn or try innovative teaching strategies.

Gradually through the early decades of the twentieth century, changes in supervision and evaluation methods took place as teaching and educational administration became established as professions. The first shift accompanied the trends toward "scientific management" in education, when a primary consideration was gaining the maximum efficiency from teachers. Ultimately supervisors came to recognize the importance of cooperation with teachers in their evaluations.

The components of a successful evaluation process consist of (a) a preobservation conference, (b) the classroom observation, (c) the analysis of data from the lesson and planning of postobservation conference, (d) the postobservation conference, and (e) the conference check-up. See Figure 6.1.

THE PREOBSERVATION CONFERENCE

Most teachers remember the first time they were officially observed. They remember because the event was pivotal in their careers, their professional developments, and especially because they weren't really sure what the process or result would be. The event is so important in the lives of most young teachers that it is usually anticipated with heightened emotions. Some regard it with dread, anxiety, or even fear, while others look forward to it as an opportunity to display their professional skills in front of the principal. It may be helpful for the principal to remember the emotion prior to his or her first evaluation by the superintendent.

Because the first official observation is so crucial and filled with so many uncertainties, it is possible, maybe even probable, that the conference will provide a distorted picture of what the teacher can and is doing. To make an assessment based on the data thus acquired could be inaccurate and ultimately damaging to the teacher, the students, and the entire school. On the other hand, when the principal is helpful and supportive, the teacher's acceptance of an appraisal and satisfaction with the principal increases.

A competent and careful principal wants to minimize these risks and get the most accurate picture possible in the observation. One of the most effective techniques to achieve this is the preobservation conference.

FIGURE 6.1. TEACHER EVALUATION PROCESS

Task		Suggested Deadline Date

Task   **Suggested Deadline Date**

I. **First Teachers' Meeting**   (August-September)
    At the first teachers' meeting the principal should review the
    evaluation process with the staff:

    A. This should be completed before the pre-observation
        conference
    B. Review the general job description with teachers and
        co-curricular supervisors
    C. Review Code of Professional Conduct or Code of Ethics
        for Teachers and School Employees — give to all employees

II. **First Observation**

    A. Pre-observation conference   (October-November)
        1. Collect information about the lesson and the
            class
        2. Discuss the teacher's lesson plans/objectives
            for the lesson

    B. Classroom observation   (October-November)
        1. Collect data based on questions posed in the
            pre-observation conference

    C. Analysis of the lesson in detail   (Within 24 Hrs.)
        1. Cite evidence from the anecdotal record
        2. Discuss the strengths and weaknesses of the
            lesson

    D. Post-observation conference   (Within 24 Hrs.)
        1. The purpose of the conference is to review the
            lesson and to point out methods and techniques
            that will improve instruction.

    E. Follow-up observations and conferences as needed

III. **Second Observation**   (February-March)

    A. Same process as first observation

    B. Teacher shares progress with yearly goals

IV. **Formal Evaluation**   (April-May 15)

    A. The formal evaluation is written sometime after the
        second observation and before May 15. (Check the laws
        and requirements of your state and/or district. They may be
        different.)

    B. Evaluation conference
        1. Share the formal written evaluation with the teacher.
        2. Initiate preliminary discussion regarding goals for
            the next school year.

Such a conference has the same function and procedure as a rehearsal has for an actor or public speaker. It is analogous to a teacher giving a sample test to students to help them know what to expect. The preobservation conference can assuage anxiety and enable the teacher to focus on the task at hand rather than on peripheral issues. It shows the teacher that the principal wants the process to be fair and wants to give the teacher every chance to do well. It demonstrates the fact that the principal and the teacher are in a collaboration to achieve the best possible outcome, rather than in an adversarial relationship whose purpose is ultimately to dismiss or humiliate the teacher.

Preobservation conferences have many other benefits, both for the teacher and the observer (Sweeney, 1989). They promote trust and positive relationships; clarify the lesson objectives; identify the teaching/learning activities that will be utilized to reach those objectives; and provide insight into follow-up lessons. The teacher can inform the principal in advance about the classroom environment and any individuals who might require special attention. The preobservation conference also affords teachers the opportunity to indicate the specific areas on which they want the principal to provide feedback.

The principal can use the preobservation conference to provide the teacher with specific information about what topics, characteristics, or issues will be focused on in both the observation and postobservation conference. Figure 6.2 is a comprehensive guide to the preobservation process which the beginning principal would do well to follow. Figure 6.3 (p. 159) is an abbreviated form that the more experienced principal might want to use.

Preobservation conferences can take many different formats. Since the needs and experiences of teachers vary, the type of conference that is best suited for one may be ill-suited for another. Moreover, the type of preconferences that are best for teachers at early points in their careers may be contraindicated for the same teachers at later stages. Thus, the wise principal will use the procedure and format that most closely approximates the specific needs of the teacher to be observed.

For example, seasoned veteran teachers who have long known and worked with the principal could be approached more informally. Most of them would probably be more comfortable dropping into the principal's office for an informal discussion about the official observation. On the other hand, a new teacher who has not yet had an extensive relationship with the principal would probably derive greater benefit from a more formal and extensive conference. This gives both the teacher and the principal a chance to

(Text continues on page 160.)

FIGURE 6.2. PREOBSERVATION PLANNING QUESTIONNAIRE

(For the principal to use with the teacher in the pre-observation conference)

1. Objective:

    a. What do you plan to teach in this period of instruction?

    b. What should the students know or be able to do as a result of instruction of this content?

2. Content:

    a. What factors were considered in selecting content for this lesson?

    b. How did you determine that students were ready for this lesson?

    c. How did you decide how much content would be taught in this period of instruction?

    d. How is the content related to previous and/or future lessons?

    e. What elements of content will be emphasized in this lesson?

3. Materials:

    a. What materials are to be used for instruction and why were these selected?

    b. What preparation of materials is required prior to the beginning of the lesson?

    c. What plans have you made for managing materials during instruction?

4. Activities:

    a. What activities will be included in this lesson and for what purpose?

    b. How will you conduct each of these activities?

    c. What is the sequence of activities to be used?

    d. How will the classes be organized for instructional activities?

After a successful preconference, the principal should use the following steps and concepts in order to provide for the continued professional growth of the teacher.

5.   Evaluation: How will you determine that the intended learning has taken place?

      a.   Analyze and label the data using the elements of instruction as the criteria.

      b.   Can the teacher: -Teach to an objective?
                                      -Select the correct level of difficulty for the
                                         learners?
                                      -Monitor the learner and adjust the teaching?
                                      -Use (not abuse) the principles of learning?

      c.   Look for: -Elements of lesson design
                                      -Organization of the materials
                                      -Effective use of audio-visuals
                                      -Good questioning techniques, wait time,
                                         delving, some higher thinking level
                                         questions
                                      -Clear directions
                                      -Recognition of learning styles
                                      -Classroom management techniques
                                      -Time-on-task
                                      -Student participation, amount and variety of
                                         students

      d.   Cite evidence for reinforcing (label +) and evidence for those things that
            need to be refined (label -).

6.   The conference takes place between the principal and the teacher. The purpose of
      the conference is to review the lesson and to point out methods and techniques
      which enhanced learning and which need to be improved.

7.   Follow-Up Observation:

      A follow-up observation is made to check improvement in the area of focus
      decided during the conference.

      The principal can see if the good skills have been maintained and if the new skill
      has been incorporated into the lesson. If change is not achieved for a new skill, the
      principal keeps teaching in an effort to reach the desired outcome.

      A conference with the teacher should follow this observation.

8.   The important keys to the success of teacher evaluations lie in the relationship of
       the principal to the staff (feelings of trust) and the ability of the principal to furnish
       the teacher with objective (hard) data.

9.   Furthermore, principals intent on improving instruction will make sure they have
       the following components included in the evaluation program each year:

       •   The pre-observation conference

       •   The observation

       •   The analysis and strategies session.
               - What took place?
               - How to present your finding to the teacher?

       •   The post-observation conference
               - Formative evaluation
               - Summative evaluation

       •   The conference check-up
               - Conclusion

FIGURE 6.3. PREOBSERVATION INFORMATION

Teacher: _____

Grade: _____

Subject/Lesson: _____

Time: _____ Date: _____

1.   What are the objectives? (skills, attitudes, knowledge)

2.   Where are you in the course or lesson? (unit, lesson, page numbers in texts, introductory, middle or culminating activity)

3.   What instructional methods are you going to use?

4.   How will you know if the students have learned?

5.   What particular teaching behaviors do you want monitored?

6.   What special characteristics of the students should be noted (unusual behaviors, group interactions, students leaving during class, lab work, etc.)?

learn more about what is to be observed, and about the conditions of the observation.

Whether the preobservation interaction is formal or informal, brief or extensive, the very least it must do is establish clearly when the evaluation is to take place and the purpose of the evaluation. In almost all instances the principal also asks for input regarding the purpose and direction of the evaluation. Beyond these minimal requirements of the preobservation, the principal uses professional judgment in determining, providing, and obtaining whatever additional information is necessary to make the evaluation beneficial for all.

A KEY IDEA

Teachers generally do good work and as such should be praised. For those who are experiencing difficulty, they need to be helped. In both cases and especially in the latter, timing is crucial. It is recommended that teachers new to the principal and the building be visited during the first two weeks of the school year. Such a visit can save a great deal of time later if the principal must deal with remediation.

THE OBSERVATION

To many less experienced teachers, the supervisor's direct observation may seem like the beginning and end of the evaluation process. After all, they might think, once it's over, there's nothing to do but go back to normal. While direct observation is important, even essential, it is by no means the whole of it. It is analogous to "data gathering" in the research process: Researchers need the raw data but until they have studied, analyzed, looked at the data from different viewpoints and in different contexts, and compared and interpreted the data objectively, the data are virtually meaningless. So, too, with the observation. It is important, but merely one step in a multistage process. As such, the teacher must be made aware that many more steps must occur for the evaluation to become truly meaningful.

What gives credence to the observation is the fact that all the subsequent interpretations that are made will be based on the information gathered during this phase. If the information is inaccurate, distorted, or unrepresentative, then all the subsequent phases in the evaluation process will also be distorted. Therefore, the careful principal must do everything possible to assure that the data obtained in the observation are valid.

Even the most capable and observant supervisor sometimes fails to get accurate information out of the observation. The teacher, who is usually very capable, might experience a sudden and atypical panic reaction to the unaccustomed scrutiny. A student, who is usually well-behaved, might disrupt the class in a way that no one had anticipated or for which they were not prepared. Or the principal might be overly tired or rushed from the press of other obligations and likely to miss details that would otherwise be noted as important. Such circumstances are common, even inevitable; so too are a myriad of other variables that influence the dynamics of a complex social group such as a classroom, especially when the principal-observer is introduced into that situation to further change it in unforseeable ways.

While such circumstances are unavoidable, they need not preclude a principal's acquisition of good and accurate data if the right precautions are taken. One precaution is for the principal to always distinguish between events over which the teacher has (or should have) control, and those events which are not controllable by the teacher. After all, the evaluation is about teacher performance, not the degree to which a classroom meets some social ideal. For example, a regular classroom teacher who has no classroom aide but is responsible for the education of a student with a severe disability and 30 other students, should not be compared unfavorably with a teacher who does have an aide or no students with disabilities.

One tool that is helpful to many principals in acquiring relevant, complete, and accurate data is the use of *scripting*. Several examples of this method are found in Figures 6.4 and 6.5. The principal should keep focused on what is relevant, and to ignore peripheral but distorting side issues. For example, a principal might be attentive to the classroom environment and forget to observe how the class members interact—until reminded by the observational guide to look for it.

Of course, no observational guide can provide the principal with all the cues and reminders of what to watch for. Continuing self-development and self-awareness are as important for the administrator as for the teacher being observed. The principal must be wary of personal biases or blind spots and must have the flexibility to recognize that many different teaching styles can be effective. If the principal has a preconceived notion that only one teaching style is the best and judges every teacher by that standard, an invalid observation may be conducted.

Objectivity is crucial in the observation process. It is important for the administrator to keep the overall purpose of the evaluation in mind and

FIGURE 6.4. SAMPLE CLASSROOM OBSERVATION

Teacher: (Elementary)
Subject: Math
Date:
Time: 1:50 to 2:22
Observer:

I.   When I entered your room, the students were ready to take a timed math test.
        A.   After the test, the students corrected each other's papers.
        B.   They turned the papers in to you, at your request.

II.   You moved from that activity to a new lesson.
        A.   You passed out worksheets for a new lesson.
        B.   You passed out some beans for the students to use on this activity.
        C.   You gave directions for the worksheet.
                1.   _____, direction-giving is one of the most important aspects of
                        setting the stage for proper and correct learning. When we give directions,
                        it is most important that we do the following:
                        1.1   Plan and think through the directions in advance to determine
                                a.   How many different things must the student remember to
                                        do?
                                b.   Which of these has been done before, and which are new to
                                        him?
                                c.   Can the student do new things if he or she tries?
                                d.   How many directions must be given at one time?
                                e.   When is the best time to give these directions?
                                f.   What is the best sequence for the directions and what must
                                        be given at the same time?
                                g.   Should the directions be written or verbal?
                        1.2   Giving directions to individual students involves these steps:
                                a.   Getting the students attention.
                                b.   Giving the directions in a way that reflects conscientious
                                        planning.
                                c.   Checking understanding.
                                d.   Modeling the behavior desired.
                                e.   Translating into action the directions.
                                f.   Redirecting if necessary.

III.   When the students started to work after the initial directions, many questions continued to
        be asked throughout the lesson.

        A.   I would suggest that you make sure you include these steps when you are teaching
                a lesson to ensure proper understanding of the intent of the objective:
                1.   _____, which involves putting the focus in the
                        mind of the learner on what it is you desire.

2.   Where you are going with what you intend for them to learn.
        2.1   An explanation of what you want them to learn. Make clear what is unclear.
        2.2   Modeling the example so that the students understand perfectly what you want.
        2.3   The instructional part.
        2.4   How you present it to them.
3.   Questions:
        3.1   What questions did students ask to make sure that the explanation is clear.
        3.2   Monitor and adjust activity to make sure that they understand and are doing it correctly.
4.   Activities:
        4.1   Have them do assignment. Monitor and rotate during the assignment to make sure they are learning also.
5.   Response to the efforts of the learners.
        5.1   Reinforcement of students' activity to make sure that their responses are being rewarded.
6.   Closure:
        6.1   To articulate in the mind of the learner what he or she has learned: putting it all together.
        6.2   Reviewing, summarizing what was learned.
        6.3   Putting the learning into practice. What is so important about what they have just learned? What did you want them to learn from that activity?
B.   This type of organization makes sure you have set the stage necessary to get the desired learning from your students.

IV.   Class Management.
        A.   During this time period, at least 10% of your time was spent correcting students.
        B.   Good class management is important and you should insist on it.
                1.   When you say I want no talking, mean it.
                        a.   Do not talk over the top of your students. Insist on quiet.
                        b.   If they are not quiet, have a consequence in mind for their actions.
        C.   You should use more positive reinforcement. I *did* not detect one incident where you praised a student during this lesson.

V.   _____, lesson planning is the most important first step of an effective lesson. I would like you to turn in your plan book to _____ every day as you leave.

VI.   Please make an appointment to discuss my observation.

Date _____   Teacher _____

Date _____   Observer _____

FIGURE 6.5. SAMPLE OBSERVATION REPORT

Teacher: School: Junior High
Date: Subject: Language Arts
Time: 9:50 - 10:40   Observer:

LESSON OBJECTIVE

The objective of the lesson was to enable students to write a response letter of a minimum of three paragraphs and to use appropriate introductory and closing and addressing procedures.

LESSON DESIGN

After the bell rang at 9:50, students were told about upcoming projects and tasks to be done in ensuing days and hours. You reviewed with the students the results of a previous project which included an analysis of a book or movie or play, etc. You reminded students that they were supposed to have taken care of adminstrivia, plot, and most importantly, opinion and substantiation for that opinion. Following that, you began a modeling activity which demonstrated how an analysis of a TV show might occur. The example used was the Cosby show; the model was to identify two issues. These issues included family values and humor. On the board, you wrote "family values," underlined it, and next to it wrote "humor" and underlined that. You then requested students to provide specific examples underneath "humor." Family values included such items as family trust, honesty, etc. Following that, you wrote instructions on the board concerning three paragraphs for the project of the day. The instructions included:

a.   An imaginary response to an imaginary person who had written a previous letter.
b.   Piece of recurrent news.
c.   An inquiry.

Then you gave instructions that you would provide the stationery. On the board also, you provided a block model of the location of the return address, the introductory remarks, the body, and conclusion. Students worked on that project until approximately 10:40.

LESSON ANALYSIS

In analyzing the lesson, it was clear that you had an objective, which was consistent with the previous day's work, and followed that activity, which was logically related to the previous assignment. You developed appropriate models and appropriate input methods to demonstrate the important points of the assignment. You demonstrated appropriate use of feedback and interest-generating devices with frequent utilization of humor. An on-task analysis was developed, and the result of that analysis showed that the class had an average on-task analysis for a ten-minute period of 71%. The on-task behavior varied from a low of 68% to a high of 88% during the appraisal period. The analysis also demonstrated that there was an increase of on-task behavior at each subsequent two-minute checkpoint to where the last checkpoint had the highest on-task behavior of 88%. This information indicates that for the plotted period, the amount of on-task behavior was below what would be wanted in that situation. The recommendation is that the students be given guided opportunity to practice the task prior to assigning the independent work which should increase the on-task behavior and decrease the number of questions that occurred during the class period. The monitoring that you did was appropriate. However, a number of the questions possibly could have been eliminated by employing one activity which would be to have the group work through a specific example prior to assigning the independent work.

SUMMARY

In summary, you demonstrated the ability to select an appropriate objective, to analyze the objective, and to provide appropriate input and models related to that objective. Increased focus on guided practice, or giving the students a specific example from which to work, should increase on-task behavior and decrease questions during the independent phase of the lesson.

Thank you for the opportunity to observe.

Date _____   Teacher _____

Date _____   Observer _____

recognize that the observation is only to gather data, not to project one's own agenda onto the event being observed. The principal must remember that the data-gathering part of the evaluation is:

- ♦ concerned with overt observable behaviors and concrete, specific facts rather than inferences, assumptions, or explanations
- ♦ based on the actual performance of the teacher, rather than the teacher's personality traits or background
- ♦ related to the present performance only, rather than past performances or reports about past performances made by different supervisors
- ♦ to determine the teacher's needs rather than the administrator's wants
- ♦ focused on specific information that can be useful, not overwhelming, to the teacher
- ♦ an attempt to distinguish between observed events that lie within the teacher's control and those over which the teacher has no control
- ♦ a process that requires objective, thorough, and well-documented notes

The principal who has taken comprehensive notes of the objective facts can later meet with the teacher and reconstruct the observation with more validity and reliability. Objective notes are important to the next phase in the evaluation process, the analysis.

ANALYSIS

...analysis exists for the sake of understanding true events in order to exercise greater control over future events.

Goldhammer, 1969

To *fail to plan* is to *plan to fail*. Since the evaluation is based on performance, the first step after the observation is to analyze what was observed. Thus, during the observation, it is critically important that an inclusive record of events be maintained. This collection of data provides the basis for decisions concerning the performance areas to be covered in the postobservation conference. It is helpful for the principal to think like a teacher during this step of the process. This part is analogous to the planning of the lesson:

you know the material and the "student." Now, how are you going to present the material so that teaching effectiveness improves and student learning takes place?

Critical questions for the principal to focus on during the analysis stage include the following:

♦ What techniques or strategies do I want to reinforce, encourage growth in, or stimulate the teacher to think about?

♦ What are the answers to the questions and concerns posed during the preobservation conference?

♦ What behavior or strategy had the greatest impact on teaching/learning behaviors?

♦ Was the lesson objective clearly stated and did the teacher stay on target by:

   • giving directions and explanations relevant to the learning task?

   • asking questions relevant to the learning task?

   • conducting activities relevant to the learning task?

   • responding to learners in ways relevant to the learning task?

♦ Were teaching opportunities outside of the stated objectives present and if so, did the instructor show flexibility and creativity?

♦ Did the instructor select objectives that were at the correct level for the students?

♦ Were there levels of opportunity for learning that met the needs of all students in the class?

♦ Were most learners able to experience success?

♦ Were behavior problems present, and if so, did the instructor

   • set standards and praise correct behavior?

   • anticipate and prevent incorrect behavior?

A form that the principal can use to prepare for communicating to the teacher is reproduced in Figure 6.6. The principal in the analysis of the lesson should select two or three items that occurred during the lesson for reinforcement and one item for refinement. If the principal provides more written information, the teacher will not be able to focus on improvement. It becomes a case of data-overload and thus paralysis by analysis.

FIGURE 6.6. ANALYSIS AND STRATEGY SESSION

(To be used by the principal in planning the post-observation conference)

Analysis of the lesson

Reinforcement (Choose 2 or 3 items)	Refinement (choose 1 item)

It is important to remember to keep it *simple* and *workable*. Don't try to impress people by digging too deep merely to show off your depth of knowledge in a given area. Work within the area of understanding of the teacher and help the teacher grow. As a principal, your analysis should be for the teacher's benefit rather than for your personal gratification.

POSTOBSERVATION CONFERENCE

...I propose that a minimum responsibility incumbent upon the observer is to discuss what he has observed with the teacher. *(This) is what earns you your right to observe.*

Goldhammer, 1969

After the lesson has been observed, the data analyzed and the postobservation conference planned, the teacher and observer should get together to analyze the observational data and set goals for improvement. This is an important occasion in the evaluation process because it allows teachers to talk in detail about their work with someone who has been in the classroom and is able to provide feedback and assistance, either directly or indirectly. It is also a time for diplomacy and candor on the part of the observer. No two conferences are going to be alike nor should they be. Teachers are different, and your approach should be designed to elicit the most favorable results from the teacher being observed. Thus, one of the most important decisions that faces a principal preparing for a conference revolves around what approach to use (Sweeney, 1989).

Maureen Zolubos, principal in Westborough, MA, considers four factors in deciding on the approach to use:

♦ What is my purpose?

   The supervisor must be very clear about the decision level to employ in discussing performance. Following are four decision levels and a guide to their use:

   • Delegate—leave the decision to change up to the teacher.

      Utilize this choice with a highly skilled, analytical, and knowledgeable teacher.

   • Suggest—suggest possible change, but leave the decision up to the teacher

      Utilize where performance is effective but alternative strategies might be helpful.

- Recommend—clearly communicate the need to change or improve present practices.

  The need for change is stronger, and the teacher *should* change present practices.

- Direct—clearly communicate that change must be made and set goals and timelines.

  This is typically employed where performance is below the district standards.

♦ What are the needs and communication or behavior style of the person being evaluated?

Augment the golden rule with the platinum rule—Do unto others as they would have you do unto them. A careful examination of the characteristics of the teacher helps to determine the approach to use in the conference.

♦ What are the situational elements to consider?

Situational factors that should be considered in planning the approach include:

- Past observation
- Recent incidents or events in the work environment
- External events

♦ What is my communication/behavioral style, and what strengths do I bring to the conference?

- Rule one in conducting a conference is to be yourself.
- Rule two is to adjust your behavior to meet the other's communication/behavior needs.

You should face this dichotomy by playing to your strengths and adjusting to your comfort zone. Following are three questions to ask in assessing your style:

- What behaviors do I bring to the conference that promote success?
- Is my primary communication style direct or indirect?
- Do I need to modify my basic behavior or communication style to promote success in this conference?

Insincerity and lack of interest will show quickly in a postobservation conference and will severely dampen the interest of those observed and lower their impression of the principal. Superficial observations should never take place; they must be avoided at all costs. If you don't think that it is important enough to do it right, then you should have a quiet little talk with yourself and rethink your priorities. One of your most important goals as a principal should be to develop well-planned and meaningful observations that show your staff that you are really concerned about their professional development, teaching effectiveness, and personal well-being. Along the same line, it is wrong to assume that feedback from the observation is just the final stage and not an important element in the growth of both parties involved. Feedback should provide results that are revealing, persuasive, caring, and creative.

Principals can make feedback more useful by eliciting information from the teacher about what transpired in the classroom during the observation. It is important to ask questions of the instructors to guide them into the areas that you wish to discuss with them and then to ask further questions that will allow them to develop solutions to their difficulties on their own, thus establishing "ownership" in the process. Questions are the ultimate tool for promoting success in a conference. Barbara Licklider, principal in Council Bluffs, IA, suggests using six types of questions:

- analysis questions
- fact-finding questions
- attitude questions
- checking for understanding questions
- agreement questions
- checking for commitment questions

Another set of questions for the principal to ask the teacher during the postobservation conference is:

- What did you do that you liked?
- If you were to teach this lesson again, what might you do differently?
- How can I help you?

Weber (1987) stated that the most important reasons for asking questions are that they help to increase the participation and involvement of the teacher, enhance the **trust, credibility,** and **rapport** between the principal

---

FIGURE 6.7. POSTOBSERVATION CONFERENCE—PRINCIPLES OF CONSTRUCTIVE FEEDBACK

---

1.   Focus on **behavior** rather than on the person. "Monitoring can increase student time on task" rather than "you're not moving around the room checking on students."

2.   Focus on behavior which the teacher can do something about. Frustration is only increased when a person is reminded of some shortcoming over which he/she has no control.

3.   Be **descriptive** rather than judgmental. By avoiding evaluative language, it reduces the need for the individual to respond defensively. "It is effective because..." rather than "I like..."

4.   Be **specific** rather than general. "When you gave directions for the activity, you wrote them on the board in logical sequential steps and you reinforced them verbally" rather than "you did a good job with your directions."

5.   Focus on **sharing** information rather than giving advice. "These are alternatives" or "can you think of alternatives" rather than "this is the way to do it."

6.   Base it on **observation** rather than hearsay. "I saw you do..." rather than "someone told me that..."

7.   Be **helpful** to the teacher rather than destructive. Comments should focus on improvement rather than being a way to release frustration by "chewing him/her out."

8.   Give the teacher the **amount** of information he/she can use rather than the amount you would like to give. To overload is to reduce the possibility of using anything effectively. When you give more than can be used, you are more often than not satisfying some need of your own rather than helping the teacher.

9.   Be **timely**. Feedback is most helpful at the earliest opportunity Reception and use of feedback involves emotional reactions. Excellent feedback presented at an inappropriate time may do more harm than good.

10.   Check to ensure **clear communication.** Have the teacher try to rephrase the feedback he/she has received to see if it corresponds to what you had mind. Feedback is often subject to distortion or misinterpretation.

and teacher. These three items (trust, credibility, and rapport) are critical because they are essential for positive communication and commitment.

- They enable the principal to check perceptions about data collected in the observation.
- They help the principal to assess the receptivity of the other person.
- They help the principal to identify personal needs, beliefs, and values about what the employee wants and believes works best.
- They stimulate the teacher to analyze performance and explore other approaches.
- They enable the principal to check for understanding, agreement, and commitment.

The more *listening* the principal can do the better it will be for the teacher as well as the principal. It is important to keep the feedback going in two directions—being a dialogue rather than a monologue (Weber, 1987). Remember the old adage: you have two ears and only one mouth. Use them in like proportion.

Another method mentioned in the "Program for Quality Teaching" urges observers to listen more and talk less. To do this, Weber suggested that the observer can:

- ask for the teacher's feelings
- ask for the teacher's inferences
- ask for the teacher's opinions
- ask for the teacher's suggestions for improvement

The nature of a principal's questions can radically affect the outcome of a conference. While two or three well-chosen, well-placed, and well-asked questions may be effective, it is by no means true that twelve or eighteen questions will be six times as effective (Hyman, 1986). Keep it *short and to the point*. If you do it right, you will be talked about as the administrator who gets it done quickly and efficiently. State your facts, ask your questions, and let the teacher draw the conclusions. If you find you are having trouble coming to an agreement with the teacher, Weber (1987) offers the following principles for consideration:

- Shut up and listen. If the other person is frustrated:
  - let him or her vent the anger or frustration

- take notes and do not interrupt
- Enhance or maintain the teacher's self-esteem.
  - praise—effort, competence, and self-worth
  - refrain from criticizing or acting defensively
- Listen and respond with empathy.
- Ask for the teacher's help in solving the problems that are holding up agreements.

Weber (1987) also offers these seven key strategies that are also helpful in overcoming postobservation conference road blocks:

- Determine the nature of the problem and the other's needs.
  - ask questions and listen
  - try to determine the nature of the problem you are dealing with
  - try to understand the other person's feelings and needs
- Explore the nature of the feelings.
  - listen for those feelings
  - reflect them back to the person
  - try to work it so that you can explore the source of the feelings
- Never lose your temper.
  - stay cool on the surface but paddle like mad underneath
  - remember, it is a professional not a personal matter
- Use "I" and not "you" statements.
  - "I" communicates what you need
  - "you" is like pointing a finger in his or her face
- Respect the others' rights and require that they respect yours.
  - set the rules
  - politely hold to the rules fairly and consistently
- Limit behavior/clarify consequences. If the person is behaving inappropriately:
  - communicate that the *behavior* is inappropriate
  - clarify the consequences of this behavior.

♦ Know when to terminate.

- calmly terminate the conference if the other person goes beyond the limits set

- terminate if you feel that you can go no further at the present time

- terminate when it is evident one or both parties need a break

- terminate when business is finished

Remember that without effective postobservation conferences, classroom observations become perfunctory in nature and produce relatively few instructional improvements because they fail to significantly modify teacher behavior (Dunkleberger, 1987).

It is hoped that eliciting information, being persuasive, and remaining open to alternatives will help instill *motivation* for the improvement within the teacher. All of the observation data is not worth much without it, as *self-motivation* is one of the critical forces in any improvement strategy. Ideally, the feedback should contribute to the accuracy of a teacher's *self-assessment*—an idea that should appeal to any teacher who wants to become more proficient (Weber, 1987). A format for working with competent and experienced teachers who are self-motivated is the annual goals approach as shown in Figure 6.8.

POSTOBSERVATION CONFERENCE CHECK-UP

Now is the time for you to model for the teacher that feedback is the Breakfast of Champions.

Now that the principal has been through the entire evaluation process, it is important to find out how he or she did. One of the best ways to accomplish this is by doing a supervisory evaluation check-up. This involves asking those who have been evaluated to let you know how they feel you are doing. It is a check-up on the principal. Following is a list of questions from Jerry Braden, a principal in the Key West (FL) School District, that he uses to help him modify his approach to future conferences:

♦ During the conference did my supervisor

- clearly communicate the purpose of the conference?

- involve me in the discussion?

FIGURE 6.8. FORMAT FOR ESTABLISHING AND ASSESSING ANNUAL GOALS

Teacher _____ Subject(s) _____ Year _____

1. In Column I list three (3) goals for the present school year, one of which may be non-instructional.
2. In Column II list the specific action plans for the teacher to accomplish the goals.
3. In Column III list the ways in which the teacher can determine when all goals have been accomplished.
4. In Column IV list the ways in which the principal can assist.

I. GOAL	II. ACTION PLAN	III. INDICATORS OF SUCCESS	IV. COMMENTS

Agreed to by _____ and _____ on _____ .

            Teacher   Principal   Date

- listen thoughtfully and open-mindedly?
- exhibit positive nonverbals—facial expression, body language, etc.?
- provide specific feedback about my performance?
- check to see if feedback or suggestions were clear to me?
- help me to analyze my performance?
- encourage or allow me to express my opinions?
- maintain a candid atmosphere?
- act tactfully in a task-oriented manner?
- really appear to be interested in my opinion?
- provide suggestions or provide help if asked?
- help me consider different strategies or approaches?
- reinforce what I did well?
- focus on important aspects of teaching?
- help me reflect on what I do?
- give me sufficient time so that I did not feel rushed?

CONCLUSION

A great deal of material has been covered in this chapter relating to the supervision and evaluation process and certain ideas have surfaced that seem to be the keys to success for the whole process:

- ◆ Attention is paid to teacher input into the process.
- ◆ Collegial observation and self-observation are allowed (using videotaping, for example).
- ◆ Feedback is frequent and observations are followed up with goal setting.
- ◆ The performance criteria are specific and subject to teachers' input when they are formed.
- ◆ Evaluators give detailed suggestions rather than vague criticism or irrelevant observations about teaching (Weber, 1987).

The following quote from Weber (1987) offers what I feel is a fitting conclusion to the material we have been studying in this chapter:

For observations to be worthwhile, the experience of practitioners and researchers indicates that they must be carried out by knowledgeable observers using a well-planned, well-recorded set of teaching criteria. Moreover, the results should be diplomatically discussed with the teacher and followed up with further observations and opportunities for teacher self-appraisal.

For the evaluation process to pay back the maximum return on the investment of time and energy, that process should be integrated with goal-setting programs and other developmental activities.

Principals should put their best effort into the evaluation process and enjoy the benefits. Remember, as principals help others become successful, they will experience success as instructional leaders and developers of teachers.

REFERENCES

Acheson, K.A., and M.D. Gall (1987). *Techniques in the clinical supervision of teachers: Preservice and inservice applications,* 2nd ed. New York: Longman.

Blackburn, R., D. Hare, and W. Kritsonis (1989). Pre-evaluation conference. *National Forum of Applied Educational Research Journal, 1.*

Bolton, D.L. (1973). *Selection and evaluation of teachers.* Berkely, CA: McCutchan.

Cascio, W.F. (1982). *Applied psychology in personnel management.* Reston, VA: Reston Publishing.

Cogan, M.L. (1973). *Clinical supervision.* Boston: Houghton Mifflin.

Darling-Hammond, L. (1986). A proposal for evaluation in the teaching profession. *The Elementary School Journal, 86,* 531–551.

Dunkelberger, G.E. (1987). Making the most of the post-observation conference. *Bulletin, 71,* 503.

Gagawski, R.A. (1980). Collaboration is key: Successful teacher evaluation not a myth. *NASSP Bulletin, 64* (434), 1–7.

Goldhammer, R. (1969). *Clinical supervision: Special methods for the supervision of teachers.* New York: Holt, Rinehart and Winston.

Huddle, G. (1985). Teacher evaluation: How important for effective schools? Eight messages from research. *NASSP Bulletin, 69* (479), 58–63.

Hyman, R.T. (1986). *School administrator's faculty supervision handbook*. Englewood Clifts, NJ: Prentice-Hall.

Iden, D., C. Fisher, and M. Taylor (1979). Consequences of individual feedback on behavior in organizations. *Journal of Applied Psychology*, 5.

Latham, G.P., and G.A. Yuki (1975). A review of research on the application of goal setting in organizations. *Academy of Management Journal*, 18.

McGreal, T.L. (1982). Effective teacher evaluation systems. *Educational Leadership*, 39 (4), 303–305.

Nemeroff, W.F., and K.N. Wexley (1977). An exploration of the relationships between the performance feedback interview characteristics and interview outcomes as perceived by managers and subordinates. *Journal of Occupational Psychology, 52*.

Peterson, C.H. (1982). *A century's growth in teacher evaluation in the United States*. New York: Vantage.

Refern, G.B. (1980). *Evaluating teachers and administrators: A performance objectives approach*. Boulder, CO: Westview.

Sergiovanni, T.J. (Ed.) (1982). *Supervision of teaching*. Alexandria, VA: Association for Supervision and Curriculum Development.

Stiggins, R.J., and Bridgeford, N.J. (1985). Performance assessment for teacher development. *Educational Evaluation and Policy Analysis, 7* (1), 85–97.

Sweeney, J. (1989). The supervisory conference: Being the best you can be. *The Practitioner*, 1.

Weber, J.R. (1987). *Teacher evaluation as a strategy for improving instruction*. Eugene, OR: University of Oregon (ERIC Clearinghouse on Educational Management).

Wise, A.E., et al. (1985). Teacher evaluation: A study of effective practices. *The Elementary School Journal*, 86 (1), 61–121.

7

ASSISTING THE MARGINAL TEACHER

REASONS FOR STUDYING THE MARGINAL TEACHER

♦ The marginal teacher can cause the principal significant problems and cause the expenditure of massive amounts of both time and money.

♦ The process of working with the marginal teacher can be a challenge to the professional skills of the principal.

♦ The students deserve a quality teacher, and it is the responsibility of the principal to improve the effectiveness of the teacher.

♦ Awareness and identification of the marginal teacher, and the willingness to confront the teacher and the behavior, will relate to the effectiveness of the principal.

The degree to which I create relationships which facilitate the growth of others as separate persons is a measure of the growth I have achieved in myself.

Carl Rogers

INTRODUCTION

This chapter provides the necessary framework for school principals in two areas: (1) increasing student learning by improving instruction, and (2) increasing their skills to work effectively with teachers identified as having professional deficiencies. While the scope of these areas is broad, schools must maintain a clear vision of their goals for instruction, and what expectations they set for teachers to continually meet those goals.

Sections in this chapter are designed to address specifically programs that effectively assist teachers in professional improvement, methods of identifying the marginal teacher, and to provide remediation for teachers found in need of improvement. Also, the steps involved in the probationary process for teachers who fail to meet improvement requirements are shown in detail. The materials included in this chapter range from sample documents and model programs, to suggested procedures and forms, all for practical use. They are provided so that a practicing principal can have access to materials which would be used in the procedures described.

THE MARGINAL TEACHER

Most teachers in our nation's schools are competent, conscientious, and hardworking individuals. All too often their efforts are overshadowed by the poor performance of a relatively small number of incompetent classroom teachers. These incompetent teachers must be identified and assisted by the principal, and if they fail to improve, they must be dismissed. Figure 7.1 lists 10 characteristics of a marginal teacher. Principals need to be alert to these characteristics and, when present, intercede in a very timely fashion in order to keep the problem from becoming more serious.

School districts that wish to confront this challenge face a formidable array of legal, technical, and human problems. These problems can be overcome if school districts are willing to adopt an organizational approach to deal with incompetent teachers in an integrated, comprehensive fashion. The eight elements comprising a useful approach are:

- ♦ Establish "excellence in teaching" as a high priority for the district.
- ♦ Adopt and publish reasonable criteria for evaluating teachers.
- ♦ Adopt sound procedures for determining whether teachers satisfy these criteria and apply these procedures uniformly to teachers in the district.

FIGURE 7.1. TEN CHARACTERISTICS OF A MARGINAL TEACHER

- Lacks "bell to bell" planning.

- Does not teach to the curriculum in general and to specific objectives in particular.

- Students become easily distracted and are off-task.

- Lacks enthusiasm for students and teaching. *and learning*

- Doesn't provide meaningful and timely feedback to students.

- Has poor personal relations with students. *and staff*

- Exhibits poor teaching skills.

- Unorganized classroom and lessons.

- Does not establish expectations for student behavior and thus, discipline is usually a major problem.

- Lacks knowledge of the subject matter.

- *Lacks accountability for lack of student learning.*

- ◆ Provide unsatisfactory teachers with remediation (assistance) and a reasonable period of time to improve.
- ◆ Establish and implement procedures for ensuring that principals have current competencies in the areas of supervision, evaluation, and in providing assistance.
- ◆ Provide principals with the resources needed to carry out their responsibilities.
- ◆ Hold principals accountable for evaluating and dealing with incompetent teachers.

♦ Provide incompetent teachers with a fair hearing prior to making the dismissal decision. (Bridges, 1990)

Principals who follow this systematic approach reap several noteworthy benefits. In districts that use this approach, principals are much more likely to confront the poor performers and to induce improvement, resignations, or early retirements if they fail to improve (Groves, 1985). Moreover, in those schools where principals are issuing formal notices of incompetence and inducing incompetents to leave, the students' achievement tends to be higher than in those schools where principals ignore the problem of poor performance (Groves, 1985; McLaughlin, 1984). Finally, the administration is much more likely to have its dismissal decisions upheld if the teacher chooses to contest the decision, rather than to resign or retire early (Bridges, 1990).

The success of any organizational program is based on the level of priority that the program holds in the school district. This is true for educational programs designed to improve teacher instruction, or provide remediation for teachers found to be marginal. The task of a school district's leadership, both at the superintendent and principal levels, is to ensure that "excellence in teaching" becomes and remains the centerpiece of the district's agenda.

When a teacher is performing in a marginally effective manner and the principal does not confront the teacher with the problem, then the principal is also performing in a very marginal manner. So just what can the principal do?

First, take time during the recruiting and selection process to make reasonably certain that you have selected a competent teacher.

A KEY IDEA

Do not be overly persuaded by special courses taken during the college experience. Instructional Theory into Practice (ITIP), whole language approaches, Math Their Way, and others can be learned later if need be. Select a teacher who cares about students and was very successful in student teaching or in previous classroom teaching.

Second, during the orientation and induction programs make sure you discuss the job description with the teacher, answer any questions regarding it, and obtain the signature of the teacher on the job description. (See Recruiting, Selection, and Induction chapters.)

Third, introduce teachers to the evaluation form and procedures so that they know what they are being evaluated on and what form it will take. In addition, introduce and explain the Teacher's Code of Ethics or Code of Professional Conduct.

Fourth, even though principals will be very busy during the first two weeks of school, they must find the time to visit the classrooms of all teachers new to their building. There are two main reasons for doing this: (1) to validate the selection process; and (2) to identify any potential problems which, if corrected early, will save substantial time and effort later. Consider Figure 7.2, which illustrates the problem that is created if the teaching deficiency is not noted early.

Fifth, check weekly with the new teachers' mentors for the first three months. If there are any early signs of problems, then the principal should intervene to assist or provide external assistance.

FIGURE 7.2. TEACHER PERFORMANCE AND PRINCIPAL INTERVENTION

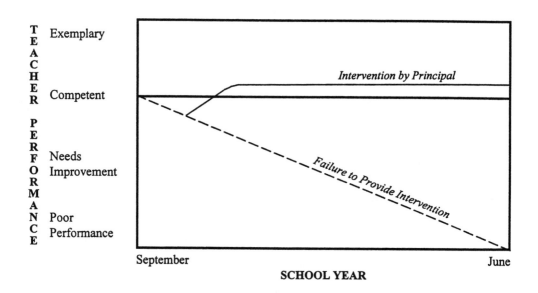

A KEY IDEA

When you make an early visit (within the first two weeks of the school year) to the classroom of a teacher there are generally two things that can happen: things are going fine or they are not. If they are going fine, you need to reinforce and affirm the teacher; if they are not going fine, then you need to provide assistance. Either way, you, the teacher, and the students are winners.

Sixth, meet individually with each teacher new to your building, ask questions regarding how things are going and provide assistance if needed.

TYPES OF REMEDIATION

Once a teacher is having serious problems regarding teaching, it is incumbent on the principal to provide timely assistance in order to make the year instructionally successful for both the teacher and the students.

The principal can do the following:

- Work with the teacher to set short-term goals which relate directly to the district's established criteria of successful teaching. Reference should be made to the district's evaluation form.

- Provide release time for the teacher to observe successful teachers, preferably out of the building, and provide time to assist the teacher reflect on the modeling.

- Examine the class in terms of its composition of difficult students. Perhaps the transfer of a couple of students could assist in making the classroom more manageable.

A KEY IDEA

The principal should always seek input regarding the placement of students from the previous teachers, but should always retain the responsibility to assign students to the teachers. Sometimes beginning or new-to-the-building teachers get the most challenging students.

♦ Provide help and support in the acquisition of teaching materials.

♦ Provide extra time for the mentor and the teacher to discuss the lessons, curriculum, and classroom procedures.

♦ Provide assistance through the Employee Assistance Program (EAP). A detailed explanation of the program is included later in this chapter.

PLANNING

Planning is one area in which principals can assist the marginal teacher. If the teacher is well-planned, then the problem shifts to the more complex phase of the lesson: implementing the plans. Figures 7.3, 7.4, and 7.5 are examples of daily, unit, and year-long plans. These provide the format to enable the principal to assist the teacher with phases of the planning process.

IMPLEMENTING THE PLANS

Once the teacher is well-planned, the implementation of these plans is critical. The following are implementation techniques with weak and strong examples of each technique. The principal should assist the teacher to internalize these techniques through modeling and discussions.

♦ Stating Concepts of Processes

Set concepts or processes and general overview for the day. Tell students what you want them to do or learn.

- *Weak example*: "We're going to work on a couple of things today."

- *Strong Sample*: "We're going to work in a large group for 30 minutes generating advertising ideas for 5 products. Then we will work in small groups for 25 minutes, where each group will write product advertising."

♦ Classroom Routine

Teach routines for all classroom activities including turning in and receiving back work, notebook organization, transitions to different-sized groups, cleanup, listening, and lecture skills, etc.

- *Weak example*: "Let's count off again today in 4s so we can work in small groups again."

FIGURE 7.3. DAILY PLAN

<u>September 10, Thursday</u>

Objective: Be able to distinguish between solids, liquids and gases.

Be able to determine melting point, boiling point, freezing point, and point of condensation of water; sublimation

Materials Needed: 2 flasks, watch glass, thermometer, beakers, mercury, water, salt, iodine, dry ice, regular ice chips, paper, pencil

Activities:

5 minutes   -   Define and show examples of solids, liquids, gases

10 minutes   -   Define and demonstrate mp, bp, fp, pt. of condensation

20 minutes   -   Students work in groups of two
                  Starting with ice in a beaker and heat and measure the temperature at which it changes to liquid, then a gas (Record data)

10 minutes   -   Demonstrate heating iodine -
                  Sublimation (gas to solid with no liquid state between)

5 minutes   -   Students measure dry ice and observe sublimation (Record data)
             -    Lab write-ups due tomorrow

5 minutes   -   Discuss results

Evaluation: Questioning
              Lab write-up

FIGURE 7.4. UNIT PLAN

CHEMISTRY OUTLINE

September 14 -
September 25
(2 weeks)

PROPERTIES OF ELEMENTS

    1. LAB, Behaviors of elements
    2. LAB, Categorizing the elements - metals/nonmetals
    3. LAB, Behaviors within the categories and He

September 28 -
October 9
(2 weeks)

ORGANIZATION OF THE ELEMENTS

    4. Periodical behaviors, Mendeleev's theory
    5. Periodical chart

October 12 - 30
(3 weeks)

ACIDS AND BASES

    6. PH levels - So what!
    7. LAB, Testing for acid and base
    8. LAB, Does Rolaids really spell RELIEF?
    9. What causes cars to rust?

November 2 - 6
(1 Week)

CHEMISTRY AT HOME

    10. Carbon units
    11. Putting strings of chemicals together, Polymers
    12. Making it go faster and cheaper
    13. Making alcohol - is it safe to drink?

FIGURE 7.5. YEAR-LONG PLAN

PHYSICAL SCIENCE OUTLINE

September 1 - 11   INTRODUCTION, CHAPTER 1
(2 weeks)

September 14 -   CHEMISTRY CHAPTERS 5, 8, 9, 6, 7, 13, 14, 10,
November 6   AND 11
(8 weeks)
                                    PROPERTIES OF ELEMENTS
                                    ORGANIZATION OF THE ELEMENTS
                                    ACIDS AND BASES
                                    CHEMISTRY AT HOME

November 9 -   LIGHT AND SOUND CHAPTERS 15, 16, 17, AND 18
December 11
(5 weeks)   WAVES AND ELECTROMAGNETIC RADIATION
                                    REFLECTION AND REFRACTION
                                    OPTICS
                                    SOUND

December 14 -   ELECTRICITY CHAPTERS 21 AND 22
January 22
(4 weeks)   STATIC ELECTRICITY
                                    MAGNETISM AND CURRENTS
                                    CIRCUITS

January 25 -   PHYSICS CHAPTERS 2, 3, AND 4
March 25
(8 weeks)   WORK'S EFFORT
                                    SIMPLE MACHINES
                                    LAWS OF MOTION

March 28 -   HEAT CHAPTERS 19, 20, 23, AND 24
April 29
(4 weeks)   SPECIFIC HEAT AND HEAT TRANSFER
                                    HEATING AND COOLING
                                    ALTERNATE ENERGIES

May 2 - May 27   EARTH SCIENCE
(4 weeks)

May 30 - June 8   TESTING AND SCHOOL CLOSING
(1 week)

- *Strong example*: "Move to your previously established small groups for group work."

♦ Directions

Keep lesson directions separate from other classroom business. Club announcements, money collecting, and so on, should be first or last. Give complete directions for each activity, so the activity doesn't have to be interrupted for additional or clarifying directions.

If the activity is long and involved, work it section by section: give directions for Section I, then have students complete Section I; give directions for Section 1I, then have students complete Section II; and so on.

♦ Directions and Planning

Plan ahead to help students behave appropriately and remain on task.

- *Weak example*: "We're all going to the library today to work on projects, so let's go."
- *Strong example*: "Because we're going to the library today, I'll take attendance twice, at the beginning and end of the period. If you have 7 or more file cards completed for your report at the end of the period, you will receive the participation points."

♦ Directions and Planning

Break down assignments into substeps to ensure students' learning and time-on-task. For example, a term paper will require a topic, an outline, note cards, and a rough draft before the finished product can be completed. Each of these substeps can have due dates and/or amounts of time in which each one can be completed, checked, and given participation points. Checking all the sidesteps along the way will greatly aid the weaker student to get the finished product completed well.

♦ Directions for Explicit Outcomes

State high expectations and make the desired outcome(s) very clear.

- *Weak example*: "Turn in a good business letter."

- *Strong example*: "Complete a business letter of three paragraphs on unlined white paper, written in black ink. It should have no mistakes and be of a quality that you would send on the job. Follow the correct form in the sample I gave you."

♦ Planning for Higher Level Thinking Skills Instead of Rote Repetition

When planning lessons, always think of ways students can demonstrate thinking instead of memorization.

- *Weak example*: "What should you wear to an interview?" Students: "Conservative clothes."

- *Strong example*: "Here are some cards where each describes an outfit a person wore to a job interview for an office job. Read the cards and be prepared to describe what is good and what ought to be improved about each of the outfits." Student: "The black suit and white blouse are fine, but the woman should not have been wearing patterned stockings and sling-back shoes."

♦ Judging Time Allotments for New Lessons

To determine how much time a new activity should take, compare it with a similar one you've already taught. If you think students may finish quickly, or you're unsure of time, plan an additional short activity that can be adjusted to use 5–15 minutes of extra time. It is always better to plan too much, than to feel anxious because you're out of material.

♦ Preparing Materials and Classroom Setting

See your materials and setting through your students' eyes and adjust accordingly. In the empty room, sit in several of the least desirable seats. Can you see the chalkboard, the overhead, and the teacher? Sit in the last seat in the room, can you see materials on the overhead? Do they look clear, attractive, and interesting, or are they poorly written, or just copies of dittos the students already have? Use colors, appropriate cartoons, graphics as attention-getters!

Look at the materials used as handouts. Do they reflect concern about quality, or do they have typing errors, and poor quality printing? If students are to write on them, do they have adequate space for neatly written answers? Are the directions explicit?

♦ Positive Attitude

Always demonstrate a positive attitude. Praise twice as much as you correct or discipline. After each class, mentally review things you liked about the class, or about the performance of individuals. Think of ways it could be shown and resolve to do it at the very next opportunity! (The formula, praise twice as much as you discipline or correct, is used very successfully in dropout programs, juvenile detention, etc.)

REMEDIATION PROGRAM

Hopefully, the principal has been successful with informal procedures to assist the marginal teacher. However, there are times when the principal must formally confront the problem and develop a Remediation Program for the teacher. A sample program follows. The five items which are unsatisfactory come from the teacher evaluation form.

Remediation Program for
John Doe, Music Teacher

The following is designed to assist you in improving your performance as a classroom teacher. My observation of your teaching indicates the following areas of performance to be unsatisfactory and in need of improvement:

I.   Professional Preparation and Scholarship

II.   Instructional Skill

III.   Classroom Management

IV.   Handling of Student Discipline and attendant problems

V.   Effort toward improvement when needed

Specifically, it is recommended that immediate attention be given to the following:

I. Professional Preparation and Scholarship

    A. Your performance reflects the following deficiencies:

1. Inability to consistently establish immediate and long-range objectives and prepare effective plans to meet objectives;
2. Inability to plan appropriately and in a timely manner for nonclassroom activities;
3. Inability to consistently start class in a timely manner.

B. We recommend that your preparation skills be improved during the probationary period to include:
   1. Ability to consistently establish immediate and long-range objectives and prepare effective plans to meet objectives;
   2. Ability to plan appropriately and in a timely manner for nonclassroom activities;
   3. Ability to consistently start class in a timely manner.

C. Suggestions which would assist you in correcting the above deficiencies include:
   1. Outline your curricular objectives in each subject area for the remainder of the second semester with the time allotted for each objective;
   2. Complete daily lesson plans by Friday for the following week.

   Components of the daily lesson plan would include:

   (a) statement of objectives

   (b) text pages to be covered

   (c) supplementary materials/handouts to be used

   (d) assignments

   (e) method of evaluation of the learning

   (f) schedule of class time use

   Following the conclusion of each school day, adjust your lesson plans for the next day and the remainder of the week, based upon the progress actually made.

   3. Begin each class by communicating to students your learning objective for the period. Write the objective on the board prior to class.

4. One month prior to the spring concert, submit an outline of planning procedures with timelines based upon criteria outlined by the principal.

5. Begin class promptly at the scheduled time which requires the timely pick-up of elementary music students from their classroom.

6. Maintain an extra set of Elementary Band Method books to be available for class use only, for students who have not brought their music to class. This music should be readily available to hand out and should be retrieved at the end of the period. Appropriate measures should be taken to ensure that students bring their music.

II. **Instructional Skill**

A. Your performance reflects the following deficiencies:

1. Inability to teach each lesson with observable objective(s);

2. Inability to adequately monitor student participation and progress and make provisions for differences in ability and interest among students;

3. Inability to implement effective home practice program for elementary band students;

4. Inability to consistently require students to properly handle music instruments.

B. I recommend that your instructional skills be improved during the probationary period to include:

1. Ability to teach each lesson with observable objective(s);

2. Ability to adequately monitor student participation and progress and then, make provisions for differences in ability and interest among students;

3. Ability to implement effective home practice program for elementary band students;

4. Ability to consistently require students to properly handle music instruments.

C. Suggestions which would assist you in correcting the above deficiencies include:

   1. Circulate among students during the class period. Monitor individual student progress periodically during class. Provide additional instruction for students requiring additional help and initiate parental cooperation and assistance.

   2. Provide elementary band students with a home practice assignment sheet after each band period. Assignment sheets would be prepared prior to class and given to students at the end of the period. Assignment sheet changes would be made after class and brought to the homeroom teacher. Parent signature would be required verifying practice, and students not returning a signed assignment sheet would be assigned a 20-minute practice session with you within one day during an optional time period, that is, P.E., student lunch time, after school.

   3. Instruct and demonstrate to students how to appropriately hold and handle instruments.

III. **Classroom Management**

A. Your performance reflects the following deficiencies:

   1. Inability to keep classroom and storage area neat and tidy;

   2. Inability to consistently prepare materials for class in advance of lesson.

B. I recommend that your classroom management skills be improved during your probationary period to include:

   1. Ability to keep classroom and storage area neat tidy;

   2. Ability to consistently prepare materials for class in advance of lesson.

C. Suggestions which would assist you in correcting the above deficiencies include:

   1. Keep classroom floor free of music and litter. Keep sheet music organized and appropriately stacked

and stored. Assign area on shelves for drumsticks. Keep desks, chairs, and music stands arranged in orderly manner. Keep piano and desk area neat and tidy. Keep instruments in their cases and on the storage shelves if possible. Keep storage shelves tidy and free of litter.

2. All sheet music, handouts, and other instructional materials should be prepared and laid out in a sequential and orderly manner in advance of a lesson for immediate distribution.

3. All audio-visual equipment and materials needed for a lesson should be obtained and ready for use prior to the start of the class.

IV. Handling of Student Discipline and Attendant Problems

A. Your performance reflects an inability to consistently establish order and discipline in the classroom.

B. I recommend that your handling of student discipline be improved during the probationary period to reflect an ability to consistently establish order and discipline in the classroom.

C. Suggestions which would assist you in correcting the above deficiencies include:

1. Communicate to students appropriate expectations for conduct and behavior. These would include the following:

   (a) students will arrive at class punctually

   (b) students will take their seats in a timely and orderly fashion

   (c) students will sit in their seats properly and remain in their seat unless otherwise instructed

   (d) students will be quiet and attentive when you are instructing

   (e) students will not be loud, disrespectful, or engage in rough housing

2. Misbehavior should result in appropriate and *consistent* consequences. This is best accomplished through a process of progressive discipline depending on the nature of the offense. Follow the adopted school sequence for dealing with discipline:

   (a) student reprimand

   (b) conference with student

   (c) detention—give notice; maximum 30 minutes

   (d) parent contact

   (e) parent conference

   (f) referral to principal

3. Maintain a current log on each student you have disciplined. Each entry should state the date of misconduct, the nature of the misconduct, and action taken.

V. Effort Toward Improvement When Needed

A. Your performance reflects an inability to consistently implement suggestions in a timely and consistent manner.

B. I recommend that you accelerate your effort toward improvement during the probationary period to reflect your ability to consistently implement in a timely manner and sustain suggestions for improvement.

C. Suggestions which would assist you in correcting the above deficiencies include:

   1. Maintain an ongoing written log of ideas and suggestions for improvement for periodic reference; and

   2. Establish and meet timelines for implementing suggestions.

Assistance Provided

A probationary team composed of the high school principal, a music teacher from the middle school, and a teacher of your choice will observe and assist you in improving your performance. In addition to the personal observations and evaluation conferences, the following assistance will be made available to you:

A. Probationary Team Assistance. The team will work with you on improving your performance as outlined in this program.

B. Visitation to other classrooms both in our school and others.

C. Consultant help. The probationary team will work with you to determine if appropriate personnel is available to assist and implement probationary plan.

D. Release time to attend workshops that might assist you in your program for improvement.

E. Additional resources shall be utilized that you and the probationary team might both deem appropriate.

Principal _____

Date: _____

I have reviewed and understand the above and agree that it represents a reasonable program to aid in the improvement of my performance.

Teacher _____

Date: _____

MEETINGS WITH THE MARGINAL TEACHER

There is no question that after the development of a program of improvement, that things are very serious. The principal would be well advised to follow these guidelines when meeting with the marginal teacher:

- Never deal alone with a teacher who has a Union Representative. Have your own witness—preferrably not another teacher, however.

- Take careful notes and have your witness take notes.

- Document everything—incidences around the building, parent conferences, and observations.

- If you request to see planbooks or correspondence, make copies.

- Review strategy of other administrators for feedback.

- Keep central office personnel and superintendent informed.
- *Know* the contract between the Teachers' Association and District.
- Know and use correct terminology. Know the law.
- Contact your attorney to review all legal documents.
- If written documentation is given to teacher, have teacher sign.
- You set meeting times and determine length.
- Avoid debate.
- If nonrenewal is evident—don't reveal decision until after the legal end of probation.
- They may resort to attacking you. Any skeletons in your closet?
- Be up front—no hidden agendas.

EMPLOYEE ASSISTANCE PROGRAM

At some time in the personal or work life of school employees, every person faces problems that are solved individually or with help from others. Some problems, however, require professional help and guidance. Approximately 5 to 8% of the nation's workers have problems which affect their job performance. These problems become even worse without assistance.

Since so much of our lives revolves around the work environment, a key to assistance for problems is often found in this setting. It is not only possible and humanitarian to help, but also it is essential for the protection, growth, and development of an important national resource, our working school employees (Melgram, 1986).

DEFINITION

The Employee Assistance Program (EAP) is a practical but responsive attempt to improve performance by constructing therapeutic strategies to help employees deal with their personal problems and thus improve their work performance (Melgram,1986). The EAP enables principals to identify employees who are having difficulties performing their jobs and refer them to the EAP if it applies. Many school districts offer confidential professional help to employees who have substance abuse, psychological, marital, family, financial, legal, or other problems (Balzer & Pargament, 1987).

HISTORY

In the late 1930s, Alcoholics Anonymous (A.A.) was founded and demonstrated that it could help alcoholics recover from their addiction. At the time, the Du Pont Corporation met with the founder of A.A. to discuss rehabilitation for alcoholic employees as an alternative to dismissal (MBA, 1993). The Eastman Kodak Company also provided assistance for their alcoholic employees through their Medical Department. Mental health programs were developed in the 1940s by the Caterpillar Tractor Company, American Cyanamid Company, and others (Melgram, 1986).

Some companies' attempts to develop employee programs were short-lived. Even though alcoholism was regarded as an occupational health problem, by the late 1950s, only 35 companies had occupational alcoholism programs. By 1973 the number of programs in the United States had expanded to 500. The number of programs increased to nearly 2,400 by 1977 and 4,000 by 1979. In 1986, 57% of the Fortune 500 companies had some type of program for their employees (Melgram, 1986).

In the early 1970s, programs began to offer assistance for a broad range of employee problems. These comprehensive programs dealt with a variety of problems and decreased the chance of participants being labeled. Currently, this kind of "broad brush" program is designed to "identify people needing assistance (for all types of problems), refer them to appropriate sources of treatment, and provide supportive services during and after the treatment period" (Melgram, 1986).

STRUCTURE OF EMPLOYEE ASSISTANCE PROGRAMS

The goals of an EAP are to:

- Assist employees with personal problems
- Provide an alternative to disciplinary action for employees who are having job performance problems
- Help company maintain a stable, well-functioning work force
- Decrease company expenses caused by the loss of well-trained employees (Melgram, 1986)

In resolving any human problem, it is essential to accurately assess the nature of the problem, provide treatment, and maintain a continuing improvement program. Teachers and school leaders should be supportive of the EAP in assisting the employee with a problem as it directly affects the school and district. They should be partners in the design and implementation of the EAP.

When an employee is identified, it is vital that the principal arrange a private meeting to relate the issues and specific concerns of job performance. At that time, a suggestion is made that the employee utilize the services of the EAP. The employee may reject or accept the offer. If the employee accepts, he or she is put in contact with an EAP counselor who assesses the problem and plans a course of action.

PROGRAM FRAMEWORK

Without altering or amending any of the rights or responsibilities of the employee of the Sample School District, it is the policy of the Employee Assistance Program to handle such problems within the following framework:

- **We recognize that almost any human problem can be successfully treated** provided it has been identified in its early stages and referral is made to appropriate care. This applies whether the problem is one of alcoholism, other forms of chemical dependency, or other personal problems. Therefore, employees having a problem which they feel could adversely affect their job performance or personal well-being are encouraged to voluntarily seek assistance on a *confidential* basis by utilizing the professional assistance of the Employee Assistance Counselor.

- **When an employee's job performance or attendance is unsatisfactory** and the employee is unable or unwilling to correct the situation either alone or with normal supervisory assistance, a personal problem may be the cause of the job performance difficulties. In such instances the employee's immediate supervisor has a responsibility to recommend that the employee utilize the Employee Assistance Program. Employees referred to the program by their principals will receive recommendations appropriate to their needs to secure services necessary to resolve the problem.

- **It is the responsibility of the employee** to comply with the referral for assistance and follow the recommendation of the Employee Assistance Program.

- Under the provisions of this policy, employees are assured that if personal problems are the cause of unsatisfactory job performance, they will receive careful consideration and an offer of appropriate assistance to help resolve such problems in an effective and confidential manner. Employees are assured that program records will be reserved in the highest degree of confidence.

♦ **In instances where it is necessary, time off** may be granted for treatment or rehabilitation consistent with the applicable benefit package.

♦ **Since employee work performance and attendance** can be adversely affected by the problem of an employee's spouse or other dependents, the employee can receive consultation from the Employee Assistance Counselor regarding problems of family members as well.

♦ **It should be emphasized that the Employee Assistance Program** and the disciplinary system each has its appropriate use. An employee's refusal to use the Employee Assistance Program is not in itself a cause for disciplinary action. The Employee Assistance Program is to be used in conjunction with applicable district policies and procedures.

Figure 7.6 graphically describes how to access and use the Employee Assistance Program.

When employees are experiencing personal problems, there are usually indications of these concerns in their interaction and functioning within the school environment.

Documentation of problems and concerns is essential in order to identify and intervene with the employee. Outlined below are areas of concern which can be identified and observed in the workplace. Principals should be alert to *early indicators of possible problems.*

♦ **Absenteeism**

   • Unauthorized leave

   • Excessive sick leave

   • Monday or Friday absences

   • Repeated absences of two to four days

   • Repeated absences of one to two weeks (five to ten days)

FIGURE 7.6. HOW TO USE THE EMPLOYEE ASSISTANCE PROGRAM

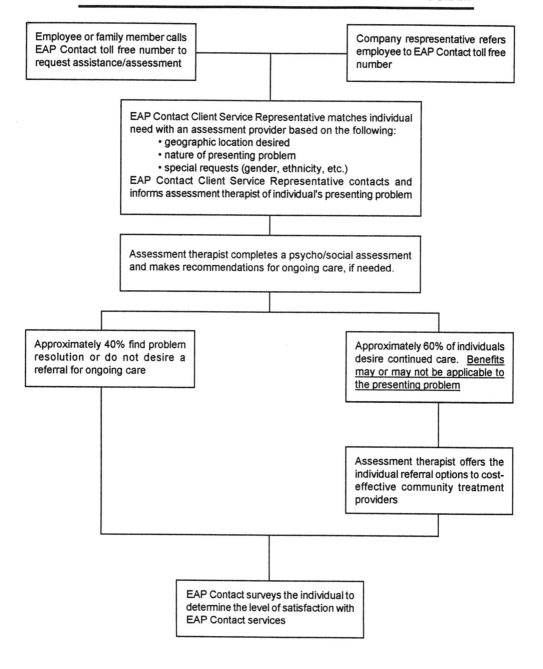

- Excessive tardiness, (especially on Monday morning or in returning from lunch)
- Leaving work early
- Peculiar and increasingly improbable excuses for absences
- Higher absenteeism rate than other employees for colds, flu, etc.
- Frequent, unscheduled short-term absences (with/without medical explanation)

♦ **"On-the-job" absenteeism**
- Continued absences from worksite (more than job requires)
- Frequent trips to water fountain or restroom
- Long coffee breaks
- Physical illness on job

♦ **High accident or mistake rate**
- Accidents on the job (whether serious enough for workman's compensation claim or not)
- Frequent trips to nurse's office
- Accidents off the job (but affecting job performance)

♦ **Difficulty in concentration**
- Work appears to require great effort
- Jobs take more time than normal
- Hand tremor when concentrating
- Frequently seems to stare off into space

♦ **Confusion**
- Difficulty in recalling instructions, details, etc.
- Increasing difficulty in handling complex assignments
- Difficulty in recalling own mistakes

♦ **Alternating work patterns**
- Alternating periods of very high and very low productivity

- ◆ **Resistance to change**
  - Doesn't change easily
  - Rigidly maintains current behavior, despite instructions to change
- ◆ **Change in employee's physical condition/appearance**
  - Comes to work impaired
  - Returns from lunch impaired
- ◆ **Lower job efficiency**
  - Takes more time to complete task
  - Increased waste
  - Damaged products
  - Lower production
- ◆ **Problems with other employees**
  - Arguments
  - Threats
  - Violence
  - Can't get along

There are numerous other concerns and problems which may be observed. It is important to document the performance problems and to discuss the behavior with the employee. Please remember, the EAP is available to discuss the work performance issues and to offer support in changing behaviors.

Principals are in the best position to know the extent of the problems on the performance of the teacher. However, few principals possess the professional capabilities necessary for diagnosing employee problems. Consequently, the principal will be expected to do ONLY that for which he has received training: SUPERVISE and REFER.

Principals should follow the steps below to assist the employee and provide appropriate assistance:

- ◆ **Document what you see**—NOT what you suspect (or what you are led to believe)
- ◆ **Diagnose unacceptable job performance**—Nothing else
- ◆ **Delegate the diagnosis of complex causes to the EAP professionals**

Personal problems that interfere with job performance are often too big to solve alone. Employers encourage their employees to maintain their physical and mental health by providing an Employee Assistance Program for the employee and their families. The EAP provides a confidential resource outside the workplace that assists employees with personal problems in a variety of areas. The initial assessment consultations are free for the employee and their immediate family members as they are paid for by the district.

The EAP is a very impressive resource for the employees of school districts who care about more than job performance—the district cares about the well-being of each employee.

REFERENCES

Balzer, W., and K. Pargament (1987). The key to designing a successful employee assistance program. *Personnel*, 48–54.

Blai, B. (1985). Staying well at work. *Viewpoint*, 120, 1–8.

Bridges, E.M. (1990). *Managing the incompetent teacher*. Eugene, OR: University of Oregon (ERIC Clearinghouse on Educational Management).

Bridges, E.M. (1986). *The incompetent teacher. The Stanford series on education and public policy*. Philadelphia: The Falmer Press.

Costa, A., and R. Garmston (1987). *The art of cognitive coaching: Supervision for intelligent teaching*. Sacramento, CA: The Institute for Intelligent Behavior.

Galleti, S. (n.d.). *Working with the marginal teacher*. Lake Stevens, WA: Lake Stevens School District.

Glickman, C.D. (1981). *Developmental supervision*. Alexandria, VA: Association for Supervision and Curriculum Development.

Glickman, C.D. (Ed.) (1992). *Supervision in transition: The 1992 yearbook*. Alexandria, VA: Association for Supervision and Curriculum Development.

Goldhammer, R., R. Anderson, and R. Krajewski (1993). *Clinical supervision: Special methods for the supervision of teachers*. Forth Worth, TX: Harcourt Brace Jovanovich.

Groves, B. (1985). An organizational approach to teacher evaluation. Ed.D. Dissertation, Stanford University.

Health Venture (HV) (1987). *Summary of services of Employee Assistance Program for Shelton School District.* Sponsored by St. Joseph Health Services.

Maschhoff, Barr and Associates (MBA) (1993). *Employee Assistance Program Supervisor Manual.*

McLaughlin, M.W. (1984). The Lake Washington School District No. 414 teacher evaluation: A study of effective practices, edited by A. Wise, L. Darling-Hammond, M. McLaughlin, and H. Bernstein. Santa Monica, CA: The Rand Corporation.

Meilleur, C.C. (n.d.). *Teacher probation.* Kirkland, WA: Lake Washington School District.

Melgram, G. (1986). Employee assistance: Policies and programs. *Rutgers Center for Alcohol Studies Pamphlet Series,* 1–22.

Parker, M.R., and M.S. Adams (n.d.). *Remediation of the marginal teacher.* Meeting Vernon, WA: Educational Service District No. 189.

8

STAFF DEVELOPMENT

REASONS FOR STUDYING STAFF DEVELOPMENT

♦ Just as developing students is the teacher's responsibility, developing teachers is a major responsibility of the principal.

♦ Education is changing rapidly. In order to keep up with those changes, school personnel must learn new techniques, methods, and procedures.

♦ If the mission of the school district contains the phrase "life-long learners" and if school personnel expect that of the students, then they should expect it of themselves.

♦ With the advent of school-based leadership, many of the previous central office responsibilities will be shifted to the principal. Staff development is one such area.

> *Staff development takes curriculum off the shelf.*

INTRODUCTION

One way to assess the quality of a school is to look at the students who are products of that district. To ensure that those students are of high quality, the principal needs to attend to the growth and development of the staff. The certified, classified, and support staff members must all be involved in an ongoing staff development process. This process must provide educational opportunities in order to cultivate both meaningful change and continuous growth toward excellence.

The primary job of educators is to teach students and to help them reach their academic potential. The better our teachers are equipped to teach, the better they will be able to provide exciting education experiences and thus improve academic achievement of their students. The education profession is always changing and there is a need to stay up-to-date. In other words, educators must continue to learn.

Mission statements in many school districts call for students to be "life-long learners." Educators should not expect anything less of themselves. Within the schools, staff development is the vehicle by which our life-long learning takes place. It is only through the continual expanding and enhancing of skills that educational personnel can maximize their ability to teach children.

THE CASE FOR STAFF DEVELOPMENT

The following is a list of reasons why we need to concentrate on staff development:

- ♦ To maintain a high quality of instruction
- ♦ To enrich and extend what is already in place
- ♦ To expand the knowledge base
- ♦ To improve instructional techniques and methods continually
- ♦ To inspire teachers and ultimately students
- ♦ To understand changing roles of teachers
- ♦ To recognize emerging needs

HOW TO ORGANIZE STAFF DEVELOPMENT

Staff development is an ongoing process that needs to grow and develop over a period of time. The successful staff development program should incorporate these essential elements:

- *Research*—Gathering of information
- *Training*—Making the subject come alive
- *Modeling*—Showing the audience
- *Practice*—Experiencing the reality
- *Coaching*—Feedback for perfection
- *Evaluation*—Improving the learning

There are five steps in providing effective staff development:

- Getting Started
- Collecting Data
- Planning
- Implementing
- Evaluation

These steps can be accomplished through the setting of goals, following the philosophy and mission statements of the district, establishing building committees, providing a plan for continuous staff improvement and evaluation, and allowing for budgetary needs. This chapter will focus on how to accomplish these steps. Figure 8.1 outlines the process.

GETTING STARTED

Figure 8.2 is helpful to use to understand and explain the staff development process to others. The goal of the staff development program is to increase student achievement through ongoing staff development. A comprehensive staff development program is for all employees of the school and district: teachers, secretaries, bus drivers, custodians, maintenance workers, instructional assistants, food service workers, substitutes, and administrators.

Further, it is helpful to think of the staff development program as a dynamic one, as represented by the "spinning top." The elements of the "top" illustrate the areas that are part of the program, while the arrows represent the process.

FIGURE 8.1. STAFF DEVELOPMENT: THE PROCESS

GETTING STARTED
Staff Development Committee
Professional Development
Principal Responsibility
Central Office Responsibility

COLLECTING DATA
Staff Development Steering Committee
Teacher Input
Administrative Input
Faculty Requests
Research
Conversations

PLANNING
Reviewing Timely Goals
Determining Needs
Brainstorming
Setting Priorities
Assuring Budget:
- Fiscal Year
- Summer
- School Year
- Grants

Setting Timelines
- Immediate
- Short-Term
- Long-Range

IMPLEMENTING
Selection of Trainers
Training Segment
Selling the Program
Support of Building Principals/Supervisors
Understanding the Adult Learners:
- *want* to be involved
- *will* resist situations suggesting incompetency
- *respond* to climate of trust, respect, and caring
- *enjoy* collegiality

EVALUATION
Regular Feedback: Daily, Weekly, Monthly
Individual Activities
Total Program Evaluation
Projections

FIGURE 8.2. STAFF DEVELOPMENT

—Teachers
—Secretaries
— Bus Drivers
— Custodians
—Substitutes

— Maintenance Workers
— Instructional Assistants
— Food Service Workers
— Administrators

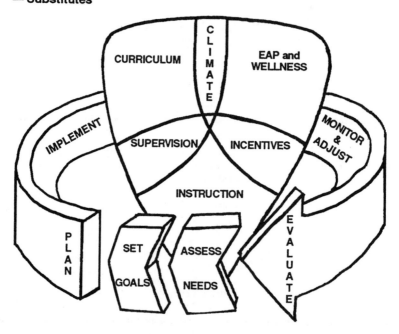

INCREASE STUDENT ACHIEVEMENT
THROUGH
ONGOING STAFF DEVELOPMENT

STAFF DEVELOPMENT COMMITTEE

Who is responsible for staff development? Traditionally, staff development has been left to the district level. Central administrators and central offices have been in charge of the entire staff development program in the district. They may organize a staff development steering committee to serve as the inservice training task force and the professional growth planning and review committee. The members can be drawn from the certified staff, counselors, union representatives, and classified staff administrators. Their **goal** will be to oversee continuous professional growth in all staff in accordance with the mission, philosophy, and belief statements of the school district. This **mission** can be accomplished by promoting effective educational changes, supporting and enhancing district goals, providing adequate time and resources to achieve desired goals, representing staff in the determination, planning, and implementation of staff development activities, and encouraging staff

Increasingly, however, school districts are phasing out their central office staff development departments in favor of site-based models. This has promoted interesting changes. Schools can now individualize and specialize their staff development to the needs of their staff. This is effective in that individual schools can do a better job of meeting their own needs. With this new freedom, however, comes the increased responsibility of schools doing their own data collection, planning, implementation and evaluation of their programs. It also opens up the reality of more than one school in the district doing the same program. This doubles the efforts that would have been made under a centralized model. Interschool collaboration can help to alleviate some of these overlapping efforts. Perhaps a model that is mostly site-based with some central office support would give us the best of both worlds. Under a site-based model, a heavy demand is placed at the building level. Despite this extra work, research shows that this method does a better job of meeting the needs of the individual staff members as well as special needs of different student populations. Goodlad (1983) found that "the individual school is the most viable unit for educational improvement." Although this assertion is not yet verified through research, the hypothesis that site-based (decentralized) decision making is "better" seems valid. As the practice of site-based management plays itself out, the research will surface to support or negate this movement.

Under this decentralized program, each building within the district also establishes a staff development committee which would consist of a member of the steering committee or leadership team, an administrator, teachers, and perhaps parents and building or district level specialists. Such a committee would report to the steering committee (leadership team or site council) on a regular basis, submitting plans to ensure continuity and coordination, plan, implement, and monitor building and staff programs, and provide opportunities for development and maintenance of skills acquired.

Regardless of who is responsible, staff development is a vital piece to a successful educational program and the committee should hold to certain standards and beliefs such as:

- Promote continued professional growth.
- Believe that adults can learn and want to improve.
- Uphold administrators as models of educational excellence.
- Renew interest in a dynamic and improving profession.
- Provide a needs-based, continuous, growth-oriented program.
- Accept and provide for the difficulty and fear of change.
- Communicate and provide a feeling of togetherness to make change less threatening.
- Develop an atmosphere of trust to encourage risk taking.
- Focus on reward, recognition, and reinforcement of excellence.

PERSONAL DEVELOPMENT OF TEACHERS

There are many suggestions to improve the knowledge and the morale of teachers. Here are several of these suggestions as a beginning:

- Professional Growth Plan (PGP)—a plan developed by each teacher/staff member to guide individual and group growth
- Inservices led by colleagues or outside speaker—sprovide inservice credit
- Staff meetings—teachers share information from summer school, conferences, or workshops attended
- Interest sessions—only those who have an interest attend
- Committee meetings—only those who have an interest volunteer and bring findings to whole group
- Informal gatherings—monthly celebration or get-together
- Professional day used to visit other schools, teachers, and programs
- Portfolio for teacher's personal papers, records, goals, etc.

THE PRINCIPAL'S RESPONSIBILITY

The principal plays a vital role throughout all of the stages of staff development. The principal must show a positive attitude. The administrator's attitudes and reactions will have a profound effect upon the success of a staff development program. The following are some items that administrators should consider when planning staff development programs:

- Believe in people from the beginning, that they have the potential and desire to succeed; then support them.
- Build on a person's strengths; you hired the teacher for a reason and are investing in him or her.
- Provide your staff with feedback; encouragement, praise, and positive criticism will help them grow.
- Build team spirit through retreats, encouraging cooperative efforts, and brainstorming sessions.
- Inspire commitment to the students, the school, the goals, and the mission.
- Set high standards and praise the results; teachers will be proud of their organization.
- Remove obstacles to teacher's success by providing the necessary resources needed and clear communication.
- Encourage teachers to ask for staff development and to take risks, to step out and try something new.
- Make work exciting with a relaxed, positive attitude.
- Let people see the results of their work being praised.
- Listen carefully to what the staff verbalizes and omits.

THE CENTRAL OFFICE RESPONSIBILITIES

One thing is clear: Expectations influence accomplishment. And high expectations start at the top with school board(s) that demonstrate through their example the importance of continuous improvement.

Sparks and Vaughn, 1994

Central office administrators should consider the following as they develop policies to recommend to the school board for staff development:

♦ Promote both the learning of individual school employees and changes in structures and processes within the district and within schools.

♦ Apply "systems thinking" to improvement efforts and be prepared for the effect of change.

♦ Heed the advice of those involved in "total quality" efforts in business and education.

♦ Have a strategic plan for the district.

♦ Recognize that the school ought to be the key decision-making unit when planning for improvement.

♦ Invest in improvement and use private and governmental resources effectively.

♦ Recognize that the most powerful forms of learning are likely to be job-embedded and that employees need at least 5% of their on-the-job time devoted to learning with additional professional days allowed.

♦ Be models of what you expect from others including special trading, risk taking, and experimentation.

♦ Remember that staff development is for everyone, not just for teachers.

COLLECTING DATA

If you don't know what you're looking for, you won't know it
when you find it.

The collection of data is the next step in providing for effective staff development. To do this, three questions should be considered:

♦ **What are our objectives?**

Our objective is the education of children. All staff development decisions would be based on the goals and mission of the district. Our schools use, and will continue to use standardized tests to measure student achievement. We are able to assess our children's academic ability. These assessments should provide one source of information for our staff development priorities. When these priorities are matched with educational objectives, we will realize the direction for our staff development program.

◆ **What objectives should we help to achieve?**

Once the objectives have been reviewed and we have looked at how well our students have done in meeting those objectives, we can generate a list of our students' weaknesses. Of course, we should not place our total faith in the ability of standardized tests to give us all of the information we need to analyze student achievement. In schools, the standardized test is the primary method by which academic achievement is measured, so whether we personally appreciate them or not, we should be able to place a fair amount of validity in their use. Once areas of need have been identified, we can begin to prioritize them and to make decisions about how and when they will be achieved.

◆ **What is the best way for us to develop our staff?**

There are very strong indications that teachers must see the need for the staff development training if they are going to "buy in" to its need. They also need to arrive at the realization that they must bear at least some of the responsibility for their students' achievement. We also know that successful staff development necessitates the commitment of all staff with a sense of ownership and representation. Seeing the need and "buying in" are vital.

Research by Porter (1981) supported the idea that teachers are willing to change their curriculum when confronted with evidence of its benefit to students, such as:

◆ Standardized tests results

◆ Principals' encouragement

◆ Parents' acceptance

◆ Other teachers' endorsement

All staff development programs should be rooted in research and should be carried out in moderation. There is no utopia, and no one program should be viewed as such. Teacher interests and needs along with student needs should be the focus. If teachers are motivated for staff development, then staff development will be successful.

The classification scheme (Figure 8.3) points out the necessity of teacher involvement in the staff development. The interest level of the individual and the interest level of the institution, be it the central office or building site, are graphed accordingly. A successful staff development presentation will have high institutional emphasis and high individual emphasis. The teacher will have "bought into" the importance of the program, and the institution will be so involved in the program that it will be pressing it with enthusiasm. Likewise, teachers will get involved when they see that something works and that others are interested. When they do, they will praise the program, be involved in its presentation, and will encourage others to do the same.

FIGURE 8.3. STAFF DEVELOPMENT CLASSIFICATION SYSTEM

	Teacher Focused • Low District • High Teacher	**School Focused** • High District • High Teacher
HIGH		
LOW	**Unfocused** • Low District • Low Teacher	**District Focused** • High District • Low Teacher

TEACHER EMPHASIS (left side, HIGH and LOW)

LOW   HIGH

DISTRICT EMPHASIS

PLANNING

Staff development programs should be established by using a set of assumptions grounded in research and best practice.

Wood and Thompson, 1993

The planning stage is a necessity for effective and successful staff development. At least in site-based models, the focus of planning staff development lies within inservice training. This type of training is usually best accomplished at the building site. When engaged in staff development planning, it is wise to have your district objectives, including mission and goals, as well as your research data readily available. Inservice planning is generally done one school year at a time; however, the recommendation is for a multiyear approach. Such short-term planning can lose focus if long-range planning is not done as well. It is important to make sure that all of your short-range planning fits into your long-range plan. When things become too fragmented, they become confusing and less useful to the staff.

Some balance should be maintained with regard to the natural overlap of different subjects. We need to realize that, if implemented, an inservice on classroom management, while not directly related to the basic skills, will have the effect of improving basic skill competency by leading to greater instructional time and a higher degree of time on task. Below are several points that should be kept in mind when planning staff development:

- Lawrence and Harrison (1980) suggested weekends, summer, and evenings are more acceptable times to teachers. One school uses the week immediately after school is out for the summer to train. The teachers are very pleased with this time block.

- The best staff development is designed as a collaborative effort by the school staff in cooperation with the principal.

- The single most important factor determining the value teachers place on an inservice education activity is its personal relevance. (Holly, 1982)

- Regularly scheduled staff development time should be allocated to protect classroom instruction and preparation time. (Ankeny, 1989)

- Budgetary allocations and constraints need to be taken into consideration before starting any project. "If school districts want improved practice, they must provide the personnel, time, materials, and dollars to support the implementation of those changes." (Wood and Thompson, 1993)

- All district employees need a sense of ownership and representation in the staff development goal-setting and decision-making process at the building and district level. (Ankeny, 1989)

- Flexibility is necessary when planning district goals and staff development programs. (Ankeny, 1989)

- All staff development decisions should be based on the premise of "what's best for kids." (Ankeny, 1989)

Often staff development programs require that staff members give up time beyond their contracted time for such programs. Although most teachers are interested in improving themselves as educators in order to help students, they are often resistant to giving up their free time to receive training. Following are some ideas for incentives that may help overcome this hurdle:

♦ Provide activities that equip teachers with the skills to increase their teaching effectiveness or gain increased feelings of empowerment.

♦ Administrators should participate in staff development activities with teachers. This is an excellent model of what is important.

♦ Provide opportunities for exchange visits between schools for sharing and discussing problems of mutual concern.

♦ Delegate responsibility for planning and presenting a workshop on a topic of interest to a group of teachers.

♦ Pay stipends to teachers who spend their own time planning, presenting, or participating in programs.

♦ Arrange staff development sessions in comfortable, attractive locations and provide refreshments for those who take part.

♦ Grant recognition in the form of certificates, plaques, and trophies to teachers who perform leadership roles in staff development projects.

Fred Wood and Steven Thompson (1993) discuss fourteen assumptions that staff development planners need to make when organizing staff development. A synopsis of them follows:

♦ The school, not the district, is the primary focus of improved practice and staff development.

♦ Significant change in educational practice takes considerable time and is the result of staff development that is conducted over several years.

♦ A school culture supportive of improved practice and professional growth is essential to successful staff development.

♦ All educators should be involved in staff development throughout their careers.

- The principal is key in any staff development effort to improve professional practice.
- Selection of the improvement goals that guide staff development should involve those who have a stake in the future of the students in that school (e.g., teachers, administrators, parents, community leaders, school staff, and the students themselves).
- Those who are changing their professional behavior must make an individual and collective commitment to, and feel ownership for the new programs and practices before they will want to participate in staff development activities.
- Staff development programs should support opportunities for both school improvement and individual professional growth.
- Staff development should enable school personnel to improve professional practice in ways that increase student learning.
- Knowledge about adult learners should serve as the basis for planning and implementation of staff development.
- Change in professional practice is difficult and requires systematic support to implement and sustain it over time.
- School districts have the primary responsibility for providing the resources and staff development necessary for a school faculty to implement new programs and instructional practices.
- Staff development should support instructional and program improvement and should be closely linked to instructional supervision, teacher evaluation, and curriculum implementation.
- School-based staff development, site-based leadership, and site-based budgeting are all important components of school-based improvement.

Wood and Thompson (1993) record the implications and conclusions they've made with regard to their fourteen assumptions, and it seems appropriate to conclude with their findings.

> These assumptions will result in staff development which is characterized by (a) school improvement goals serving as the focus for staff development; (b) long-range, multiyear planning; (c) development of a school climate and culture supportive of change and staff development; (d) ongoing staff development for all

educators in a district; (e) principals actively participating in all aspects of staff development; (f) involvement of all stakeholders in selecting improvement programs for their school; (g) support for both school and individual professional learning goals; (h) selection of research-based programs; (i) staff development based on the principles of adult learning; (j) follow-up support to implement and sustain changes in professional practice; and (k) staff development functioning as a component of instructional, program, and school improvement systems. We cannot continue to practice staff development and school improvement as if we are not aware of the knowledge base in our field. As staff developers, we call on others to change and behave in new and more effective ways. We must "practice what we preach," examine our assumptions, and learn new ways of behavior that are consistent with research and best practice.

IMPLEMENTATION

*Staff development is the active ingredient in the recipe for
school and student improvement.*

Implementation is the next step in an effective staff development program. How a staff development program is implemented will vary from school to school, year to year, and audience to audience. Different people have different needs and require a different approach. This important step should be addressed in the planning stage as well as in the implementation stage. When considering the audience, consider the level of expertise of your teachers. Beginning teachers need more structure in presentations and, in general, a more directive approach. On the other hand, teachers with more experience would much rather learn new ways to work together in teams and add variety to their instructional techniques.

A survey study done by McBride, Reed, and Dollar (1994) indicated that teacher attitudes towards staff development are mixed. The teachers agreed with reason and needs for staff development but were often dissatisfied with the results. Teachers wanted staff development, but they wanted it to be tailored to their needs. This last aspect is all too often ignored.

Another problem that needs to be addressed is how much is going to be presented to the audience. Principals and staff developers often make the mistake of trying to do too much in one session. With the cost involved and time constraints, leadership often feels pressed to present as much information as possible during each session. They must keep in mind the resources, the time, the caliber of presenters and the presenters' energy before proceeding. A word of caution, if you don't have these necessary resources, don't tackle the project; it will probably not be successful.

One of the more common themes of a staff development program is to show teachers how to use a new instructional technique. Stallings (1985) recommended the following four-step technique:

- Baseline/pretest: Teacher observation for target teacher behavior; profiles are prepared, and goals are set.

- Information: Information provided that links research and practice.

- Guided practice: Teachers adapt the new techniques to their own context and style.

- Posttest: Teacher observation; new profile made; set new goals; assess the training for effectiveness.

Using this basic format, or something similar, will help to ensure the success of your staff development program. There are no unimportant elements.

Much has been said about school restructuring and change. It seems most of the focus has been on changes in policies and procedures. While it is true that those changes will have to be made, change is really about people. If authentic change is to take place, then we must invest in people. When attempting to implement change, training is essential for all employees, students, and parents in areas such as group processes, decision making, team building, and leadership in order for site-based human resources to be effective.

Staff development is not a one-time or even a short-term project. Staff development for change must be viewed as a long-term program. The new way of doing things can easily slip back into the old way of doing things. There needs to be a commitment of support for all involved if change is to be sustained. Research by Hall and Loucks (1980) found that "When innovation is complex, major components should be phased in one or a few at a time." A study done by Gersten, Carnine, and Williams (1982) concurs with those findings. This research seems to indicate that staff development programs given in stages are more successful than one-time presentations. Research done by Lawrence and Harrison (1980) adds that staff development programs presented in this manner allow teachers to try things out a little at a time.

Staff development must be relevant. "Research and experience have shown that unclear expectations are one way to guarantee nonimplementation. Teachers appreciate clear objectives. They need to know what they are expected to do and how their roles are to change" (Hall and Loucks, 1980).

This methodology supports current research in the area of staff development. Consider the following:

- During their staff development, teachers need time to reflect upon their present way of doing things.
- It is easier for teachers to make gradual changes, one or two aspects at a time, and then move toward full implementation.
- Teachers need to know how to implement change.
- Follow-up is imperative to successful staff development.

To reiterate and add to what was stated at the beginning of this chapter, it is imperative to note the importance of the role of the principal. What the principal does is critical to the success of an implementation effort. The principal must play that leadership role in staff development. The principal's attitude is being watched! Some recommendations and implications for the principal to heed are:

- Provide time for sharing ideas and activities. If common planning time is impossible, consider a peer sharing group which meets during lunch or outside of school time.
- Choose school goals that encourage cross-curricular or cross-grade level planning.
- Encourage teachers to teach each other. Have teachers share information from conferences and workshops they attend.
- Provide opportunities for teachers to observe each other. Facilitate the logistics involved to make it easy to occur.
- Formalize ways for teachers to work together to solve problems. Make asking for help an acceptable practice.
- Celebrate small successes. Recognize that change occurs slowly and that small steps can lead to a collaborative culture.

All of this takes time and effort and cannot be forced. The ultimate benefits of improved instruction for students and an improved climate for teachers are worth the time it takes (Jakicic, 1994).

In conclusion, teachers trying new instructional approaches for the first time need staff development experiences which link theory to practice, address the problems associated with change, and give them the opportunity to work with other teachers. Through a workshop process in which teachers acquired new instructional strategies, reflected upon the change process, and experienced collaboration, participants found themselves well prepared for many of the day-to-day difficulties of innovation implementation. Through the preparation provided by the workshop, participants became more empowered teachers (Jakicic, 1994).

EVALUATION

Staff developers can use the concept of "return on investment" to document the effectiveness of their programs.

Todnem & Warner, 1993

Perhaps the most overlooked step in an effective development program is evaluation. All too often staff development ends with the end of the presentation. We all need feedback to know how we are doing. We are very good at giving immediate feedback to our students, but we often fail to do so with each other. Just as our students work toward outcomes and objectives, so must our staff development program. These outcomes are the criteria by which our staff development program should be evaluated.

With all of the research and planning involved in setting up a staff development program, not to mention the time and expense of getting a presenter and your staff together, it is imperative that some time be spent in evaluation.

Without an effective evaluation process there is little chance for you or your staff to know if your program is working. We all want to know if what we did, worked. Waiting for the results of your academic testing is too long a time span and it does not give us all of the answers.

Follow-up is a must. Coaching and feedback must be part of the program. It does take time and money to do follow-up and to do it right. We want to move on, but we need to realize that we are better doing a few things well than lots of things poorly.

As has been stated before, the most important reason for doing staff development is to learn how to better teach students. Unfortunately not a lot of work has been done to help us match student achievement with staff development. Orlich et al. found that "While the use of some instructional practices have resulted in improved student achievement, the direct link between teacher staff development and student achievement has not been supported by statistical data from several major studies" (Orlich et al., 1993). Orlich also stated, "School practitioners and theoreticians tend to be too simplistic in their assumptions about the scope and influence of teacher staff development on student performance."

School budgets are becoming increasingly tight. With many programs already being squeezed out, increased advocacy for staff development is necessary. Within this advocacy, the "powers that be" at the district level want to know what they are hoping to get for their money. Schools are increasingly coming under the pressure of validating how each dollar is spent. Principals need to find the best way to use their money. There are at least four levels at which the impact of staff development training could be measured. If we are going to evaluate effectively our "return on investment" (ROI) for our staff development program, we must follow through all four levels:

- Participants' reaction to the staff development—usually done immediately after the program.
- Participants' implementation of their new skills and knowledge while performing their jobs.
- Measurement of the organization's results.
- Measurement of student learning.

In their article, "Using ROI to Assess Staff Development Efforts," Todnem and Warner (1993) offered these conclusions in using the ROI concepts:

> The current climate of accountability requires that staff developers become fully informed about and skilled in several assessment models. ROI provides a valuable tool to demonstrate impact. In order to determine ROI educators must first define what constitutes ROI. We offer the concept of "meaningful change" as a starting place for expressing the units by which ROI is to be calculated. In schools, ROI needs to be expressed in units that relate to the program goals, express the interest areas of planners and stakeholders, and also are quantifiable. Some staff development efforts may not be readily assessed with the ROI concept. It is our experience, however, the concept of ROI opens up a variety of assessment approaches our colleagues and stakeholders will find acceptable. We invite staff developers to explore the concept of ROI with their constituencies and to share their experiences with others. Together, we can show how staff development benefits

students and educational organizations. (Todnem and Warner, 1993)

It is very important for the participants in a staff development program to be involved not only in the planning phase, but all the way through including evaluation. Gelareh Asayesh (1994) concurs, "When participants in staff development are involved in the evaluation of their own training, they become involved in shaping their own growth rather than passively submitting to a third party, the staff developer." All vested parties should be involved in all phases of a staff development program. Do not minimize or eliminate the evaluation component as no staff development program is complete without a thorough evaluation.

Figure 8.4 is a sample middle school staff development plan. Features of this plan include goal statements, performance requirements (*who* is going to do *what* for *whom* by *when*), and indicators of success (evaluation). Further, teachers, secretaries, educational assistants (EAs), substitutes, and administrators are part of the staff development program. Still further, all biweekly staff meetings have 15–20 minutes devoted to staff development topics.

INCENTIVE PROGRAMS

Incentive programs in education can be divided into three major categories: (1) programs with monetary incentives for improved performance; (2) programs that provide extra pay/extra responsibility for extra work; and (3) programs that offer nonmonetary/recognition incentives. Since the monetary incentives for improved performance are not very prevalent and a discussion of them often generates more heat than light, the focus of this section will be on the other two categories and the relation of incentives to staff development. Although the thrust here is on the teaching staff, other school employees should be able to participate as well.

The case can be made that in a comprehensive staff development plan, as illustrated by Figure 8.1, incentives are a part of the staff development program of a district. Incentives can be thought of as anything that encourages teachers to grow professionally and to enhance their skills. Principals will want to do all that they can to encourage teachers in this growth and, therefore, must be knowledgeable about the role of incentives.

There are a wide variety of programs that fall into the extra pay/extra responsibility category. Some examples are: department or grade level chairs;

(Text continues on page 236.)

FIGURE 8.4. SAMPLE MIDDLE SCHOOL STAFF DEVELOPMENT PLAN

I.   GOALS:

1.   **Policy:** to continue to reinforce and support all personnel with implementation of the discipline procedures.

2.   **Curriculum:** to study scheduling and elective options to meet the needs of increasing student enrollment.

3.   **Climate:** to support staff morale and student motivation.

4.   **Quality Teaching:** to continue to provide encouragement and support for ITIP, Peer Coaching, and Cooperative Learning.

II.   PERFORMANCE REQUIREMENTS:

1.   WHAT: "Needs Assessment Survey"
      FOR: All building staff — classified, certified, and substitutes
      BY: Building Principal and Staff Development Coordinator
      WHEN: Spring

2.   WHAT: "Clerical Staff (Secretaries) Inservice" - welcome, review goals, expectations, changes, clarify responsibilities and discuss building climate.
      FOR: Secretaries
      BY: Building Principal
      WHEN: August 20--return to buildings

3.   WHAT: "Orientation" - charactertistics of SMS students, discipline policy, schedule, building procedures, materials, supplies, expectations, etc.
      FOR: New teachers, E.A.s, substitutes
      BY: Building Principal, with counselor, librarian, head secretary, and vice principal
      WHEN: August 29 (before school opens)

4.   WHAT: "Collaboration & Team Building" - share goals for the year and skills of collaboration.
      FOR: All building staff (substitutes invited)
      BY: Building Principal with vice principal and 2-3 teachers
      WHEN: August 30 (half day inservice before school opens)

5.   WHAT: "Preparing for the First Day" - review discipline policy, classroom management, tips for motivating students, and student expectations.
     FOR: All building staff
     BY: Staff Development Coordinator or teacher designate with building principal.
     WHEN: 10:00 am - noon, August 31- (following all-district meeting and preceding catered staff lunch)

6.   WHAT: "Presenting a Positive Image: Handling Parent, Teacher and Student Interactions" (district offering)
     FOR: Clerical and classified staff
     BY: District or ESD Trainer
     WHEN: Mid-September

7.   WHAT: "E.A. Inservice" - welcome back, clarify duties, responsibilities, legal rights, expectations, discipline policy, etc.
     FOR: Building E.A.s
     BY: Building Principal
     WHEN: Afternoon—1 hour, August 31

8.   WHAT: "Peer Coaching" (district offering) ten-hour, one-credit class to set up coaching teams in each building to support implementation of effective teaching strategies.
     FOR: All certificated staff (administrators also)
     BY: District Trainer
     WHEN: Late Sept.-Early Oct. (Jan., Mar., May, follow-ups)

9.   WHAT: "Beginning ITIP" - (district offering)
     FOR: All teachers, E.A.s & substitutes
     BY: District Trainer
     WHEN: Fall — October

10. WHAT: "Scheduling & Electives Appropriate for Middle School Students"
     FOR: Middle School Staff
     BY: Consultant
     WHEN: Early October - delayed start (consultant to remain in the building all day to observe classes, students, study physical site, demographics, and later meet with a building study group who will take his recommendations into consideration as they make school visitations, review research and prepare a recommendation for the staff in March.)

11.   WHAT: "EA. Follow-up" - check on assignment of duties, address concerns, seek feedback.
       FOR: E.A.s
       BY: Building Principal
       WHEN: October — Friday am — before school coffee hour

12.   WHAT: "Motivation & Self-Esteem" - (district offering)
       FOR: All staff
       BY: District or ESD Trainer
       WHEN: November — once a week 10 hours, one credit

13.   WHAT: "Integrating Curriculum: Writing Across the Curriculum" - An examination of the writing process.
       FOR: Teachers, E.A.s, Secretaries
       BY: District Instructor
       WHEN: Nov., Jan., Mar., May (2-hour sessions, twice a month)

14.   WHAT: "Cooperative Learning" - (district offering)
       FOR: All staff
       BY: District Trainer
       WHEN: January

15.   WHAT: "Advanced ITIP" - (district offering)
       FOR: All interested staff
       BY: District Trainer
       WHEN: February

16.   WHAT: "Presentation of Scheduling & Electives Options"
       FOR: All building staff
       BY: Building study group
       WHO: Early March — Early Release

17.   WHAT: "Computerized Scheduling and Report Cards" - training on computer management.
       FOR: All building staff — teachers, secretaries, administrators
       BY: E5D computer trainer
       WHEN: April-May 20 hours, two credits

STAFF MEETING COMPONENT OF STAFF DEVELOPMENT

Bi-weekly staff meetings will devote 15-20 minutes to staff development topics. The following list is a guide to the topics that will be led by various staff members.

SEPT:	Team Building Souls — follow-up (invite parent advisory)
SEPT:	Motivating Students for Success
OCT:	Update: Revise/Reflect on Discipline Policy
OCT:	Collaboration: Input on Scheduling Options
NOV:	Implementing ITIP: Tips
NOV:	Writing Across the Curriculum: Tips
DEC:	Celebrating Our Gifts — Principal acknowledges each staff member for his/her special gifts to the school.
JAN:	Peer Coaching Progress Report: Implementing ITIP, Discipline, Writing
JAN:	Tips to Handle "End of the Semester Stress"
FEB:	Motivating Students for Success: "What Works" — presentation by Students.
FEB:	Progress Report for Scheduling/Electives by Study Group Members
MAR:	Teacher Feature: Selected by parent advisory group to acknowledge special efforts by particular teachers.
APR:	Model Cooperative Learning with staff meeting agenda
MAY:	Present Plan for Schedule & Elective Changes
MAY:	Motivating Students: Keeping Them Going Through the End of the Year
JUNE:	Celebrating our Successes: Reflection and Evaluation of our Year

III.   INDICATORS OF SUCCESS

1.   Completion of the above-listed staff meetings, inservice programs, classes, and workshops.

2.   The level of staff participation

3.   Evaluations of each staff development inservice

4.   Feedback, formal and informal regarding staff development activities, and staff meetings.

curriculum coordinators; cocurricular assignments such as coaching, advising, and supervising; mentoring new teachers; extended contracts for curriculum development; teaching extra classes; teaching beyond the school day (drivers' education); and asking the teacher to serve as a consultant in the district or outside the district. These activities can be good for the teacher as well as the district. The pay for this category should be thought of as an investment rather than strictly as an expenditure. A caution here is for the principal to be alert that the extra responsibility does not take the place of the classroom instruction and that teaching the students does not become secondary to the extra assignment.

Recognition can be a strong incentive to grow professionally. Some examples are: recognition in the newspaper and/or with the school board; a letter or certificate of appreciation; the Golden Apple Award from the Parent-Teacher Association; release from duties to attend professional conferences; naming facilities after the staff member: Jones Field, Smith Auditorium; teacher of the year, new teacher (rookie) of the year, coach of the year. Other examples are: printed business cards, frames for teaching certificates, lapel pins for number of years of service, and printed note pads. Still others are: thank you notes sent to the home address for extra impact, audiotapes, and semimonthly breakfasts to hear a motivating speaker or discuss a book or article. There are innumerable opportunities for the alert principal to recognize members of the staff if time is taken to focus on it. This activity should not be thought of as an addition to the principal's job but a vital part of it. It is also important to be timely with the recognition so that the recognition is connected to a specific deed.

The recognition program can develop awards for completion of the wellness program of the district. This is the next topic to be discussed as a part of the staff development program.

WELLNESS PROGRAMS

Another staff development program that can pay dividends for all employees of the district is the wellness program. The wellness program is a series of health measures and activities designed to support the employees in meeting their personal wellness goals. It is a voluntary program and can make a difference in classroom instruction and in the work life of district employees. When employees feel good and are healthy they can be more effective employees and coworkers. The activities generally fall into two categories: *preventive checks* and *wellness activities*.

The *preventive check* category includes:

- physical examination
- cholesterol screening
- blood pressure screening
- body composition screening
- prostate screening
- colon screening
- mammogram/medical doctor breast examination
- PAP smear
- flu shot
- one-mile walk test
- annual dental check-up
- biannual vision check
- hearing check
- personal health history
- breast self-exam
- testicular self-exam

The *wellness activity* category includes:

- fitness/exercise program—3 times a week for 30 minutes.
- nutritional assessment—keep a nutrition diary, low-fat cooking classes, etc.
- develop one leisure/hobby activity
- regular meditation and reflection time
- recycling/composting
- healthy back workshops
- skin mapping
- seat belt use 100% of the time
- positive behavior change
- water consumption

Besides being good for the individual some of the activities can bring about a positive climate in the school. Aerobics classes and faculty-staff volleyball games are just two examples.

CONCLUSION

Designed to make a significant difference in the teaching lives of the staff, and thus, make a similar difference in the learning lives of students, the staff development function will take on a greater role in the improvement of instruction and the achievement of students. The principal, likewise, will have greater responsibilities for the development of the staff. The principal is the key person in the staff development process, much like the teacher is for students. As district office staff members are eliminated, this is a responsibility which the principal should eagerly accept. If done correctly, staff development will not be seen as merely a collection of various inservice activities but rather a carefully planned, research-based, curriculum-oriented program.

REFERENCES

Ankeny Community Schools (1989). *Staff development plan.* Ankeny, OH: Ankeny Community Schools.

Asayesh, G. (1994). Effective advocacy for staff development. *Journal for Staff Development*, 15 (2).

Asayesh, G. (1993). Staff development for improving student outcomes. *Journal for Staff Development*, 14 (3).

Burden, P.R., and D. Wallace (1983). *Tailoring staff development to meet teacher needs.* Paper presented at the Association of Teacher Educators meeting, Wichita, KS.

Ellis, S.S. (1994). Principals as staff developers. *Journal of Staff Development*, 15 (2).

Gall, M.D., et al. (1985). *Effective staff development for teachers.* Eugene, OR: College of Education, University of Oregon (ERIC Clearinghouse on Educational Management).

Gersten, R., D. Carnine, and P. Williams (1982). Measuring implementation of a structured educational model in an urban school district: An observational approach. *Educational Evaluation and Policy Analysis.*

Goodlad, J.L. (1983). The school as workplace. In G.A Griffin, *Staff Development.* Chicago: University of Chicago Press.

Hall, G.E., and S.F. Loucks (1980). *Program definition and adaptation: Implications for inservice.* Austin, TX: Research and Development Center for Teacher Education, University of Texas.

Holly, M.L. (1982). Teachers' views on inservice training. *Phi Delta Kappan,* Bloomington, IN.

Jakicic, C. (1994). Taking small steps to promote collaboration. *Journal of Staff Development,* 15 (2).

Joyce, B.R., K. Howey, and S. Yarger (1976). *ISTE Report I.* Palo Alto, CA: Stanford Center for Research and Development in Teaching.

Kirkpatrick, D.L. (1975). *Evaluating training programs.* Alexandria, VA: American Society for Training and Development.

Lawrence, G., and D. Harrison (1980). *Policy implications of the research on the professional development of education personnel: An analysis of fifty-nine studies.* Washington, DC: Feistritzer Publications.

Loucks, S., and H. Pratt (1980). A concerns-based approach to curriculum change. *Educational Leadership.*

McBride, R.E., J. Reed, and J. Dollar (1994). Teacher attitudes toward staff development: A symbiotic relationship at best. *Journal of Staff Development,* 15 (2).

Nolan, J.F., and T. Huber (1989). Nurturing the Reflective Practitioner Through Instructional Supervision. *Journal of Curriculum and Supervision,* 4 (2), 128.

Orlich, D.C., A.L. Remaley, K.C. Racemyer, J. Logan, and Q. Cao (1993). Seeking the link between student achievement and staff development. *Journal of Staff Development,* 14 (3).

Porter, A. (1981). Curriculum content influenced by many factors. *IRT Communication Quarterly.*

Rogers, C.R. (1983). *Freedom to learn for the 1980s.* Columbus, OH: Merrill Publishing Co.

Sadowski, L.L. (1993). Staff development 101 for administrators: alternatives for thirteen management myths. *Journal of Staff Development,* 14 (3).

Seyfarth, J.T. (1991). *Personnel management for effective schools.* Boston: Allyn and Bacon.

Sousa, D.A. (1992). Ten questions for rating your staff development program. *Journal of Staff Development,* 13 (2).

Sparks, D., and S. Vaughn (1994) What every school board member should know about staff development. *Journal of Staff Development,* 15 (2).

Stallings, J. (1985). *How effective is an analytic approach to staff development on teacher and student behavior?* Nashville, TN: Vanderbilt University, Peabody College.

Stallings, J., and E.M. Krasavage (1986). Program implementation and student achievement in a four-year Madeline Hunter follow-through project. *The Elementary School Journal.*

Sullivan, R. (26 Jan. 1981). City's teacher training program criticized in 1977–1978 state audit. *New York Times.*

Todnem, G., and M. P. Warner (1993). Using ROI to assess staff development efforts. *Journal of Staff Development,* 14 (3).

Wenatchee Public Schools. *Staff Development.* Wenatchee, WA.

Williams, R. (1993). Initiatives for systemic change. *Journal of Staff Development,* 14 (2).

Wood, F.H., and S.D. Caldwell (1991). Planning and training to implement site-based management. *Journal of Staff Development,* 12 (3).

Wood, F.H., and S.R. Thompson (1993). Assumptions about staff development based on research and best practice. *Journal of Staff Development,* 14 (4).

9

COLLECTIVE BARGAINING

REASONS FOR STUDYING COLLECTIVE BARGAINING

♦ Principals work with teachers. Teachers belong to groups that bargain. Therefore, it is important for principals to understand bargaining.

♦ An understanding of the art of negotiating will help principals in their daily tasks.

♦ Failure on the part of the principal to be knowledgeable about the bargained contract and process can lead to leadership difficulty.

♦ The principal's role on the district management team can provide a site-based emphasis to the bargaining process.

Principals and teachers in a conflict situation should come to see themselves as working cooperatively, attacking the problem, not each other.

Fisher and Ury

INTRODUCTION

The National Education Association (NEA) was formed in 1857. However, it was formed as a professional association rather than a labor union. Its development into a labor union is a rather recent development and, in some cases, can be traced to the unilateral, authoritarian action by administrators. In fact, some states retain laws which prohibit collective bargaining by public school employees. In Washington State, a bill was introduced to the legislature that would severely limit the scope of collective bargaining. In the words of the Washington Education Association, it would "...drag education employees back into the pre-1965 'meet and confer' era when the balance of power in all employer-employee matters lay with the school boards." Even in the current conservative political climate, the bill is viewed as having little chance of being enacted. However, it serves as an illustration of a political reaction to the perceived power of the labor unions that represent school employees.

In the 1960s the National Education Association (NEA) developed a bargaining agenda which had met with initial success in some of the Great Lakes states such as Michigan and Wisconsin. This bargaining agenda was exported to other states. The state and local affiliates pressed for representation rights and, subsequently, for greater control over terms of employment and working conditions. The bargaining style which emerged was positional and confrontational. It pitted a teacher agenda, which was often heavily influenced by the state and national organization, against that of the district. Districts had been accustomed to dictating terms and conditions to employees. Thus, the typical initial response to bargaining was for positions to be directed by school boards and the administrators of the district. The limited roles of principals on the bargaining team were to defend the prescribed district positions and to lend credibility to those positions by virtue of their position on the front lines with the teachers. Things in this arena are changing.

The trend toward revised governance structures in schools is having a profound influence on the bargaining process. As we are in the midst of this change, it is difficult to predict the long range effects. However, some changes are clear and easy to describe at present. These include an emerging consensus that the management of schools is not and should not be the exclusive province of the board, central office administrators, and principals. Rather, it is increasingly accepted that those closest to the educational process should have an increasing and perhaps dominant voice in decisions. Thus, teachers and principals are beginning to assume more influential roles. This is beginning to be felt in the area of collective bargaining. The principal now serves as much more than a source of credibility. The principal is a partner in the development of language that creates terms and conditions of employment which facilitate new management-teacher relationships. We are beginning to see the emergence of a partnership designed to create the new educational structures needed to deliver services to our changing clientele. Principals no longer seem willing to serve as spokespersons for a board of directors which is detached from the educational process. Rather, they are stepping up to a lead position in collective bargaining.

Principals sense the shift in the importance of their role in the bargaining process and they attribute that shift to changing governance structures. However, districts are slow to recognize this shift and continue to relegate principals to a secondary role in the bargaining process. This seems to support the contention that this is an emerging change.

TRANSITION FROM POSITIONAL TO COLLABORATIVE BARGAINING

Bargaining between professional educators and boards of eduction is shifting from the positional bargaining which developed in the 1960s and 1970s to the collaborative bargaining model. A comparison of the models is set forth in Figure 9.1.

PRINCIPAL'S BEHAVIORS AND THE COLLABORATIVE BARGAINING MODEL

Principals, whether or not in the collaborative bargaining arena, should develop a thorough understanding of the collaborative model and the behaviors that promote a climate of trust. Figure 9.2, beginning on page 246, outlines an integration of the four steps of collaborative bargaining and the appropriate behaviors that reinforce collaboration. When the collaborative model breaks down, principals would be wise to first consider their behavior and whether it was a contributing factor before looking at either the process or the other professionals involved in the conflict.

COLLABORATIVE BARGAINING PRINCIPLES AND ASSUMPTIONS

The principal needs to develop an operational model which differs from positional bargaining in order to develop positive and trusting relationships with others. This is true not only when the principal is on the bargaining team but also when performing normal day-to-day leadership and

---

FIGURE 9.1. COMPARISON OF BARGAINING MODELS

Positional Bargaining	Collaborative Bargaining
• Follow rituals	• Be flexible
• Stake out positions	• Focus on interests
• Vague and closed about interests	• Open and direct about interests
• Backward looking	• Forward looking
• Content expert	• Process expert
• Emphasize risks	• Emphasize potential for mutual gain
• Leverage deadline to force movement	• Allocate time in relation to importance of issue
• Focus on quick fixes and closure	• Focus on lasting solutions
• Allocation of resources	• Expansion of resources

management duties. Figures 9.3, on page 248, lists key elements of the principles and assumptions.

MUKILTEO SCHOOL DISTRICT: A CASE STUDY OF COLLABORATIVE BARGAINING

What is the best way for school districts and associations to deal with their differences? After having the longest teacher strike in the history of the State of Washington (about 33 days), the Mukilteo School District and the Mukilteo Education Association were able to work out a three-year contract by using collaborative bargaining. Negotiation is a fact of life. We do it every day of our lives in varying settings from deciding where to go to dinner

FIGURE 9.2. THE COLLABORTIVE BARGAINING MODEL

Stage 1 — Moderating Culture

- *Control Emotional Expression*
  Avoid posturing, confrontation, and personal attacks and remain calm in
  the face of volatile or provocative behavior.

- *Promote Positive Group Climate*
  Develop ground rules for how labor/management committee meetings will
  be conducted and enforce constructive behavior in these meetings.

- *Suspend Judgment*
  Actively try to understand the other side's point of view by listening
  before joining arguments, by not taking rigid positions, and by exhibiting a
  willingness to collaborate.

- *Apply Interpersonal Skills*
  Use verbal and nonverbal cues to help structure committee members'
  understanding of agendas, decisions, and action plans and give committee
  members supportive feedback to encourage active, balanced, and creative
  participation.

Stage 2 — Building Relationships

- *Acknowledge Systems*
  Understand and respect relevant aspects of organization/worksite policies
  and procedures, union structure, and the bargaining agreement.

- *Accept the Bargaining Process*
  Respect the differences between labor and management and actively
  support the negotiations team as a legitimate forum.

- *Project Commitment*
  Exhibit confidence in own judgment. Take and change positions based
  upon an analysis of factual information and stand up to negative or
  confrontational people.

- *Maintain Credibility*
  Demonstrate reliability by honoring agreements, avoiding surprises,
  sharing constraints, and communicating without hidden agendas.

Stage 3 — Integrate Interests

- *Combine Systematic and Creative Thinking*
  Define issues clearly, gather relevant information, explore alternative remedies, and strive for innovative/imaginative solutions.

- *Integrate Formal and Informal Activities*
  Use an appropriate balance of formal and informal meetings and settings to address issues, formulate solutions, and build support.

- *Emphasize Mutual Benefits*
  Formulate solutions that address the other side's underlying interests and concerns and emphasizes benefits to the other side when presenting solutions.

Stage 4 — Agreements

- *Build and Protect Alliance*
  Identify key players on both sides. Anticipate their positions and reactions and take steps to gain their support.

- *Make Efficient Use of Resources*
  Maximize committee effectiveness by using relevant subgroups and individuals inside and outside the committee to help define and resolve issues and problems.

- *Press for Closure*
  Focus on issues and problems that both sides want to resolve and do whatever it takes to assure that committee decisions and agreement are implemented.

- *Use Feedback to Improve Results*
  Evaluate committee process and outcomes regularly and initiate remedial actions needed to assure achievements of committee goals.

FIGURE 9.3. COLLABORATIVE BARGAINING ASSUMPTIONS AND PRINCIPLES

Assumptions	Principles
• All can benefit • Relationships can be enhanced • Synergy is key—the whole is greater than the sum of its parts • Feelings are facts • The process never ends—although there may be a pause	• Focus on issues or problems—not on people • Focus on interests of each party—not on position • Focus on options or choices • Focus on fairness

with our spouse to setting a curfew for our kids. Negotiation is a back and forth communication designed to reach an agreement between two sides.

With the advent of site councils, a trend has emerged where everyone wants to participate in decisions that affect them and fewer people are willing to accept decisions dictated by someone else. Standard strategies for negotiation often leave people dissatisfied and alienated. This was the situation that faced Mukilteo after the strike.

Standard strategy consists of two ways to negotiate: soft or hard. Soft negotiation tries to avoid conflict by willingly making concessions to reach an agreement with the other side. Soft negotiators often end up feeling exploited and bitter about the negotiations.

The second common strategy is hard negotiation. In this type of negotiation, the negotiator sees every situation as a contest of wills where the side that takes an extreme position and holds out the longest wins. Hard negotiators want to win, which will elicit a tough response from the other side that ends up harming the relationship between the two sides.

As the Mukilteo School District found, there is a better way. It is neither hard nor soft. It is based on deciding issues on their merits, not on what each side says what it is willing to do and not do. With this method, you look for mutual gains and, if there is a conflict of interests, the outcome is based on a fair standard independent of the will of either side. Collaborative bargaining is hard on problems but soft on people.

Using collaborative bargaining principles and assumptions together with the stark realization that positional bargaining did not work very effectively, the Mukilteo School District and Mukilteo Education Association built a more positive climate which led to a more trusting relationship and to the development of site-based school councils. The collaborative negotiation brought out an "us" attitude rather than the previous "we–they." This process took time, but as one of the participants summed up the feelings of all sides, "it was worth it." The students, teachers, parents, district, and community all benefitted. Much work remains to be done to make these gains part of the culture, but there is a good start. Other school districts and education associations would be well advised to adopt this model. Principals can play a key role in the establishment of the collaborative model.

STEPS TO SUCCESS

Prior to any new approach to bargaining, members of both parties and other significant leaders should be involved in training sessions so that they understand the approach and devleop new skills. Such training is best done by an outside facilitator agreed upon by both sides and should be done in a retreat setting of two days, followed by a one-day retreat immediately prior to the commencing of the process.

The following steps are key to *the process*, *the agreement*, and the *length of the agreement*:

- ♦ **Ground Rules**

    After the training and after the general assumptions and principles have been agreed upon, the Collaborative Bargaining Team members (both labor and management) must act on those agreements. One of the first places to do this is to develop the ground rules. Figure 9.4 is a list of possible topics for ground rules.

    An example of the ground rules is Figure 9.5. These ground rules were arrived at collaboratively.

- ♦ **Agree on the List of Issues**

    All team members should meet with the groups they represent in order to develop the issues important to the members of the

FIGURE 9.4. POSSIBLE TOPICS FOR GROUND RULES

1.   Scope of Agenda Issues — Scope of Issues

2.   Use of Caucus

3.   Participation by Negotiating Team

4.   Alternates

5.   Visitors

6.   Interruptions/Messages

7.   Communication/Connections to Constituents/Media

8.   Targeted Completion Date

9.   Frequency of Meetings/Length of Meetings

10.   Potential Use of Sub-Committees

11.   What to Do If This Process Breaks Down/Stalls Out
      (Notifying other party of concern, etc.)

12.   All "Agreements" Tentative until Final Agreement Reached

13.   Tentative Agreement Must Be Ratified

14.   Preparing Language Before/After Reaching Tentative Agreement

15.   Facilitator Role; Sharing of Role of Facilitator

16.   Adding Issues; Jointly Developing New Issues

17.   Note Taking/Record Keeping; Record Maintenance

18.   Meeting Location

19.   Adapting/Accommodating Work Schedules

FIGURE 9.5. SAMPLE COLLABORATIVE BARGAINING GROUND RULES

1. Meetings will be held on Thursdays from 5 to 7 p.m. beginning February 3, 1994, in the Excellent School District Board Room, unless otherwise agreed to.

2. Issues presented will represent the legitimate goals and purposes of each party. Each party will respect the legitimacy of the other party's issues.

3. Negotiating Team Members will:

    - Arrive at the meetings on time.
    - Keep the discussion focused on the issue being addressed.
    - Let one Team Member speak at a time with no interruptions.
    - Pay attention to whomever is speaking.
    - Make constructive comments and suggestions, avoid value judgments, and try to suggest alternatives.
    - Be open to new ideas and explore other Team Members' ideas.
    - Exercise patience with the process and the people involved.

4. Each Negotiating Team Member agrees to participate in the process, and no Team Member will dominate the discussions. There will be no chief spokesperson for either party, and there will be no alternates for absences.

5. A caucus may be held at any time. The Facilitator will assist if requested.

6. Visitors are welcome as observers and to attend caucuses; however, they will not participate in the Negotiating Team discussions. Visitors will be asked to contact the Association President or the District's Human Resources Manager before they attend a session.

7. Each Team Member will be mindful of the impacts of his or her public and private statements about the negotiations on the efforts of the Negotiating Team.

8. As issues are resolved, proposed language for the agreement will be written by a subcommittee of the Negotiating Team, the whole Negotiating Team, or a caucus of either party.

9. If new issues are generated as a result of developing options for original issues, they will be addressed at a time agreed upon by the members, consistent with the issue topic as it relates to other issues.

10. The Human Resources Manager's Secretary will be the custodian for all tentative agreements.

11. Both parties agree that the role of the Facilitator is to keep the Negotiating Team Members on the process.

12. Each Team Member should feel free to remind other Team Members to follow these guidelines.

13. If the process breaks down, Negotiating Team Members agree to discuss the reasons why and attempt to resolve the problem and return to the process.

group and to inform them of the process to be used during collaborative bargaining. After the team members come together and establish the ground rules, the issues should be listed on easel paper and taped around the room. Make sure that each member has one chance to speak before any member has the second chance. Repeat this process around the room allowing members to pass if they have no more issues or if their issue has already been mentioned. The list can then be refined by combining like issues, and adding or deleting others. When deleting, always obtain absolute concurrence from the entire group and anyone who suggested that issue.

♦ **Prepare and Present Interest Statements**

An interest statement is one party's concern about an issue. These interest statements are best developed during caucus or between meetings. It is helpful to enlist other members of your party in this process so they also develop an understanding.

All interest statements should be presented, then paraphrased by the nonpresented parties to ensure good communication.

♦ **Develop Options**

An option is one of several solutions that can satisfy an interest or an issue. It is important here to attempt to develop many options to satisfy the interest. This should be done by each party separately, then jointly. An example of issues, interest, and options is given in Figure 9.6.

♦ **Test Options Against Standards**

After the many options have been developed, they should be tested against objective standards. Standards could be legal; mission-driven; good for students; and financially responsible, among others.

♦ **Choose the Best Solution**

This is the final step to success of the contract language. From among the many options the team chooses the best possible solution that meets the standards at the current time. The best approach to the choosing is a consensus approach. Consensus means that all members can honestly say:

FIGURE 9.6. AN EXAMPLE OF ISSUES, INTEREST, AND OPTIONS

ISSUE

Seniority

INTEREST

We are interested in a system where
length of service with the organization shall be
considered a criterion for promotion.

OPTIONS

1. Strict Seniority
2. Experience
3. Qualifications
4. Trial Period
5. Performance Evaluations
6. Length of Service in Other Positions

- I believe that you understand my point of view and that I understand yours, and
- Whether or not I prefer this option, I support it because it was reached fairly and openly, and it is the best solution for us at this time.

COMMUNICATION SKILLS

Communication is often the key problem in negotiations. Without communication, there is no negotiation. Communication in negotiations has three major problems to overcome.

First, negotiators may not be *talking to each other in a way that can be understood.* If hostile and suspicious feelings are being harbored on one or both sides, you should expect that the other side will almost always hear something different than what you said. Frequently, when distributive win/lose bargaining is taking place, both sides are not attempting any serious communication; instead they are just talking to impress their own association or district. This leads to the **second** problem—*listening*. Even when you are talking directly to them, they don't hear you because they are so busy thinking about how they are going to reply. This is referred to as "shoot and reload" syndrome.

The **third** problem is *misunderstanding*. Negotiations can be compared to sending smoke signals in a high wind: what is said is often misinterpreted by the other side. To solve these communication problems, you need to become an active listener. Standard techniques are to pay close attention, to ask the other party to spell out what they mean in a clear and careful way, and to request the other party to repeat their ideas if there is any ambiguity for you. The other side will feel comforted by your questions because they will know that they are being heard and understood.

Another factor to consider in communicating when participating in collaborative negotiations is perception. It is alright to discuss each other's perceptions. Make the perceptions explicit and discuss them with others in an honest manner without blaming another for the problem. A discussion like this can go a long way toward clarifying perceptions between associations and school districts. If people are not involved in the process, they are not likely to approve of the outcome, so give them a stake in the outcome by making sure that they can participate in the process. Figure 9.7 lists some communication skills that need to be part of the training and used in bargaining as well as daily management of a school.

Listening is critical to the collaborative bargaining process as well as school leadership. If you are good at listening, you are a good communicator who takes time to acknowledge other people's ideas and feelings.

Some people, especially those in authority positions, tend to be better at talking than listening because they are used to being "listened to." Other factors such as mood and timing can undermine our ability to listen to and hear what someone else is saying. Figure 9.8 presents techniques for developing listening skills.

PRODUCTIVE GROUP BEHAVIORS

The quality of a group's relationship can frequently be directly linked to the quality of the communications. There are identifiable communication behaviors which can be shown to have either a positive or negative influence on the interactions of the groups. Individual group members can have a positive impact on the group's function by monitoring the nature of the

FIGURE 9.7. TECHNIQUES FOR DEVELOPING COMMUNICATION SKILLS

- Use "I" not "You" Messages

  Ex: "I am upset that I can't schedule a meeting in the next week" versus "You never are available to meet with me."

- Ask Questions for Clarification First

  Ex: "I need clarification on how you understand the assignment of overtime in this department" versus "Isn't overtime always given to the same people in this department?"

- Paraphrase

  A)   For Accuracy

  Ex: "I hear you saying that in calculating overtime if the employee works four (4) hours and 22 minutes that will be considered as four and one-half (4 1/2) hours of overtime."

  B)   For Understanding

  Ex: "Are you saying that sick leave can be used for bereavement for five (5) days guaranteed and more could be granted if needed?"

- Check Assumptions/Perception

  Ex: "Are you concerned that people will use bereavement leave for a family member they barely know?" versus "You always assume that people will use any excuse to get out of work."

FIGURE 9.8. TECHNIQUES FOR DEVELOPING LISTENING SKILLS

- Focus on the ideas being presented, on the speaker, and on the delivery.

- Get the meaning behind the words. Ask questions to clarify.

- Resist the urge to respond immediately. Even though you may want to express something, it's better to listen first.

- Don't rush or interrupt the speaker. And don't change the subject until the speaker is finished.

- Don't plan a response while the speaker is talking. You'll be thinking and not listening.

- Acknowledge that the speaker has been heard before responding.

- Avoid getting provoked by strong words. Hear the speaker out.

- Connect feelings and emotions to the words. They are part of the message.

- Work at listening. It requires energy and attention.

- Watch body language. It often tells more than the words.

contributions, including their own, and working to ensure that interactions contribute to, rather than inhibit, successful outcomes.

The following framework of communication behaviors is adapted from the work of Schein (1969), who summarized the work of Gordon, Rogers, Ginott, and others. The "Roadblock" behaviors are those that impede the accomplishment of group goals. "Productive" behaviors are those that must occur conssitently for satisfactory progress to be made (see Figure 9.9).

- ◆ **Roadblock Behaviors**
  - **Avoiding:** Diverting the topic, bird walking and "stonewalling"

FIGURE 9.9. GROUP COMMUNICATIONS BEHAVIORS

PRODUCTIVE BEHAVIORS	ROADBLOCK BEHAVIORS
⟶	⟵
+ Initiating	– Avoiding
+ Information Giving	– Personal Attacks
+ Active Listening	– Poor Listening
+ Maintenance	– Directing
+ Proposing Closure	– Judging

CAVEAT:

Some effective behaviors can be dysfunctional if not balanced with other effective behaviors.

Examples:

Over-Defining the Problem
*
"Hyperactive" Listening
*
Opinion Overload
*
Excess Maintenance Behavior (process over substance)

- **Personal Attacks:** Put-downs, "sharp" humor, false humor, and name calling
- **Poor Listening:** Planning ahead, daydreaming, and assuming
- **Directing:** Use of positional power and authority through ordering, threatening, paternalistic advising, and monopolizing time
- **Judging:** Unsolicited diagnosing and criticizing before the appropriate time for evaluation

♦ **Productive Behaviors**
  - **Initiating:** Identifying issues and defining the problem
  - **Information Giving:** Offering facts, data, ideas, opinions, perceptions, or feedback
  - **Active Listening:** Seeking first to understand by soliciting opinions and information, clarifying, summarizing, and remaining open to feedback
  - **Maintenance:** Process checking, harmonizing, management of the environment, encouraging, "gatekeeping," and timekeeping
  - **Proposing Closure:** Using techniques for closure, including: evaluation against interests, "straw" designs, testing for consensus, and intuitive summaries

CONFLICT

Whatever the skill, training, or intent of the team members, conflict is inevitable. Jandt and Gillette (1985) make the following assumptions about conflict:

♦ Conflict is inevitable and not necessarily harmful.

♦ Some kinds of conflict can contribute immeasurably to the health and well-being of the organization—for example, by stimulating productive competition.

♦ No matter what the conflict, it can be managed in such a way that losses are minimized and gains maximized.

It is beneficial for the principal to think of *managing* rather than *resolving* conflict. Some conflicts can be solved, others need to be managed because the resources of time and money to resolve them plainly are not worth it.

It is also helpful to think of satisfying the conflict along three dimensions: **Procedural**, **Substantive**, and **Psychological**. To satisfy the parties to the conflict the principal must attend to the *process*, the *content* of the agreement, and to how the parties *feel* about the "solution" to the conflict (see Figure 9.10).

A comprehensive list comparing the elements of a relationship that may promote conflict and collaboration is detailed in Figure 9.11, which begins on page 260. The principal and others can check their behaviors against these contrasting elements.

FIGURE 9.10. ELEMENTS OF CONFLICT MANAGEMENT/RESOLUTION

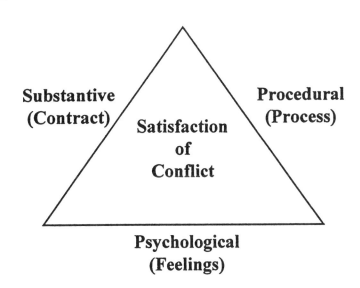

FIGURE 9.11. ELEMENTS OF THE LABOR RELATIONSHIP THAT PROMOTE CONFLICT AND COLLABORATION

Promote Conflict

Promote Collaboration

Attitudes

1. Managing is done "around the contract."

2. "Distributive" bargaining of separate interests with compromise.

3. Mediation takes place only after impasse is formally declared.

4. The other side is viewed as a problem in an involuntary relationship.

1. Managing is done "through the contract."

2. "Collaborative" bargaining of mutual interests.

3. Informal mediation processes are built in so they happen continuously.

4. The other side is accepted as a necessary part of a bilateral process.

Financial Structures

5. Budgetary information is restricted by the district.

5. Open budget processes and/or financial formula are used.

Bargaining Processes

6. Bargaining is done from positions.

7. One person talks for each side, or communication is restricted.

8. Caucuses are frequent, and the purpose and outcome is kept secret.

9. Bargaining chips are used frequently.

10. Bargaining consists of a "package" of small tentative agreements into which each side is fixed.

11. Bargaining planning involves the selection of positions.

12. Each side sits directly across the table from the other.

13. Communications to the constituencies and general public are frequently conflicting and divisive.

6. Bargaining is done from problem statements.

7. Open communication with everyone encouraged to talk.

8. Caucuses are held less frequently, with each side openly explaining the reason for the caucus and the outcome.

9. Both sides strive for consensus and the elimination of bargaining chips.

10. Bargaining involves conceptualizing the "bigger picture."

11. Process planning tools are utilized to analyze interests, options, and parameters.

12. Participants are arranged in a circle around a mutual focal point such as a flip chart.

13. Communications with constituencies and the general public are developed together.

Working Relationships

14. The labor-management relationship evolves as a by-product of the collective bargaining process.

14. The two sides work together to plan and develop a relationship which supports the achievement of mutual goals.

15. Relationship issues and substantive issues are mixed and traded off for one another.

15. Relationship issues and substantive issues are addressed separately and independently.

16. Field representatives and consultants are perceived as outsiders.

16. Field representatives and consultants are perceived as insiders, or as bringing unique mediation and dispute resolution skills.

17. Formal bargaining is the only problem-solving mechanism.

17. Mechanisms for solving problems are developed, including communications and issue-focused committees and brainstorming strategies.

18. The superintendent and board are insulated from the labor relations process.

18. The superintendent and board are involved in the labor relations processes, although not at the table.

19. There is a positional approach to work-site problems.

19. There is a "consensus" approach to work-site problems.

20. There is a reliance on format grievance procedures, unfair hearings, and concerted job actions for resolving conflict.

20. There is a reliance on problem-solving techniques for resolving conflict.

Shared Decision Making

21. Bargaining is narrowly confined to scope.

21. Discussions and decisions address all aspects of the mutual relationship (even beyond scope).

22. Employee groups feel excluded from decision making.

22. Employee groups feel included in relevant decisions.

COMPENSATION

The principal's role in compensation programs is minimal. This is an area for centralization with the district office staff. Centralization provides standardization and equity as well as accurate information in a sensitive and critical area. Nevertheless, the principal should have a general understanding of the salary schedule and the benefits program in order to provide assistance which must be confirmed by the district office staff.

A KEY IDEA

The principal should refer all inquiries regarding salary and benefits to the policy manual or to the staff at the district office.

In addition, the principal must also provide information to the superintendent when the salary and benefits for teachers do not allow the school to compete for outstanding teachers. Membership of the principal on the collaborative collective bargaining team can be beneficial to both teachers and the district personnel. The principal can often view potential conflict from another position and thus, improve communication among all participants.

MARYSVILLE (WA) SCHOOL DISTRICT CASE STUDY

The Marysville School District developed the six, 10-year goals through the collaborative process as shown in Figure 9.12. In addition, the district and the association developed their respective roles in the achievement of those goals, as shown in Figure 9.13 on page 264. This is an excellent example of the collaborative bargaining process.

CONCLUSION

The role of the principal in collaborative bargaining can be critically important, directly to the success of the process, and indirectly to the district. The principal's understanding of the collaborative process and the roles that the elements of trust, communication skills, and conflict management play in the process can help both the teachers' association and the district management team fashion an agreement which will serve everyone well. Further, in learning and refining these skills, the principal becomes more skillful in the day-to-day leadership of the school.

FIGURE 9.12. MARYSVILLE SCHOOL DISTRICT—10-YEAR GOALS

1.   Financial security

2.   Quality facilities

3.   Culture of collaboration and cooperation within the
      educational community (trust, respect, honesty, and caring)

4.   Plan to address rapidly changing student needs

5.   Recruit, retain, and develop a quality, culturally diverse
      staff

6.   Ongoing flexible strategic planning process
      •   Technology
      •   Shared decision making
      •   Performance-based education

One of the best ways for the principal to become knowledgeable about the contract and its significance at the building level is to be a member of the collaborative bargaining team. It is in this role that the principal can assist other members of the team realize the impact that the contract has on students and teachers, as well as on principals and parents.

REFERENCES

Adams, J.L. (1974). *Conceptual blockbusting; a guide to better ideas.* San Francisco: W.H. Freeman.

Attea, W.J. (1993). From conventional to strategic bargaining: One superintendent's experience. *The School Administrator,* 16–19.

FIGURE 9.13. MARYSVILLE SCHOOL DISTRICT—DISTRICT AND ASSOCIATION ROLES IN 10-YEAR GOALS

GOAL 1: FINANCIAL SECURITY

DISTRICT ROLE

- Ensure that resources support district priorities
- Ensure communications and involvement in fiscal planning and management
- Assemble budget
- Provide leadership for levies

ASSOCIATION ROLE

- Seek ongoing sharing of financial information by the district
- Review information from Association's perspective
- Make members aware of the financial realities that exist
- Become partners with the District in planning and prioritizing the budget
- Active involvement in levy campaigns
- Actively participate in legislative lobbying efforts
- Participate in grant writing

GOAL 2: QUALITY FACILITIES

DISTRICT ROLE

- Develop long-range facilities plans through collaborative process
- Maintain and update existing facilities

ASSOCIATION ROLE

- Keep district informed of facility needs
- Help plan healthy facilities and see them through
- When costs meet needs, we get to help decide what to give up

GOAL 3: TRUST, RESPECT, HONESTY, AND CARING

DISTRICT ROLE

- Build trust
- Create a climate that values trust, respect, honesty
- Adhere to operating principles and model these qualities

ASSOCIATION ROLE

- We commit to you that we will be honest with the district and to our members
- Be ambassadors out in the community with the public
- Active participation information of District committees

GOAL 4: DEVELOP A PLAN TO ADDRESS
RAPIDLY CHANGING STUDENT NEEDS

DISTRICT ROLE

- Stay abreast of current research and proven models / programs / strategies
- Provide continuous staff development

ASSOCIATION ROLE

- Identify needs of teachers for coping effectively with changing needs of students
- Provide resources for staff development to meet those needs
- Design a staff development plan cooperatively with the District
- Be pro-active, not obstructionists

GOAL 5: RECRUIT, RETAIN, AND DEVELOP
QUALITY, CULTURALLY DIVERSE STAFF

DISTRICT ROLE

- Implement community developed recruitment and training plan that ensures a quality, diverse staff
- Model lifelong learning

ASSOCIATION ROLE

- Provide resources and help plan for staff development
- Be role models for students and peers with regard to racial and gender issues
- Encourage minority students to pursue careers in education

GOAL 6: STRATEGIC PLANNING

DISTRICT ROLE

- Participate with staff and community in the goals and process
- Provide information and support
- Base decisions on priorities of the strategic plan

ASSOCIATION ROLE

- Be participants on implementation committees
- Analyze and inform the district of anything that would potentially impact the contract

Bluestone, B., and I. Bluestone (1992). *Negotiating the future:A labor perspective*. New York: Basic Books.

Conley, D.T. (1993). *Roadmap to restructuring: policies, practices, and the emerging visions of schooling*. Eugene, OR: ERIC Clearinghouse on Educational Management.

Covey, S.R. (1991). *Principle-centered leadership*. New York: Summit.

Covey, S.R. (1989). *The seven habits of highly effective people*. New York: Simon and Schuster.

Decker, R.H. (1991). Helping the board of education and negotiating team understand their roles in collective bargaining. *School Business Affairs*, 6–10.

Fisher, R., and S. Brown (1989). *Getting together*. New York: Penguin Books.

Fisher, R., and W. Ury (1981). *Getting to yes*. Boston: Houghton Mifflin.

Jandt, F.E., and P. Gillette (1985). *Win-win negotiation: Turning conflict into agreement*. New York: Wiley.

Janes, L., and N.B. Lovell (1982). A systematic labor-relations model: Returning the principal to the driver's seat. *NASSP Bulletin*, 66 (451), 73–78.

Kerchner, C.T. (1988). Professional negotiations: The critical role of administrators. *Thrust*, 10–14.

Kerchner, C.T. (1993). Building the airplane as it rolls down the runway: Administrators discover labor relations as the linchpin to school change. *The School Administrator*, 10–14.

Malito, R.T. (1992). A new era in negotiations. *The Clearinghouse*, 51–52.

Peters, T.J. (1987). *Thriving on chaos*. New York: Knopf.

Schein, E.H. (1969). *Process consultation*. Reading, MA: Addison Wesley.

Sharp, W.L. (1993). *Collective bargaining in the public schools*. Madison, WI: WCB Brown and Benchmark.

Smith, S.C., D. Ball, and D. Liontos (1991). *Working together: The collaborative style of bargaining*. Eugene, OR: ERIC Clearinghouse on Educational Management.

Weisbord, M.R. (1987). *Productive workplaces: Organizing and managing for dignity, meaning, and community*. San Francisco: Jossey-Bass.

10

CONTINUITY AND LEGAL ISSUES

REASONS FOR STUDYING CONTINUITY AND LEGAL ISSUES

- ◆ Our contemporary society is a very litigious one. Staying out of legal troubles is critical to your success as a principal.
- ◆ Your teachers, staff, students, and parents will, from time to time, ask you about the legality of certain actions. You will want to know the legal basics.
- ◆ The failure to follow certain statutes on your part is *prima facie* evidence to revoke your certificate as principal.
- ◆ One element of treating people fairly is to treat them legally.

> *School-based leadership makes the principal more vulnerable in the legal arena.*

LEGAL ISSUES IN SCHOOL HUMAN RESOURCES ADMINISTRATION

INTRODUCTION

This chapter provides a reference guide to legal issues concerning human resources administration. Following an outline of legal sources, this chapter includes six major sections which address specific areas of concern in human resources administration: recruiting and hiring, contracting, working with staff, dealing with conflict, employee discipline, and dismissal. Each section includes three subsections: a list of the most common problem situations, guidelines for preventing legal problems, and a reference list of applicable legal references. Omitted from this chapter are the state statutes that apply to human resources administration. These must be examined to have a more complete understanding of the legal issues. Since these statutes vary from state to state, no effort has been made to include them here. However, the building handbook outline which can be found in Figure 10.2 (beginning on page 283) will provide guidance that principals may find helpful.

LEGAL SOURCES DOCUMENTS

The purpose of this section is to orient the reader to the sources of legal requirements and highlight those of most concern in human resources

FIGURE 10.1. SOURCES OF LAW

	Constitution	Statutory Law	Administrative Rules
United States	Constitution	Federal Statutes	Federal Agencies
State	Constitution	State Statutes	State Agencies
Local District		Board Policy Contracts	Administrative Regulations & Procedures
Building		Governance Council	Building Handbooks

administration. The major sources of law, and other legally related requirements, include constitution, statutory, and administrative rule.

In addition, case law, arbitration decisions, and attorney general opinions give guidance on which personnel actions are acceptable and which are not. To avoid conflict, each level is subject to the laws at all higher levels. Principals must follow their own school rules plus their district rules, state laws, and federal laws. Within a given level, administrative rules are subject to statutes which in turn are subject to the constitution.

THE UNITED STATES GOVERNMENT

Federal laws include the U.S. Constitution, federal statutes enacted by the Congress, and administrative law put into place by federal agencies.

Constitutions, both federal and state, limit the powers of the legislative, the judicial, and the executive branches of government. The U.S. Constitution is the supreme law of the land. Any rules or laws found to conflict with the U.S. Constitution would be declared unconstitutional and, therefore, not legal. Although the U.S. Constitution does not address education directly, several of its provisions affect school human resources administration:

- *Article 1, Section 10*: Contracts with employees or bargaining units, once agreed to by the board, must be honored.

- *First Amendment*: Personal freedoms of religion, speech, and assembly are protected.

- *Fifth and Fourteenth Amendments*: Employee contracts are considered to be contract rights which cannot be taken away without following due process requirements which include, at a minimum, the right to: know the charges being brought against you, confront your accuser, tell your side of the story, and have representation present.

- *Fourteenth Amendment—Equal Protection Clause*: Discrimination on the basis of race, sex, and handicap is prohibited.

Statutes are those laws passed by legislative bodies like Congress or the state legislature. Examples of statutes passed by Congress include:

- The Occupational Safety and Health Act (OSHA) requires employers, including schools, to provide a safe working environment.

♦ The Civil Rights Act (CRA) requires employers, including schools, to ensure fair treatment of those in "protected classes" based on race, gender, age, disability, and veteran status.

The concept of "states' rights" limits Congress' ability to impose federal statutes on the states, therefore, Congress often makes receipt of federal funding contingent upon following the statutes enacted by Congress. Examples of these are found in the exhibits at the end of the chapter.

Administrative law comes from federal or state agencies with authority to regulate public functions. Federal agencies most concerned with education include: the U.S. Department of Education (USOE) and the National Institute of Education (NIE). Other agencies that impact laws related to school personnel administration include: the Department of Labor, which administers the Occupational Safety and Health Act (OSHA), the Office of Civil Rights (OCR), and the Equal Employment Opportunity Commission (EEOC). Examples of these are found in the exhibits at the end of the chapter.

THE STATE

The State Constitution limits state laws in the same way that the U.S. Constitution limits Federal laws. The most important parts of a state constitution from a personnel perspective relate to equity. Two examples are:

♦ Schools must make ample provision for the education of all children residing within its borders, without regard to race, creed, religion, or sex.

♦ Schools must remain forever free of sectarian control or influence.

Most statutory laws affecting school personnel administration come from state legislatures. Each principal should develop a good working knowledge of those laws.

Administrative laws are rules and regulations adopted by state agencies with the power to regulate public schools. In most states, administrative laws are adopted by the State Board of Education and by the Office of the Superintendent of Public Instruction.

SCHOOL DISTRICTS

Schools and school boards, although administered locally, have been consistently found by the courts to be under the authority of the state. State governments delegate to school boards specific authority for operation of the schools. Boards are given the authority to pass *policies* to implement those laws which they have been charged with implementing. School boards, in turn, sometimes delegate to the superintendent the responsibility of writing *administrative regulations and procedures* which give further direction for carrying out board policies. Policies enacted by local school boards have the weight of law for that specific school district and it is the responsibility of district employees to act in ways consistent with adopted policies and procedures.

In addition to adopting policies and procedures, school boards regularly approve at least two kinds of *contracts* which have a direct bearing on the role of the principal. School boards bargain with and subsequently enter into formal negotiated agreements, or contracts, with formally recognized bargaining units. By approving these contracts, the board pledges itself and its employees to abide by these agreements. The second type of contract that the board approves is the individual employment contract. These contracts, made with each certificated employee (and some supervisory classified employees), set forth the terms and conditions of employment which usually include the salary and the term and length of the contract. The U.S. Constitution and other laws require that, once agreed to, the terms of the contract be adhered to by the district and by the administrative representatives of the district.

LOCAL SCHOOL BUILDINGS

Individual school buildings may also set forth a variety of administrative rules. *Handbooks* may outline rights and responsibilities for staff and/or students. Schools with local decision-making councils may adopt *bylaws* or other self-governance rules. Once adopted, schools may be expected legally to abide by those rules. School rules that conflict with district procedures, board policy, administrative law, statutory laws, or state and federal constitutions will be overturned. An outline of topics to be included in a school building handbook is shown in Figure 10.2 beginning on page 283.

OTHER RULES

The laws and rules listed above create an array of rules to follow. Although they may not be readily available to the principal, each of the above laws and rules may be found in written form in standard reference works. In addition to the foregoing sources, there are at least four other sources of laws and guidelines which may regulate the actions of the well-informed school principal.

What each of the four sources have in common is that, although they can be found in writing, they are not easily found in standard reference guides. Knowing about these sources of information is therefore more difficult, but sometimes necessary, to the well-informed principal. The four sources are:

CASE LAW

Case law (also called *common law*) comes from the court decisions made over decades and centuries in a given area. **Due process** and **just cause** are two examples in the personnel area. The U.S. Constitution guarantees due process in the fifth and fourteenth amendments. No definition is provided in the Constitution. Hundreds of court cases have since helped define what is meant by due process. Other cases have helped define just cause. These two terms will not be defined in any statute, but case law—the collection of previous cases in this area—will define what principals can and cannot do in disciplining or dismissing employees.

ADMINISTRATIVE RULES

In addition to rules adopted by agencies that directly control schools, the U.S. Department of Education, and the State Board of Education for example, there are many other agencies concerned with public health, safety, and welfare. These agencies write rules regarding fire drills, food preparation, use of pesticides, and other activities which go on in schools.

ARBITRATION DECISIONS

When an employee files a grievance under the terms of the negotiated agreement, that grievance may eventually be decided by an arbitrator. The arbitrator's decision then reinterprets the negotiated agreement in the same way that case law defines terms found in statutory or constitutional law. Once decided, the arbitrator's ruling becomes a precedent, meaning that the district and the association must abide by that ruling in future cases.

ATTORNEY GENERAL OPINIONS

Occasionally a district or a state agency will ask the attorney general to offer an opinion about laws that are hard to interpret clearly. An attorney general's opinion (AGO) is just that, an opinion. It does not have the weight of law, however, it does serve as a useful guideline for how that law can best be interpreted.

RECRUITING AND HIRING

Recruiting consists of all activities designed to attract potential employees to the school or district. Activities may include brochures, job announcements, advertisements, and initial interviews.

POTENTIAL PROBLEMS

Any exclusionary or discriminatory recruitment practices or failure to safeguard against such practices present the greatest potential problems in recruiting. The administrator must make special efforts to avoid discrimination against individuals in a protected class: females, minorities, disabled, those over age 40, and/or veterans.

HOW TO PREVENT PROBLEMS

The following information provides a practical guide for preventing potential legal problems in the recruiting process and comes largely from information by Shoop and Dunklee (1992).

- ◆ **Position Analysis:** When a position becomes available:
  - Perform a job analysis to determine the critical work behaviors to be used as criteria for measuring employee performance. Include supplemental needs such as coaching and supervising.
  - Develop a job description—see Recruitment in Chapter 4, for examples.

    Make sure the job standards allow for a beginner in the job.

    Every job standard specified must be verifiable as a valid requirement for the job.

For nonteaching positions, every job specification should include levels of skills or abilities necessary for progressively higher-level positions in the same job family.

- Evaluate the qualifications for all positions to ensure that there are no excessive or unnecessary requirements that might have the effect of disqualifying a disproportionate number of minorities, women, or others in a protected classification.

◆ **Recruitment:** Include as many possible sources of qualified applicants as possible when recruiting.

- Use representatives of both protected and nonprotected classifications of employees as part of the overall recruitment team.

- Add colleges and universities with predominately minority and female populations to contact lists of sources of qualified applicants.

- Maintain records of recruitment methods for the dual purposes of evaluating effectiveness and documenting practices.

◆ **Initial Applications and Screening:**

- Make sure not to ask preemployment questions that may lead to a charge of discrimination.

  All required information, whether asked on the employment application or in an interview, must be related to the job and the applicant's qualifications for the job.

  All applicants must be asked the same questions. Follow-up questions may differ, however, if the intent is to seek clarification or expansion.

  If the applicant volunteers information that is illegal to ask, do not reject the applicant based on that information. Liability exists for discrimination whether or not the information was volunteered.

  If the applicant volunteers information regarding a handicapping condition which directly relates to the job requirements, the employer may be obligated to investigate whether the applicant can be reasonably accommodated to perform the job.

- Be sure that notes or summaries of interview with job applicants:

Refer only to job-related aspects of the position.

Are stated in neutral, objective terms.

Have no negative inferences.

Do not include coded information.

◆ **Interviews:**

- Be careful with "ice-breaking" small talk and comments. Case law has demonstrated that these aspects of the interviewing are the most susceptible to legal problems. Only job-related and legally allowable questions may be asked in the interview. Consequently, the principal who is completely familiar with the job being filled should lead the interview.

- Document the interview including the date of the interview, the interviewer's name, and the results (e.g., "eliminate" or "application processed further").

- The most important principle in interviewing, at any stage, is to ask only questions which are related to job requirements.

- Questions better left alone deal with:

Health

Income

Marital status or lifestyle

Race, religion, or politics

Age, date of birth, height, weight, gender

Nonwork-related issues

Children and family plans

◆ **Preemployment Testing:**

- Preemployment tests must not limit any protected class from consideration for employment unless the employer can prove that the test is job-related and properly validated.

- Physical testing may only be used for jobs clearly requiring physical standards. All applicants for such a position must be given the same test.

  Drug testing law remains an unclear legal area.

  Employers may not test prospective employees for HIV, ARC, or AIDS.

♦ **Reference Checking:**
  - Any personal characteristics known to be important for job performance should be included in the listed qualifications for the job. Typical characteristics include honesty, dependability, and ability to work with others.
  - All questions asked in a reference check must be related to the applicant's past performance.

    Make sure to obtain all information from someone knowledgeable about the applicant's work performance.

    Have all applicants sign a form authorizing release of the information requested from references to protect against potential defamation suits.

    Gather the same information from references for all applicants and use the information consistently.

♦ **Hiring Decisions:**
  - Make all decisions without regard to race, color, national origin, sex, or religion. An exception here are private church-related schools.
  - Evaluate all aspects of recruiting and hiring to detect biases that might adversely impact protected groups.
  - Any restrictions related to race, color, national origin, sex, religion, or protected groups must be based upon a bona fide occupational qualification necessary to job performance.
  - Document each stage of the selection process for purposes of evaluation.

LEGAL REFERENCES FOR THE PRINCIPAL

- ◆ Title VII of the Civil Rights Act of 1964
- ◆ The Equal Pay Act of 1963
- ◆ The Age Discrimination in Employment Act (ADEA)
- ◆ The Rehabilitation Act of 1973
- ◆ The Americans with Disabilities ACT of 1990 (ADA)
- ◆ The Veterans' Re-employment Act
- ◆ The Immigration Reform and Control Act of 1986 (IRCA)
- ◆ Title IX of the Education Amendments of 1972

CONTRACTING

Contracting consists of ensuring that the employee meets all hiring criteria, clarifying all terms and conditions of the contract, obtaining school board approval, and adhering to the terms of the contract.

POTENTIAL PROBLEMS

EMPLOYEE QUALIFICATIONS

In addition to the job-related requirements listed in the previous section, there may be several additional checks designed to ensure against the hire of noncitizens, pedophiles, or those with criminal records. Several checks may need to be carried out either before the contract is signed or with the clear written understanding that the successful completion of these checks will be required to fully enact the contract.

All employees are now required to provide proof of citizenship (Form I-9) or other documentation showing entitlement to be employed in the United States. Fingerprinting may be required by your district as a basis for running a criminal background check to ensure against the hiring of those convicted of child molestation or other crimes. Checking certificate numbers against those recorded at the state level may be required to ensure that certificates are current and have not been revoked. Each state maintains computer links to other states for lists of certificates which have been revoked. In addition, a call to the state office can often tell whether there is a current investigation of the teacher in question. Checking driving records may be required in the case of hiring bus drivers.

CERTIFICATION

Schools make a distinction between two categories of employees: certificated and noncertificated, or classified. Certificated employees are those who hold state certificates as requirement of the position they hold. All other employees, who are not required by their position to hold certificates, are usually referred to as classified employees.

Teachers must be certificated and, depending on the state, have an endorsement for each area in which they teach. This creates two potential problems. The first is that the teacher must have a certificate. Schools are also required to make sure that classrooms are under the supervision of a certificated employee. Teachers who have not yet been granted a certificate or those whose certificates have expired cannot continue to teach.

The second potential problem may come from hiring teachers who lack the proper endorsement. Failure to check for the proper endorsements may mean that the district is obligated to employ individuals but may not be able to assign them to teach the courses for which they were hired. This is a recurring problem in smaller high schools where teachers are expected to teach a variety of subjects. Care must be exercised in checking for valid certificates and the necessary endorsements for the position being filled.

WRITTEN CONTRACTS

Employment contracts must be written, define an offer by the school board and acceptance by the employee, and involve consideration (a legal term denoting an exchange of value, in the case of employment contracts, services for money). Principals and human resource administrators must be aware that any written correspondence, statements on application forms, job descriptions, position posting, advertisements, or personnel manuals may be construed as contractual. Care must exercised in all written documents. Care must also be exercised in all discussions, being careful not to offer or appear to offer anything more than is explicitly stated in the contract.

Only school boards have the authority to enter contracts. School principals and human resource administrators are cautioned to condition all offers of employment upon approval of the school board.

SUPPLEMENTARY CONTRACTS

A supplementary contract is a contract for work being done above and beyond the regular school day. A coaching contract, for example, could be included in a supplementary contract. Supplementary contracts are similar to regular full-time teaching contracts in that both must be fully adhered to during the term of the contract. Supplementary contracts differ from regular full-time contracts in one important aspect—there is no guarantee of continued employment for supplemental duties after the expiration of the current contract. Regular contracts carry an implied right to continued employment, after the teacher has been tenured, from year to year (more details on continuing contracts are included in the next section). Supplementary contracts may not imply any right to continued employment from year to year.

HOW TO PREVENT PROBLEMS

Openness and quality communication prevent legal problems arising from contracts. To prevent problems in the area of contracting:

- Make sure that employees know *all* terms and conditions of employment, including such conditions as citizenship and criminal checks.

- Exercise care in hiring and assigning teachers only in the areas for which they have the proper certificates and endorsements.

- Exercise care in all written communication. Make sure to include conditions of employment in writing. Take care to avoid putting into writing or stating verbally any implied promises which you cannot guarantee as a part of the contract. Avoid, for example, implying that a supplemental coaching contract will be extended later. Condition any offer of employment upon formal approval by the board of directors.

- Clarify for the benefit of employees that any supplemental contracts are extended only for the term of the current year and that the district may choose to renew or not renew the supplemental contract for the following year.

LEGAL REFERENCES FOR THE PRINCIPAL

- Certification Laws
- Contract Law
- Theory of Contracts
- Any Offer or Claim May Be Construed as a Contract

WORKING WITH THE STAFF

Courts recognize the need and the desirability for order and control to be maintained in the school environment. The principal is the state's representative in the school building. This section on *working with the staff* includes an overview on board policy and areas about which the school staff need to be well informed.

POTENTIAL PROBLEMS

SCHOOL BOARD POLICY AND RESPONSIBILITY

The School Board (and its superintendent) is a most important entity in an administrator's life. School Boards are officials of the state, and are given powers expressed and implied in the state statutes. The school district is formed under the policies of the Board. Boards establish rules, regulations, and school district policies whose only limitation is that they cannot be contrary to state and federal laws.

In personnel matters the Board is considered to do the actual hiring, transfer, and termination of employees. It is responsible for Equal Opportunity Employment, Affirmative Action, union contracts, and many other activities that impact the terms and conditions of employment. Boards which have objective, current, written policies covering these actions and follow them will have the fewest problems.

Policies, regulations, and procedures, once in writing, can then be studied with an eye toward assuring that federal and state laws, rules, and regulations are satisfied. Compliance with procedures will thus reduce the majority of complaints and legal actions to a minimum. Inevitably, there are situations where the conditions of the case are not clearly answered by current policies and laws. In those situations, administrators are often called upon to make decisions, handle problems, and make recommendations to the Board. In the current climate there is always some danger that legal action will result if a decision is not favorable to all concerned.

Therefore, it is very important that principals be aware of the basics of educational law. District insurance generally protects administrators from personal liability as long as they act in good faith. Administrators can be found to be personally liable when they neglect their duties by ignoring violations that they should have known about, or if they cause harm through deliberate violations of law. The administration must be conversant with the law.

The importance of all this is that the principal is a representative of the School Board and therefore, the state. The majority of the actions performed by the principal for the school district reflect the School Board policies set out by the Board. While the Board has ready access to legal counsel, the administrator will more frequently have to rely on their own immediate understanding of educational law. The principal must know the law well enough to follow the basics and well enough to know when the district administration and/or the district attorney need to be consulted.

HANDBOOKS AND TRAINING

As the representative of the board and therefore the state, the principal has a duty, not just to be informed, but also to inform others who work under their supervision. This is best done through putting rules into writing in the form of a building handbook which can provide one single source of the legal information needed by the majority of staff. This information can then become the basis of further training, emphasis in the daily bulletin as needed, or personal follow up in the course of the administrator's daily supervision of the staff.

The section that follows is a practical, hands-on checklist that building principals can use to make sure that their building staff are aware of the laws and policies of the district in which they are employed. The handbook becomes a useful guide when making decisions regarding the building personnel. In addition, the personnel administrator must have access to the full and current board policy manual, the laws of the state, and a copy of the negotiated agreement. These will provide direction for the school administrator.

School administrators may find that it has been some time since a particular section of the board policy has been changed. If the policy is out-of-date, or nonexistent, then it needs to be brought to the attention of the Superintendent. And when board policies are being reviewed and revised, the school administrator needs to be involved in helping to shape policies that are legal and that will aid in the administration of the schools. Likewise, staff, parents, and students should be involved in shaping the content of district policies.

The section that follows is intended to be an outline for your building handbook (Figure 10.2). Many entries come from state and federal law and should be a part of every handbook. Other entries must be customized for your particular district. Figure 10.3, which begins on page 287, presents acceptable preemployment inquiries under EEOC guidelines.

FIGURE 10.2. OUTLINE FOR SCHOOL BUILDING HANDBOOK

❑ **Federal/State Posting Requirements**
There is a long list of Federal and State Posting Requirements that need to be posted in:
(1) Hiring location - a conspicuous place, usually the place where applicants are first
received; and (2) Work location - where the notice can be readily observed by the
employees in the course of their activities, i.e., faculty lounge, or department location.
Contact state officials for the requirements of your state.

❑ **Personnel Records**
These files are confidential to school district employees authorized by the Superintendent
to access them. Any other persons or agencies may not see these files without the written
consent of the staff member, or when subpoenaed by a court of law. These files are kept at
the district office under supervision.

❑ **Professional Organizations**
Do your staff members have to belong to the union? Some districts have this negotiated
into the contract. Are there any other restrictions on other professional organizations that
they might join?

❑ **Professional Research and Publishing**
Most districts encourage research and publications on the part of staff members. But make
sure it is clear that a situation doesn't occur where proprietary rights to materials are in
doubt because the employee worked on them during school hours.

❑ **Reduction-In-Force (RIF)**
Know the district's policy on how a reduction-in-force is processed in the district.

❑ **School Calendar**
Make sure your staff is aware of the school calendar and copies are always available in the
school office. This is usually a negotiated item with the union.

❑ **School Day**
Know the contracted school day that is set down in negotiations, or if flex time or any
other adjustments to the school day can be made for individual staff members.

❑ **Sexual Harassment**
Make sure your staff knows what does and does not constitute sexual harassment and
what the complaint procedure is if they are involved. Remember, it can be verbal,
sex-oriented "kidding" or insults, or at the other end of the spectrum, demands for sexual
favors. No matter how innocent it seems, make sure your staff knows it will not be
tolerated at any level.

❑ **Staff Complaints and Grievances**
Discover and practice effective means to resolve differences that may arise among your staff. Maintaining open communication and reducing potential areas of complaint are important, and resolving issues in a timely fashion helps staff members focus on their teaching. Make sure you know your district's grievance command channel.

❑ **Staff Conduct**
Most school districts have a policy that requires all staff members to conduct themselves in a manner that not only reflects credit to the school system, but that also sets forth a model worthy of emulation by students.

❑ **Staff Conflict of Interest**
This could deal with the hiring of "immediate family" within the same building, or a conflict of interest in the hiring of outside contractors or consultants.

❑ **Staff Development**
Know what staff development is available, and whether it is a required or optional part of your staffs needs.

❑ **Staff Code of Ethics**
You and your staff should be knowledgeable of any requirements that the Board has set as policy. This deals with transactions in school business, making sure the staff uses the proper channels, etc. The Code of Ethics or code of conduct should be given and discussed with all staff at least once per year.

❑ **Staff Evaluations**
Know the dates of completion that your district requires of all staff observation and evaluations.

         First-year teachers: 1st Observation by _____
                                   2nd Observation by _____
         Returning teachers: Evaluations due by _____

❑ **Staff Extra Duty**
Know if any part of the staff's day is considered extra duty. Is it contracted? Is it extra pay?

❑ **Staff Health and Safety**
Make sure the required health and safety posters are displayed, and beyond that, make sure your staff is aware of any programs offered to them in the form of assistance in any personal difficulties, such as Employee Assistance Programs (EAP).

❏ **Staff Hiring**
Know that you are always looking to attract, secure and hold the most highly qualified personnel for all professional positions and that the selection process should be based on an alertness to candidates who will devote themselves to the education and welfare of the children attending your school. Know your EEOC requirements, and that federal law prohibits discrimination against protected classes of people. The protected status categories are: age (40 years and above), sex, race, color or national origin, religion, disabled, Vietnam veteran, citizenship, pregnancy or related medical conditions. Many states also prohibit discrimination on the basis of other categories including: sexual orientation, marital status, appearance, and medical conditions such as AIDS. See Figure 10.3 for acceptable pre-employment inquiries under EEOC guidelines.

❏ **Staff Leaves and Absences**
Know the district policy on leaves and absences. This includes sick leave, bereavement leave, emergency leave, personal leave, district business, etc. Know if a precedence has already been established in the district as to how some of these leaves can and cannot be used.

❏ **Staff Meetings**
Make sure your staff knows your expectations for staff meetings, and whether or not they are required to attend.

❏ **Staff Nonschool Employment**
Does your district have a policy on outside employment for full-time certificated staff members?

❏ **Staff Participation in Community Activities**
Most districts encourage staff members to participate in community activities. If yours does, are they representatives of the school system or are they on their own?

❏ **Staff Participation in Political Activities**
Individual and personal rights and freedoms cannot be dictated by school districts, but some school districts do have policies whereby a staff member's political activity must not compromise his or her professional integrity. The academic process must not be influenced in the interests of the staff's own political ambitions or those of a political group.

❏ **Staff Protection**
Beyond the required postings, schools are now posting "Gun Free and Drug Free Zone" signs. Every precaution must be taken to protect all employees from physical and/or psychological abuse.

❑ **Staff Status**
Know the status of all of your staff members, whether they are on a probationary or continuing contract, etc. Know the date (usually in April) when termination letters need to be delivered.

❑ **Staff Visitations and Conferences**
Because most school districts want their staffs to stay abreast of current trends, does the district budget allow for staff visitations and conference attendance?

❑ **Staff Work Load**
Whether it be number of preps or class size, know the contract language regarding both. Make timely adjustments when these are not in compliance.

❑ **Staff-Student Relations**
Know the district's policy on the professionalism of staff in regards to their relationship with their students.

❑ **Suspension and Dismissal of Staff Members**
Make sure you know the steps required in the suspension or dismissal of one of your staff. Make sure there is complete documentation, and that there is just and reasonable cause. Know the timeline for written reports, and response times allowed by law.

❑ **Transfers**
Know how your district feels about transfers within the district. How is the transfer process handled?

Figure 10.3. Acceptable Preemployment Inquiries Under EEOC Guidelines

Subject Area	Acceptable	Unacceptable
Name	For access purposes, whether applicant's work records are under another name.	To ask if a woman is a Miss, Mrs. or Ms., or to ask for maiden name.
Residence	(a) Place and length of current and previous address. (b) Applicant's phone number or how applicant can be reached.	None.
Age	After hiring, proof of age by birth certificate.	(a) Age or age group of applicant. (b) Birth certificate or baptismal record before hiring.
National Origin	None	(a) Birthplace of applicant, parents, grandparents, or spouse. (b) Any other inquiry into national origin.
Race	Race for affirmative action plan statistics, after hiring.	Any inquiry that would indicate race or color.
Sex	Inquiry for affirmative action plan statistics, after hiring.	Inquiry which would indicate race sex unless job related.
Religion or Creed	None	(a) Birthplace of applicant, parents, grandparents, or spouse. (b) Recommendations or references from church officials.
Citizenship	(a) If U.S. residence is legal. (b) Required proof of citizenship, after hiring.	(a) If native-born or naturalized. (b) Proof of citizenship before hiring. (c) Whether parents or spouse native-born or naturalized. (d) Date of citizenship.
Marital Status	(a) Status (only married or single) after hiring for insurance and tax purposes. (b) Number and ages of dependents and age of spouse after hiring for insurance and tax purposes.	(a) Status before hiring. (b) Number and age of children, who cares for them, and if applicant plans to have children.

Subject Area	Acceptable	Unacceptable
Military Service	(a) Service in the U.S. Armed Forces, including branch and rank attained. (b) Any job-related experience. (c) Require military discharge certification <u>after hiring</u>.	(a) Military service records. (b) Military service for any country other than U.S. (c) Type of discharge.
Education	(a) Academic, professional, or vocational schools attended. (b) Language skills, such as reading and writing foreign language.	(a) Nationality, racial or religious affiliation of schools attended. (b) How foreign language ability was acquired.
Criminal Record	Listing of convictions other than misdemeanors.	Arrest record.
References	General and work references not relating to race, color, religion, sex, national origin, or ancestry.	References typically from clergy or any other person who might reflect race, color, religion, sex, national origin, or ancestry.
Organizations	(a) Organizational membership — professional, social, etc., so long as affiliation is not used to discriminate on the basis of race, sex, national origin, or ancestry. (b) Offices held, if any.	Listing of <u>all</u> clubs to which applicant belongs or has belonged to.
Photographs	May be required <u>after hiring</u> for identification purposes.	(a) Request photograph before hiring. (b) To take pictures of applicants during interview.
Work Schedule	(a) Willingness to work the required work schedule. (b) Whether applicant has military reservist obligations.	Willingness to work any particular religious holidays.
Physical Data	(a) To require applicant to prove ability to do manual labor, lifting and other physical requirements of the job, if any. (b) Require a physical examination after a job offer is made.	To ask height and weight, impairment, or other non-specified job-related physical data.
Disability	If the applicant can perform the essential functions of the job with or without reasonable accommodation.	To exclude disabled applicants as a class on the basis of their disability. Each case must be determined individually.
Other Qualifications	Any area that has a direct reflection of the job applied for.	Any nonjob-related inquiry that may present unlawful discrimination.

Source: Civil rights act of 1964, Title VII as amended; Equal Employment Opportunity Act of 1972; Education Amendment of 1972, Title IX; Age Discrimination in Employment Act of 1967; Equal Employment Opportunity Guidelines, 1978 and revisions.

In addition to general board policies and the more specific collective bargaining agreement, if any, the implied obligations of a teacher are considered to be: duties related to subject matter, duties inherent in contracts with all teachers, appropriate dress, behavior, and speech, moral obligations, cooperation with administrators when given reasonable requests, and helping to maintain discipline and order when special circumstances occur in a school. School staff are also responsible for promoting civic virtues and understanding in their classes. These are areas which you may wish to add to your building handbook to ensure good, clear communication of expectations.

HOW TO PREVENT PROBLEMS

To prevent problems in the area of working with staff:

♦ Take your role as representative of the Board and state seriously; remain well-informed on changes in district policy and state law; take an active role in influencing Board policy.

♦ When in doubt, ask. Don't be afraid to ask for legal advice from district administrators or from the district attorney.

♦ Put it in writing. Create and constantly update a building handbook which will serve as a summary of the responsibilities of staff. Keep your calendar current and record notes which may serve you better. Besides a subject file for letters and memos, create a chronological file for each year which contains all correspondence for one school year.

♦ Reinforce key expectations through formal training, daily bulletin, faculty meetings, and daily one-on-one supervision.

LEGAL REFERENCES FOR THE PRINCIPAL

♦ State School Law Manual
♦ School District Policy Manual
♦ Master Agreement with the Teachers' Association
♦ Other negotiated agreements
♦ Department of Labor and Industries
♦ Human Rights Commission
♦ Occupational Safety and Health Act of 1970 (U.S.)
♦ Family and Medical Leave Act of 1993 (U.S.)

+ Civil Rights Act of 1964, Title VII as amended
+ Equal Opportunity Act of 1972
+ Education Amendment of 1972, Title IX
+ Age Discrimination in Employment Act of 1967
+ Equal Employment Opportunity Guidelines, 1978 and revisions.

DEALING WITH CONFLICT

Hiring the right staff and clearly communicating rules and expectations go a long way toward the effective operation of schools for students. Conflicts over differing opinions and interpretations are a reality of life and resolving those conflicts is one of the duties of the principal. This section on dealing with conflict addresses: balancing demands, avoiding lawsuits, and dealing with employee grievances.

POTENTIAL PROBLEMS

BALANCING DEMANDS

The principal is responsible for virtually everything that occurs in and around the school building and grounds. Every aspect of the public school system is regulated in one form or another by some federal or state law. The principal is expected to do his or her best to comply with each and every law. It behooves the principal to devote adequate time to evaluating decisions and balancing competing demands of government, board policy, politics, parents, students, staff, and union. Throughout any given day the principal is likely to encounter any or all of these demands. They influence every decision, and every course of action taken.

The interaction of these demands necessitates constant compromise as competing forces push to influence decisions and actions in their favor. Ultimately, the principal is responsible for running the school efficiently and effectively for the achievement of students. This is a responsibility carried out in the public's interest. To that end it is imperative that as many of the basic policies and procedures of the school be in writing as possible. This is to ensure consistency.

LAWSUITS

Schools can be sued in civil court to collect damages that result in injury received as a result of the action or inaction of the district. Technically, a lawsuit brought by a parent or patron is known as a tort. Torts are also known as private wrongs. They do not involve contracts. To be successful in this type of suit, there must be: (1) a duty on the part of the district, (2) failure to exercise reasonable care, and (3) injury. If the school has no duty to provide care, as in a fight between two students on the way to school, there is likely to be no school liability. If there is a duty to provide care and the district did in fact exercise proper care, as in an accident on a properly supervised play field, there is likely to be no liability. And if no injury occurred, physical or emotional, there is no liability.

The biggest pitfall in this area is failure to supervise students properly. All student activities must be supervised. The nature of the activity and number of students involved influence the number of staff required. Staff need to be informed of the importance of providing proper supervision. The state holds that teachers have a definite legal duty to the students and that duty is the protection of the students from reasonably foreseeable risks. The school may be liable if evidence indicated that there was sufficient time for the teacher to know what was going on, or should have known, or was inattentive.

Another major pitfall in this area is proper maintenance of facilities. Playground equipment, athletic equipment, shop, and science laboratory classes are potential targets for this type of action. If the school or the principal creates a hazardous environment that presents unusual dangers to students, they can be found liable. The risk of liability goes up sharply when the principal knew of the danger and did not correct it in a timely fashion. Each principal should develop a safety committee and see that it meets regularly.

One additional area that involves risk comes from teachers physically harming students by intervening in a fight, forcibly restraining students, or striking students in anger. Increasingly, teachers are also bringing suits against students for physical injuries caused by student violence.

Principals can reduce liability by training new teachers and staff for their assignments. Staff need to be trained in the importance of proper supervision, the best ways to reduce the risk of injury to students, and the dangers of using physical force on students. Staff, in turn, may need to provide special training for students who will be using science, shop, or P.E. equipment that increases the risk of injury. Failure to follow stated policies and guidelines increases the risk of harm and therefore the charges of negligence and/or malpractice.

The defense of principals or teachers, as public officials and at public expense, depends on whether or not it can be shown that they were performing their duty in good faith and in the furtherance of their responsibilities. School staff do not enjoy total immunity from lawsuits. There is the potential that staff may be held personally liable for damages if they acted knowingly to endanger students.

COLLECTIVE BARGAINING AND GRIEVANCES

In addition to the individual contract between an employee and the district, there often is another master contract between recognized bargaining units and the district. Traditionally, the areas that are subject to the collective bargaining process are: salaries, fringe benefits, hours of work, and working conditions. The district has a continuing duty to bargain with a union over these subjects before any rules or rule changes can be made.

Since no contract can specifically address all the details regarding rights and obligations of the parties, there is always room for different interpretations. The principal, therefore, as the representative of the Board, will often have to decide on the meaning of key parts of the negotiated agreement. To monitor the interpretation of the contract, most collective bargaining agreements include a grievance procedure whereby employees who are "aggrieved" by actions of the district can file a complaint. Contracts usually specify a standard grievance procedure and state whether grievances apply to only the master contract or whether grievances can also be filed over Board policy, administrative rules, and past practices. Unions usually favor broad definitions while Boards tend to favor narrow definitions of what can be grieved. If not defined as grievable in the current contract, then it is not grievable.

Because of the stigma attached to grievances and the time they consume, even the master contract in which they are found encourage resolution through informal processes. When informal processes prove to be insufficient, knowing and following the formal procedures become essential. Your district's process may vary, but most grievances include the following steps:

- *Step One—Informal:* An informal meeting and discussion takes place between the teacher and the principal in an attempt to solve the alleged problem. If unsuccessful, then the teacher (aggrieved) moves to Step One—Formal.

- *Step One—Formal:* A grievance form (usually found in the master contract) is completed by the aggrieved and submitted to the principal. The principal has a set amount of time in which to respond to the grievance. If no response is given before the deadline, or if the grievance is not resolved to the satisfaction of the aggrieved, the grievance proceeds to the next step.

- *Step Two:* At this level the grievance is appealed to the school district superintendent or a designated representative at the district level. The district has a set number of days in which to respond. Again, if no response is given or the grievance is not resolved, it goes to the next step.
- *Step Three:* Some contracts call for Step Three to be heard by the school board. Others call for an outside arbitrator. Some call for final and binding arbitration while others leave open recourse to the courts.

Failure of either side of the disputed grievance to follow the negotiated procedures is classed as an unfair labor practice and is subject to legal action. While the procedures for handling grievances vary widely, many grievances are best resolved at the administrative level through sincere efforts to find resolution. Most grievances seek to clarify contract language, procedures, and potential safety issues and expectations.

HOW TO PREVENT PROBLEMS

To prevent problems when dealing with conflict:

- Seek first to understand the needs of the parties involved and then the nature of legal requirements that apply.
- Know that you can't always please everyone; take care to provide first for the safety and welfare of the student.
- Reduce the risk of law suits by providing for proper supervision at all times, by inspecting and repairing hazardous equipment and by providing adequate staff training.
- Seek to resolve grievances informally if possible; take care to follow the procedural requirements when formal grievances are filed.
- Follow the advice of Walter Baer, *Do's and Don'ts in Handling Grievances* (Figure 10.4).

LEGAL REFERENCES FOR THE PRINCIPAL

- State School Law Manual
- Master Contract(s)
- Grievance Procedures

FIGURE 10.4. ADAPTED FROM *DO'S AND DON'TS IN HANDLING GRIEVANCES* BY WALTER E. BAER

In most school districts, the building principal or program supervisor is given responsibility and authority to deal with the problems and grievances of employees — and to resolve them by application of the proper remedy.

In most cases, the principal or supervisor had no hand in negotiating the contract nor did he or she share in drafting its provisions. Nevertheless, the principal is the one who deals most frequently with employees and with the association — and must be equipped to represent the district's interests and preserve the district's rights, or they will quickly go down the drain.

The following checklist pinpoints the major practices and pitfalls that the principal or supervisor should be familiar with in handling the grievance machinery. Naturally, all these points are not applicable in every case, but if the principal or supervisor is familiar with all of them — and observes them in handling the grievances — he or she will be prepared for almost any kind of case that may arise.

DO

- Do investigate and handle every case as though it will eventually result in an arbitration hearing.

- Do talk with the employee about his or her grievance. Give the employee a good and full hearing.

- Do require the grievant to identify the specific contractual provision allegedly violated. Determine whether the matter can properly be constituted a grievance — as deemed by the agreement.

- Do determine whether the grievance was filed, appealed, and processed from step to step.

- Do examine the contract negotiations record for new or changed contract provisions on the grieved matter. If there is a <u>new</u> provision, which party proposed the language, and for what reason? Which party's language was eventually adopted? What do the negotiation minutes reveal regarding discussions on the provision in dispute — whether it is new, changed. or unchanged? Who was present during discussions on the relevant provision?

- Do record all results of your investigation.

- Do determine whether there is a political connotation to the grievance. Is the grievant a deposed union official, or is he or she now aspiring to a union office? What is the grievant's relationship with current union officials? If unfriendly, why?

- Do control your emotions — control your remarks — control your behavior.

- Do pass along to your district's personnel supervisor your experience with any troublesome contract clauses.

- Do remember your case may result in an arbitration hearing. Fully inform your supervisor of all discussions about the grievance.

DON'T

- Don't discuss the case with the association representative alone — if the (grievant) employee is at work and can be present during the discussion.

- Don't argue with the association representative in the presence of employees. Hold your discussion privately.

- Don't admit to the binding effect of a past practice — for settlement of the grievance — until you have first discussed it with your district's personnel supervisor.

- Don't forget that the association is a political institution — it must sometimes attempt to justify itself. Some grievances are irreconcilable.

- Don't assume a judicial role. Hear the association's case, then be an advocate. Represent management's interests.

- Don't argue the merits of the grievances first, if grievance was untimely raised or filed. If untimely:

  1. Present your arguments on that issue first — give reasons for considering it untimely.

  2. Be very clear — you are denying it first on that basis.

  3. Do not excuse or waive the timeliness issue on untimely filed grievances (unless you have caused employee or union delay).

- Don't withhold any relevant facts — if they reveal weaknesses in your case, prepare logical and persuasive defenses.

- Don't make settlements that obligate the district to prior approval, mutual consent, or joint consultation with the association before management can act.

- Don't ask favors of the association. They won't forget — they will someday expect a reciprocal concession.

- Don't give lengthy written answers on grievance forms when denying a grievance. If the grievance should be legitimately denied — after exhausting all persuasive efforts to resolve it — give the simple written answer, "No contract violation. Grievance denied."

- Don't make any settlement "outside" the terms of the agreement — unless you have first discussed it with your district's personnel supervisor.

- Don't hold back a remedy if the district is wrong. Make correction in the amount you calculate to be proper — even if it is less than the relief sought by the association.

- Don't settle grievances on the basis of what is "fair" — the contract determines what is fair.

- Don't pay the grievant if the grievant was the improper employee to file the grievance — even if an actual contract violation has occurred. Instead, determine the employee who was wronged by the contract violation and apply the remedy to that employee, even if such action does not resolve the original grievance.

- Don't count on the association to assume authority for resolving your problems; exercise authority and dispose of issues.

- Don't interrupt or stop the educational program to convenience an association representative demanding instant handling of a grievance — but don't postpone or delay grievance handling beyond the time when such procedure will no longer interfere with the educational program.

- Don't, by action or inaction, cause the employee or association to default on their compliance with any time limits. If you do, don't later deny the grievance for reason of their noncompliance with such time limits.

- Don't settle the grievance — if in doubt. Discuss the case with your district's personnel supervisor.

+ Torts
+ Liability
+ Negligence

EMPLOYEE DISCIPLINE

Staff have the right to be treated with respect and they have a right to be informed of the duties that are expected of them. Principals have a duty to provide proper training, informal correction and, if needed, formal discipline when rules or duties are not performed properly. This section on employee discipline addresses the concept of progressive discipline, due process procedures, and just cause requirements.

POTENTIAL PROBLEMS

PROGRESSIVE DISCIPLINE

Discipline of staff may come from documented negligence, inadequate supervision, assault and battery, failure to perform specific duties, insubordination, abuse of sick leave, failure to maintain proper discipline, inappropriate dress or language, chronic lateness, or violation of any other known rule. Incompetent performance is usually dealt with through evaluation and probation (addressed in the next section) rather than discipline.

Discipline procedures are designed to protect the employee from arbitrary or unfair action by management. Following proper procedures is also important to the district in that it reduces the risk of loss to the district. Most districts have adopted a series of discipline steps that are progressive. That is, the steps progress from mild corrective actions to more severe actions which could result in dismissal:

+ *Oral Warning*—a clear verbal statement of the rule, the expectation that the rule be followed, and the consequences that can occur if the rule is not followed in the future. The time, date, and substance of the warning should be noted in your daily calendar or some other informal written record (NOT the personnel file).

+ *Written Warning*—a clear written statement similar to the above delivered personally to the employee. Technically, these two steps are not discipline. Rather they are warnings that give notice to the employee as to the existence of the rule and expectation that it be followed.

♦ *Reprimand*—This is a formal discipline step (see Figure 10.5) . A reprimand cannot occur unless there has been:

- notice—ensuring that the employee knew of the rule and the charges;

- investigation—to determine if, in fact, the rule was broken; and

- hearing—to ensure that you hear the employee's side before deciding.

   If justified, a reprimand giving the above details is put in writing, delivered in person to the employee, and placed in the employee's personnel file at the district office. Figure 10.6 is an example of a reprimand.

FIGURE 10.5. THE REQUIREMENTS OF AN OFFICIAL WRITTEN REPRIMAND

---

1. The reprimand must be individually written stating specific material facts such as date, time, place, witnesses to, and actions of the individual(s) involved.

2. The reprimand must include a quotation of the rule or regulation violated or breached, or the misconduct if not in the written rules.

3. The reprimand should outline all previous oral warnings. These should be usually limited to the current school year, or immediate past year.

4. It must be explicit and to the point. Avoid using hearsay evidence or assumptions or conclusions of third parties. Tell what you saw, heard or investigated, and found to be true. Findings of fact are the usual way these are presented.

5. It should state that the staff member is being given another opportunity to improve his/her conduct and express the hope that he/she does so.

6. It should state that if the staff member is found guilty of repeated misconduct he/she will be subject to further disciplinary action. This is a critical point, but the principal must remain flexible by not stating what the exact further action will be.

7. The staff member must be given a copy of this letter; do not mail it.

8. Forward a copy of the letter to the central administration office to be included in the employee's official personnel file.

FIGURE 10.6. LETTER OF REPRIMAND–NEGLECT OF JOB DURING WORK HOURS

(date)

Mr./Ms. _____

_____

_____

Dear Mr./Ms. _____:

I am giving you this written reprimand as disciplinary action for your improper conduct and failure to fulfill the duties and responsibilities required of you and your teaching assignment. Our Evergreen School rule on page 11 of the manual states "students are not to be left unattended."

On December 15, 19___, at 10:35 a.m., I came to Room 102, your assigned room, and found you not in your room. Your students were making an excessive amount of noise and creating a disturbance for surrounding classrooms. Two of your students, Anthony Able and Joe Benson, were leaning out of the windows in your room. Gertrude Cable and Myrtle Denson were pulling each other's hair. I found you in the teachers' lounge, reading the newspaper, unaware that your students had returned from their physical education class in the multipurpose room at 10:30 a.m. as scheduled. I stated to you my concern for the safety and well-being of your students if they were left unattended. You indicated you shared that concern and that in the future you would meet your students at the multipurpose room and return to your classroom with them. You were given a verbal warning by me at 10:45 a.m., December 15. 19___. I stated that unless you were able to be at your assigned classroom when your students returned from their class with Ms. Everhart, the Physical Education Teacher, you would be subject to further disciplinary action. On January 3, 19___, only two weeks after the verbal warning given to you on December 15, I went to your room following the afternoon recess at 2:15 p.m. Once again your students were in your room unattended. The door to your classroom was open and the noise being made by your students was disturbing nearby classroom teachers. I found you at 2:20 p.m. in the boiler room with the building engineer. You informed me that you were requesting the engineer to repair the dripping drinking fountain. This excuse as a reason for leaving your students is not acceptable to me as this matter could be taken care of at a time other than when your presence in your classroom to teach your students was essential to their safety and to the instructional program in this school.

It appears from your improper conduct that you have not corrected your actions and remain negligent in meeting the responsibilities of your teaching assignment. By this written reprimand, I am giving you an opportunity to correct your improper conduct and perform the duties and responsibilities required of you and your teaching assignment. Unless you correct your conduct and perform your duties and responsibilities equally with other teachers in this building, you will subject yourself to further disciplinary action.

Very truly yours,

(Administrator)

cc: Central Administration Office
        Personnel files

◆ *Suspension*—Suspension with pay is often a nondisciplinary step that provides time for an investigation to determine if discipline is justified. Suspension with pay can also accompany a second reprimand to emphasize the seriousness of the infraction. Suspension without pay can be used with salaried employees but is not easily used with contracted employees. Contracts are considered a property right. The U.S. Constitution states that we cannot be deprived of property without due process of law (see next section).

◆ *Termination*—Employees who have not responded to the earlier discipline steps above may eventually be terminated. For contracted employees termination may be made effective at the end of the contract (for the reasons outlined above) with the employee placed on administrative leave with pay until the end of the contract term. Courts generally demand more exact procedures and extensive documentation the closer an action gets to depriving an individual of income or the right to continue in the job.

In all of the previously mentioned steps, the burden of proof lies with the school district to demonstrate the actions taken are warranted. For less severe kinds of misbehavior, or for a long-time employee, the district may have to go through the above steps more slowly, more frequently, or more thoroughly. For more severe kinds of misbehavior, such as criminal activities or immoral behavior, the process may begin and end with the termination step.

DUE PROCESS

The fifth and fourteenth amendments to the U.S. Constitution state that no one is to be deprived of life, liberty, or property without due process of law. As stated above, a contract is considered to be property. Therefore, school districts cannot take any action which may have an adverse effect on an employee's contract without providing due process. Based on case law from hundreds of previous court cases, due process includes:

◆ **Charges**—The employee must know what he or she is accused of doing or not doing. This is best done through a written memo delivered directly to the employee stating the nature of the charges, the time, date, and location of a meeting with the principal, and (recommended but not required) the right of the employee to bring a representative to the meeting.

+ **Time to Prepare**—There must be some reasonable time period between the date of the notice and the time of the meeting. The notification of charges also needs to be specific enough for the employee to prepare a defense.

+ **Hearing**—The employee must have the opportunity to hear the specific charges, confront the accuser(s), and give his or her side of the story.

Following the previously mentioned steps, the principal may choose to render a decision at the meeting, take the time to write out a decision and hand-deliver it to the employee, choose to investigate further, or decide that discipline is not justified in this case. If formal discipline is being given, the decision must be put into writing, delivered personally to the employee (could be certified mail with return receipt requested), and filed in the employee's personnel file.

The definition of due process is flexible depending on how likely it is that the action will adversely affect the employee's contract. Lower levels of discipline, known as pretermination hearings, require steps similar to those listed. In a termination hearing, all facts and evidence applicable to the action must be presented so that the person can respond to them. This includes documentation of the warning steps, subsequent discipline steps that reiterated the deficiency in performance, and the events leading up to termination proceedings. This means that the principal must have documented evidence over a long period of time including names, dates, occurrences, and any other data. The staff member has the right to confront the principal bringing the charges and make a defense of his or her actions. The staff member has the right to appeal the action taken to terminate his or her employment. The master contract may specify that the appeal is to a hearing officer, to an arbitrator, or may give to the employee an "election of remedy"—the employee's choice of hearing officer or arbitrator.

The school district has several options that fall short of termination. The position can be modified to allow the strengths of the staff member to be capitalized upon. The employee can be retained and provided with additional training. The position or assignment may be changed; however, any reduction in pay requires due process to justify the change or adjustments. Transfers may be an option if the system is large enough. Here it is best if the staff member volunteers for the transfer rather than being forced into the move, again because due process procedure is required.

JUST CAUSE

Just cause, like due process, means far more than is meant by any literal definition. Like due process, just cause has been defined by many court cases. Again the definition is flexible depending on how severe the punishment. Generally, the following steps are required to ensure that there was just or good cause for the discipline being meted out (Figure 10.7).

HOW TO PREVENT PROBLEMS

To prevent problems when dealing with employee discipline:

- *Notice*—Make sure that employees know what is expected of them.
- *Investigate*—Make sure that an infraction has occurred; never discipline without an investigation.
- *Due Process*—Always have a hearing before disciplining employees; let the employees know in advance what the charges are, invite them to bring a representative with them, give them an opportunity to confront their accuser and give their side of the story.
- *Progressive Discipline*—Give lower-level discipline for first time offenses and more severe discipline for repeated infractions or more severe misbehavior.
- *Just Cause*—Make sure that employee knew the rule, verify that a violation occurred, be even-handed in administering discipline, and make sure that the punishment fits the crime.

LEGAL REFERENCES FOR THE PRINCIPAL

- Due Process
- Just Cause

EMPLOYEE EVALUATION AND DISMISSAL

The previous section on employee discipline dealt with misbehavior by the staff. This section deals with employee performance, or nonperformance, in the classroom. Ensuring staff competence is one of the most important and most difficult roles of the principal. This section

FIGURE 10.7. TESTS FOR DETERMINING "JUST CAUSE" FOR DISCIPLINARY ACTIONS

A basic principle underlying most disciplinary procedures is that management must have "just cause" for imposing the discipline. This standard often is written into negotiated labor-management agreements or read into them by arbitrators. Even in the absence of a negotiated agreement, it sums up the test used by employees in judging whether management acted fairly in enforcing company rules.

While the definition of "just cause" necessarily varies from case to case, one arbitrator has listed these tests for determining whether a company had just cause for disciplining an employee.

1.   Was the employee adequately warned of the consequences of his conduct? The warning may be given orally or in printed form. An exception may be made for certain conduct, such as insubordination, coming to work drunk, drinking on the job, or stealing company property, that is so serious that the employee is expected to know it will be punishable.

2.   Was the company's rule or order reasonably related to efficient and safe operation?

3.   Did management investigate before administering the discipline? The investigation normally should be made before the decision to discipline is made. Where immediate action is required, however, the best course is to suspend the employee pending investigation with the understanding that he will be restored to his job and paid for time lost if he is found not guilty.

4.   Was the investigation fair and objective?

5.   Did the investigation produce substantial evidence or proof of guilt? It is not required that the evidence be preponderant, conclusive, or "beyond reasonable doubt" except where the alleged misconduct is of such a criminal or reprehensible nature as to stigmatize the employee seriously and impair his chances for future employment.

6.   Were the rules, orders, and penalties applied evenhandedly and without discrimination? If enforcement has been lax in the past. management can't suddenly reverse its course and begin to crack down without first warning employees of its intent.

7.   Was the penalty reasonably related to the seriousness of the offense and the past record? If employee A's past record is significantly better than that of employee B, the company properly may give A a lighter punishment than B for the same offense.

addresses employee contract status, employee evaluation, probation, and dismissal.

POTENTIAL PROBLEMS

EVALUATION

One of the most important duties of a school principal is the evaluation of staff. Board policy and the union contract may provide other requirements as to when and how evaluations are to be conducted. In some states, failure to ensure that evaluations are performed is *prima facie* evidence for the dismissal of the principal.

STATUS

Several teachers teaching side by side in the same building may have different contractual status and therefore be entitled to different levels of evaluation and supervision. In Washington state, teachers fall into one of the following categories (other states may have similar categories):

- **Noncontinuing**—A noncontinuing contract can be issued only when the teacher hired is replacing a teacher who is on leave of absence. The contract is good only for the one year and states that it expires at the end of the year.

- **Provisional (nontenured but tenured track)**—During the first two or three years, a new teacher is said to be "provisional." The new employee must be evaluated during the first 90 days of employment. Your master contract may require that provisional employees be placed on probation if found to be unsatisfactory. In some states the power is vested almost entirely in the school district. The district may choose to give reasons for its decision or it may choose not to give reasons. The employee may be entitled to a hearing before the Board but may not appeal the decision.

- **Continuing Contracts (tenured)**—Contracts given to employees during the third or fourth year are said to be "continuing" or "tenure" contracts. The employee has the reasonable expectation that the contract will be continued from year to year unless there is good cause.

- **Probation**—If there are problems with competence in the classroom, the administrator must evaluate the employee, identify areas to be improved, and send a recommendation for probation to the superintendent. The superintendent reviews the recommendation and notifies the employee. During the probation period, the employee must be observed every two weeks, be given oral and written feedback, and assisted in the improvement process. If adequate progress has not been made, the district may notify the employee that the contract will not be renewed for the following year. The employee is entitled to a hearing and may appeal the decision.

DISMISSAL STEPS

Care must be exercised in giving fair consideration to all employees. Although this section is titled "dismissal steps," the principal must remain open to improvement up to the final step when improvement has failed. Failure on the part of the administrator to keep an open mind may provide the employee with evidence of prejudice and denial of due process.

- **Observation**—All contractual steps regarding evaluations must be completed and completed on time. Union contracts may call for prenotification of the employee prior to observing the classroom. They may call for 30 minute observation. Care must be taken to do the evaluations exactly as required. The follow-up conferences also need to be held on time and provided in writing. If performance is of continued concern, additional observations may be required in order to document deficiencies.

- **Deficiencies**—Due process requires that the employee be given detailed information on deficiencies along with the opportunity for improvement. For continuing contract employees in Washington state, the principal will need to prepare detailed evidence of deficiencies for the probation when sending the recommendation to the superintendent.

- **Probation**—The evidence is reviewed by the superintendent and a decision is made regarding probation. The employee being placed on probation receives a detailed letter outlining the deficiencies, notifying him or her of their probationary status and what assistance will be provided, and that failure to improve by a certain date may result in nonrenewal of the contract.

- **Observations**—During the probation period, the school principal must observe the employee every two weeks, meet subsequently with the employee for a postobservation conference,
  and put observation evaluations in writing. The employee has
  the right to have a union representative present during the
  postobservation meetings. Completing these steps represents a
  major commitment in time and energy for the principal.

- **Assistance**—Additional assistance toward improvement is required. This might take the form of visits to other classrooms,
  demonstration units in the teacher's classroom, and/or provision
  of a support team consisting of master teachers and union
  representatives.

- **Recommendation**—At the end of the probationary period, the
  principal must carefully review the documentation of the last
  several months, comparing the observations to the deficiencies
  stated in the letter of probation. If deficiencies continue to exist,
  they must be documented as observed on specific occasions and
  dates in the classroom. Efforts for assistance also need to be
  documented. All of this is included in a letter and sent to the superintendent. A copy should be shared personally with the employee and his or her representative.

- **Pretermination Hearing**—The superintendent may elect to
  hold a pretermination hearing (or may consider that the principal has already done this at the building level). The employee
  would have already received a copy of the recommendation outlining the continued deficiencies. The employee and his or her
  representative would be invited to meet with the superintendent to present any evidence that argues against dismissal. They
  would have the right to question the principal recommending
  dismissal.

- **Dismissal Notice**—Prior to the legal and/or contractual date
  the superintendent must notify the employee that the contract
  will not be renewed for the following year. The letter would include similar details as were included in the building administrator's letter of recommendation for dismissal.

- **Appeal**—The employee has 10 days in which to appeal the decision of the superintendent to the school board. If requested, the

Board will have a hearing (open or closed at the choice of the employee) in which both sides present arguments and have an opportunity for rebuttal. To preserve the fairness of the process, the superintendent must not have previously discussed the case with the Board. The Board has a limited time in which to make its decision.

♦ **Remedy of Election**—Following the Board's decision, the employee again has 10 days in which to appeal the decision. Depending on the terms of the contract, the employee may elect to have a hearing before a hearing officer (someone licensed to practice law; often a retired judge) or an arbitrator. Generally, decisions by the hearing officer are appealable in the courts while arbitration decisions are final.

The process previously described applies to "nonrenewal" of a continuing contract. Terminating a contract in mid-year would require much more evidence because it would be depriving an employee of a property right in an unexpired contract. Even when employees are removed from a classroom mid-year, they are usually paid for the remainder of the year to avoid meeting the higher standards required for mid-year termination.

UNCOMMON TERMINATIONS

There are a few unusual forms of termination that do not fit the preceding issues.

♦ **Voluntary Resignation**—An employee may, in the midst of probation or other stages of dismissal, volunteer to resign or retire at the end of the year. If a resignation is indeed provided, this may allow any dismissal proceedings to be concluded. Caution is advised here. A resignation is complete only when reduced to writing, signed AND accepted by formal action of the Board. Suspension of any dismissal proceedings prior to that time may cause a due process flaw in the dismissal case.

♦ **Counseling Out**—Although some principals do this well, caution is advised. Due process requires an open mind on the part of the supervisor. Encouraging an employee to resign gives evidence that you do not think that the employee can improve. If you later begin probation or dismissal proceedings the employee may be able to prove that you were biased against him or her.

♦ **Disability**—If the employee is no longer capable of performing his or her duties due to reasons of impaired health, the employee may qualify for disability or a disability retirement. The principal should coordinate with district policies and state requirements and be sensitive to the feelings of the employee.

♦ **Negotiated Settlement**—Administrators may not pressure an employee into resigning. However, after dismissal notice has been given, the two sides may enter into negotiations that would conclude the dismissal without lengthy (and costly) appeals. This is also a way in which assistance can be provided in outplacement, counseling, or continuation of benefits.

♦ **Death**—The other form of termination is that brought on by the death of a staff member. The administration will be expected to represent the school to the family, assisting them in meetings with the district and the retirement system regarding salary and benefits. Other school employees will have to be notified as will students. Care must be taken, depending on the circumstances around the death. Counseling for students and staff may be needed.

HOW TO PREVENT PROBLEMS

To prevent problems when dealing with evaluations and dismissals:

♦ **Evaluations**—Make sure that all employees are evaluated in a timely fashion according to provisions of state law, Board policy, and master contract.

♦ **Deadlines**—Due process requires that all timelines be met. Key timelines are evaluation of first-year employees within the first 90 days, recommendation for probation by January 20th, and notification of nonrenewal by May 15th.

♦ **Documentation**—Dismissal proceedings place a heavy burden of proof on the district. The school administrator must document time, date, and location for deficiencies.

+ **Open Mind**—The administrator must keep an open mind about the employee's ability to improve. Failure to do so may cause the case to be lost.

LEGAL REFERENCES FOR THE PRINCIPAL

+ State Law
+ Negotiated Contract

RECORD RETENTION

Maintaining records efficiently can be difficult. The first step is to know the requirements of the law. Figure 10.8 lists federal laws pertaining to recordkeeping.

CONCLUSION

There are many aspects of school law which have implications for the principal. Knowledge and awareness of legal requirements are assets in running a well-managed building. To assist the principal, terminology commonly used in personnel law is listed and defined in Figure 10.9, which begins on page 313, at the end of this chapter. In this chapter we have reviewed ways in which the principal can use knowledge of the law in recruiting and hiring staff, contracting with staff, notifying staff of expectations, dealing with conflict, disciplining employees, and evaluating and dismissing employees.

The potential problems, legal guidelines, and strategies reviewed tend to be specific to certain portions of the human resources process. There are many principles, however, which are more generic, applying to many aspects of the process and provide a suitable summary.

+ **PRINCIPLE #1: BE COMPASSIONATE**—Hope. Trust. Work toward improvement. Go the second mile. Believe in people. People don't care how much you know (or how right you are) nearly as much as they want to know that you care.

+ **PRINCIPLE #2: BE A GOOD STEWARD**—Do the right thing. The right decision may not always be the easy one. It may be unpopular to support the employee, but still be the right thing to do. Or it may be necessary to remove a popular employee. Do

FIGURE 10.8. PERSONNEL RECORD RETENTION

Law	Records	Retention
ADEA	Payroll records	3 years
	Personnel records used in hiring, termination, and promotion. Results from employment tests. Job advertisements and training records.	1 year from date of personnel action
	Employee benefit plans, written seniority systems, and written merit plans.	1 year longer than duration of plan
	Personnel records for temporary positions	90 days after personnel action
Equal Pay Act	Records regarding the work week definition, the number of hours each employee works, pay rates, total wages, and total deductions.	3 years
	Collective bargaining agreements.	3 years
	Timecards/sheets, merit system and seniority system records, wage rate tables.	2 years
Title VII	Personnel records (résumés, applications, records on promotions, demotions, transfers, layoffs, and compensation information).	1 year
	All information pertaining to discrimination charge.	Until charge is resolved
	Apprenticeship records including: applicant names and addresses, dates of application, applicant sex, minority group i.d., test scores.	2 years or duration of apprenticeship program, whichever is longer.

Executive Order 11246 (Affirmative Action)	Test records and results, job group analysis, affirmative action program evaluations.	(Law applies to certain government contractors) Law specifies no retention period. Recommended: 7 years
	Written Affirmative Action program.	Recommended retention: 7 years
OSHA	OSHA Form 200 and OSHA Form 101.	5 years
	Records of medical exams used to monitor exposure to hazardous materials.	Duration of employment plus 30 years.

the right thing. Act for the greatest good, the safety and well-being of all.

♦ **PRINCIPLE #3: BE FAIR**—Listen to both sides. Seek out the truth. Investigate. Follow due process. Be consistent. Be even-handed.

♦ **PRINCIPLE #4: BE A GOOD EXAMPLE**—People follow what you do, not what you say. Treat people the way you would want to be treated.

♦ **PRINCIPLE #5: LOOK FOR WIN-WIN SOLUTIONS**—There are ALWAYS, ALWAYS, ALWAYS options. Too many issues go to court because of stubborn people. Think about what is most needed, consider the pros and cons of your best two options, and make a decision that will be best for all concerned.

♦ **PRINCIPLE #6: GIVE CLEAR NOTICE OF EXPECTATIONS**— Most people want to do the right thing—and will if they know what it is. Be clear on expectations. Involve staff in setting expectations. Review expectations frequently. Enforce expectations fairly.

♦ **PRINCIPLE #7: BE PROACTIVE**—He who hesitates is lost. If negative evidence is accumulating, do something about it. Begin an investigation, seek counsel, talk to the employee. Don't assume that it will get better on its own.

- **PRINCIPLE #8: KEEP AN OPEN MIND**—Truth is often stranger than fiction. Give the employee the benefit of the doubt but be open to information that may prove otherwise. And as evidence accumulates, be open to the need to act, but remain open to the possibility of improvement.

- **PRINCIPLE #9: GET THE BEST ADVICE POSSIBLE**—Build a personal support team. Seek out those who have been there. When in doubt, ask. Listen. Hire the best experts available.

- **PRINCIPLE #10: SEEK FIRST TO UNDERSTAND**—Investigate. Listen to both sides. Be fair. Ask tough questions.

- **PRINCIPLE #11: DON'T USE A SLEDGE HAMMER WHEN A FLY SWATTER WILL DO**—Punishment causes resistance and resentment. Look for a better way. Use small doses. Use greater force only when other options have been exhausted.

- **PRINCIPLE #12: BE PREPARED**—Time is of the essence. Better early than late. Use your calendar. Document everything. Do your homework. Stay informed.

- **PRINCIPLE #13: HOPE FOR THE BEST, PLAN FOR THE WORST**—Everything will become public. People will turn against you. Morale will plummet. Things will go wrong at the worst possible moment. Prepare for the worst case scenario. Always have a fall-back position.

- **PRINCIPLE #14: GIVE THE BENEFIT OF THE DOUBT TO THOSE WHO LIKE KIDS AND WANT TO IMPROVE**—Those who don't like kids or don't want to improve are hard to change.

- **PRINCIPLE #15: CHECK YOUR SUPPORT LEVELS DAILY**—Stay in constant communication with your superiors. Say it four times. No surprises. Ask for needed support. Don't assume anything. Communicate more—not less—when the going gets tough.

- **PRINCIPLE #16: TRADE SHORT-TERM COST FOR LONG-TERM BENEFIT**—Pay now or pay (usually more) later. Why is there never enough time to do it right the first time but always enough time to fix it later? Invest time up front. Cut your losses. Don't double up on your bets or go for broke.

- **PRINCIPLE #17: PICK YOUR BATTLES**—What you stand for and what you fall for are both important. Know when you can make a difference and have the courage to do so. Know when you have to cut your losses and have the courage to do so. Pick the ones that are most necessary and the most doable.

- **PRINCIPLE #18: DON'T TAKE IT PERSONALLY**—People will attack you personally. Stay out of the kitchen if you can't take the heat.

- **PRINCIPLE #19: AIM FOR JOINT DECISION**—Make time your ally. Meet often. Take small, steady, consistent steps. Telegraph your thinking. Say it four times. Find a way to get the message across. Be honest. Give the employee time to see the true situation.

- **PRINCIPLE #20: SHOW RESPECT**—Let people disagree with what you did but not how you did it. Treat everyone with respect.

- **PRINCIPLE #21: COUNT THE COST**—Know in advance what you stand for, what you will bleed and die for. There are things that are worth fighting for. And others that are not.

Two concepts run through this list. There is forever dynamic tension between knowing when to bend and when to stand. Kenny Rogers put it brashly in *Know When to Hold 'em and Know When to Fold 'em*.

The Serenity Prayer may say it aptly:

> *God grant me…*
> *The courage to change that which I can change,*
> *The humility to accept that which I cannot change, and*
> *The wisdom to know the difference.*

REFERENCES

Castetter, W.B. (1992). *The personnel function in education administration.* New York: Macmillan.

Contract administration: Understanding limitations on management rights. (n.d.). Eugene, OR: Center for Educational Policy and Management, College of Education, University of Oregon.

Drake, T.L., and W.H. Roe (1994). *The principalship,* 4th ed. New York: Macmillan.

Huges, L.W. (1994). *The principal as leader.* New York: Macmillan.

Hunt, J.W. (1984). *The law of the workplace.* Washington, DC: BNA Books. (Available from BNA Books, BNA Inc., 2550 M St. NW, Westbridge, Suite 699, Washington, DC 20037).

Jackson, G.E. (1986). *Labor and employment law desk book.* Englewood Cliffs, NJ: Prentice-Hall.

Ramesey, R.D. (1984). *Management techniques for solving school problems.* West Nyack, NY: Parker Publishing.

Reutter, E.E., Jr. (1985). *The law of public education,* 3rd ed. Mineola, NY: The Foundation Press.

Schoop, R.J., and D.R. Dunklee (1992). *School law for the principal: Section II.* Boston: Allyn and Bacon.

Smith, S.C., and P.K. Piele (Eds.) (1989). *School leadership: Handbook for excellence,* 2nd ed. Eugene, OR: College of Education, University of Oregon (ERIC Clearinghouse on Educational Management).

The school personnel management system. (n.d.). Alexandria, VA: National School Board Association. (Available from National School Board Association, 1680 Duke St., Alexandria, VA. 22314.)

Understanding personnel law. (1994). Council on Educational Management: Borgman Associates.

Webb, D.L., A. Metha, and K.F. Jordan (1991). *Foundations of American education.* New York: Merrill, Chap. 11.

APPENDIX: TERMINOLOGY COMMONLY USED IN PERSONNEL LAW

ADMINISTRATIVE REMEDY—Nonjudicial remedy provided by an agency, board, commission, or the like. In most instances, all administrative remedies must have been exhausted before a court will take jurisdiction of a case. For example, U.S. District Courts will not consider a claim of employment discrimination arising under Title VII unless all remedies before the EEOC have been exhausted. Collective bargaining agreements typically contain an administrative remedy in the form of procedures for the resolution of grievances. For this reason, employers operating with labor contracts have reduced exposure to lawsuits filed by employees in civil court.

ADVERSE IMPACT—A term used to describe a substantially different rate of selection in hiring, promotion, transfer, training, or other employment decision that works to the disadvantage of members of a protected class. If such rate is less than 80% of the selection rate of the race, sex, or ethnic group with the highest rate of selection, it is generally regarded as evidence of adverse impact. (This "80% rule" is also referred to as the "4/5ths" rule.)

AFFIRMATIVE ACTION PLAN (AAP)—Written employment programs or plans required by federal statutes and regulations. Such plans are designed to eliminate discrimination or the effects of past discrimination, and to create systems and procedures to prevent further discrimination. They apply to hiring, training, and promotion which consider race, color, sex, creed, national origin, and handicap. AAPs are required for employers holding over $50,000 in federal government contracts and who have 50 or more employees. Employers holding over $10,000 in federal government contracts must develop and implement AAPs for disabled veterans and Vietnam-era veterans.

AT-WILL EMPLOYMENT—A traditional American rule in private sector employment stating that the employer is free to fire an employee for any reason—or for no reason at all—and the employee is free to leave employment for any reason for or no reason at all. In the past, there have been only four types of exceptions to "at-will" terminations:

- Employees covered by a union agreement.
- Employees with individual employment contracts.

- Members of a "protected class" under antidiscrimination laws.
- Public sector employees, generally considered to have constitutionally protected "property" interest in their jobs and due process rights.

While these exceptions continue to apply, new limitations on the employers right to discharge have emerged over the last few years, including:

- Discharge in violation of public policy.
- Discharge in breach of an implied contract.
- Discharge breaching an implied duty of good faith and fair dealing.

BONA FIDE OCCUPATIONAL QUALIFICATION (BFOQ)—"Bona Fide" means genuine, honestly or in good faith. The employer who regards sex, age, religion, or another protected characteristic as a bona fide qualification for a job must be able to demonstrate business necessity. For example, sex is a BFOQ for modeling dresses or work in a men's locker room. Sex is not a BFOQ, however, for heavy physical work because some women are physically strong. Customer or employer preference may not be considered in determining BFOQ. There is no race BFOQ.

BUSINESS NECESSITY—Policies or practices essential for the safety or efficiency of an organization. If an employer's practices or policies tend to result in a disparate impact affecting members of a protected class, then the employer must be able to demonstrate that these practices or policies are a compelling (i.e., essential for safety or efficiency) business necessity. The employer may be required to show that no alternative, nondiscriminatory practice with a lesser impact can achieve the same required business results.

CIVIL CASE OR CIVIL ACTION—A lawsuit brought by private parties to enforce or protect private rights (such as medical malpractice, divorce, or breach of employment contract). A criminal case is one involving a charge by a state or federal government against a defendant alleging a public wrong, such as murder.

CLASS ACTION—A lawsuit where one or more persons are suing as representatives of a class in a pertinent matter. Every member of the class need not be named. It is brought on behalf of, or names as defendants, others in similar circumstances. Members of the class must be so numerous that it is impracticable to bring them individually before the court. Named representatives must fairly and adequately represent the members of the dress.

COMMON LAW—The body of principles and rules of action relating to the government and security of persons and property, which come solely from traditional usage and custom. This "unwritten law" is recognized, affirmed, and enforced by court decisions. Common law in the United States was inherited from England and enlarged and changed by our courts. The rule, "one is presumed innocent unless proven guilty beyond a reasonable doubt," is from the common law, as is "employment-at-will."

CONSTRUCTIVE DISCHARGE—An end of employment caused by actions of an employer, or employer's representative, which make an employee's job so unbearable or onerous that the employee, acting prudently, has no other reasonable choice but to quit. Some jurisdictions have ruled that a demotion involving a substantial reduction in compensation and status is a constructive discharge.

CONTRACT—An agreement between two or more persons or entities that creates an obligation to do or not to do a particular thing. Contracts are the body of law governing the agreement process in business. Some kinds of contracts are:

 ◆ Implied Contract—An agreement which is implied by the acts or conduct of the parties, and not evidenced by express agreement. The circumstances surrounding the transaction imply the parties understood that a contract or agreement existed. In some states, courts have held that a long period of employment combined with the absence of employer criticism of employee behavior or performance gives rise to an implied contract of continued employment.

 ◆ Oral Contract—A contract that depends on spoken words, all or in part. It can be a written contract that was later orally changed. Offer and acceptance of employment in an interview is an example of an oral contact for which the employer can be held responsible. Similarly, representations by a manager contradicting the employee handbook may amount to an oral modificationn of a written contract.

♦ Written Contract—A contract that has all terms and conditions set down in writing, for example, a collective bargaining agreement between a union and an employer. In many states, an employee handbook is considered a written contract.

DEFAMATION—Holding out a person to ridicule, scorn, or contempt in the community; that which tends to injure the reputation. Defamation is a civil wrong and includes both libel and slander.

♦ Libel—Defamation by means of print, writing, pictures, or signs; publication that is injurious to the reputation of another.

♦ Slander—The speaking of false, malicious, and defamatory words harming the reputation, trade, business, or means of livelihood of another.

DISCRIMINATION—In personnel law, discrimination refers to the adverse treatment of an employee or group of employees, whether intentional or unintentional, based, for example, on race, color, national origin, religion, sex, disability, age, or veteran status. The term also includes the failure to remedy the effects of past discrimination.

DISPARATE IMPACT—The result of an employer's action or policy which is not unlawful on its face, but affects one or more classes of employees differently than other classes of employees. In antidiscrimination law, concern with disparate impact deals with unequal treatment received by members of a protected class or classes. For example, a policy requiring that all applicants for employment possess no greater than 2 years experience, while not unlawful on its face, could have a disparate impact on persons over age 40.

DISPARATE TREATMENT—Different treatment of employees or applicants based directly an race, religion, sex, national origin, deity, age, or veteran's status.

EQUAL EMPLOYMENT OPPORTUNITY COMMISSION (EEOC)—A federal enforcement agency created by Title VII of the Civil Rights Act of 1964. The purposes of the Commission are to end discriminatian based on race, color, religion, age, sex, or national origin in hiring, promotion, firing, wages, testing, training, apprenticeships, and all other conditions of employment, and to promote voluntary action programs by employers, unions, and community organizations to put equal employment opportunity into actual operation.

EEOC GUIDELINES—Positions expressed by the EEOC that don't have the force of law when issued, but tend to be supported by the courts and hence become law. These positions are outlined in various EEOC publications such as "Discrimination Because of Sex," and "Discrimination Because of Religion."

EEO-I REPORT—The Equal Employment Opportunity Information Report is an annual report filed with the Joint Reporting Committee (composed of the OFCCP and the EEOC) by employers subject to Executive Order 11246 or to Title VII of the Civil Rights Act of 1964. The EEO-I report details the race, sex, and ethnic composition of an employer's work force by job category.

EXEMPT—A term used to describe the status of employees whose positions meet specific tests established by Fair Labor Standards Act (FLSA). Employees who meet certain standards are not subject to (i.e., are exempt from) overtime pay requests.

GOOD FAITH AND FAIR DEALING—A concept employers use which has no technical or statutory definition. Basically, it means acting on the basis of honest intentions and beliefs. Employers who are thought to act in bad faith may have a lawsuit brought against them. In such a case, the court looks to see whether the employer acted out of malice toward the employee, and whether there was an attempt to defraud or seek an unconscionable advantage over the employee. The courts in a few states, including California, have accepted good faith and fair dealing as a theory on which to base an exception to "employment-at-will."

HANDICAPPED INDIVIDUAL—Under federal law, any individual who (1) has a physical or mental impairment that substantially limits one or more of his or her major life activities; (2) has a record of such impairment; or (3) is regarded as having such an impairment. A handicap is substantially limiting if it is likely to cause difficulty in securing, retaining, or advancing in employment. The term Qualified Handicapped Individual refers to a handicapped individual who is capable of performing the essential functions of a particular job with reasonable accommodation to his or her handicap.

JUST CAUSE—Labor arbitrators have long applied a definition of "just cause." A definition useful in personnel law is: "Good and sufficient reason related to the needs of business operations and supported by demonstrable fact."

NONEXEMPT—A term used to describe employees whose positions do not meet Fair Labor Standards Act (FLSA) exemption tests, and who must be paid 1½ times their regular rate of pay for hours worked in excess of 40 per week computed at an hourly rate.

PROTECTED CLASS—Any group (or member of that group) specified in, and therefore protected by, antidiscrimination laws.

PUBLIC POLICY—Generally, this term refers to standards for behavior that the court believes are necessary to support the common good and maintain the fabric of our society in its critical dimensions. Public policy is of reflected in a statute, a constitution, or, less clearly, in commonly-accepted values. Perhaps the most vague and unpredictable standard in personnel law today, the definitions of public policy change as society changes.

PUNITIVE DAMAGES—Punitive damages are sums of money awarded by a court to punish a party because of that party's acts of violence, oppression, malice, fraud, or wanton and wicked conduct. They are intended to provide solace to the wronged party for mental anguish and exacerbation of the wrong. Unlike compensatory or actual out-of-pocket damages, punitive damages are based on a different public policy consideration—that of punishing a particular defendant or of setting an example for others. Punitive damages are awarded in addition to compensatory or actual damages, and punitive damages are not covered by insurance policies.

REASONABLE ACCOMMODATION—Alterations, adjustments, or changes in the job, the workplace, and/or terms or conditions of employment that will enable an otherwise qualified disabled individual to perform a particular job successfully, as determined on a case-by-case basis.

SYSTEMIC DISCRIMINATION—Employment policies or practices which, though often neutral on their face, serve to differentiate in terms or conditions of employment between applicants or employees because of their race, color, religion, sex, national origin, age, disability, or veteran's status. Systemic discrimination relates to a recurring practice rather than to an isolated act. Intent to discriminate may or may not be involved.

TORTS—The law of private wrongs, other than breach of contract, governing the behavior of persons and setting out their obligations to each other. The courts provide a remedy for these wrongs in the form of an action for damages. Assault is an example of a tort, as are intentional infliction of emotional distress and personal injury. Civil suits can be filed for such wrongs.

VALIDATION—The study of an employer's tests or selection standards which proves that those who score high turn out to be successful on a specified job and those who score low turn out to be unsuccessful. The study requires a large sample of applicants and must include representatives of protected groups in the employer's labor market.

11

TECHNOLOGY AND HUMAN RESOURCES

REASONS FOR STUDYING TECHNOLOGY AND HUMAN RESOURCES

- ◆ Technology is a new and emerging area of human resources which will play an increasingly prominent role in the future.
- ◆ As teachers and students become more technologically literate, principals need to model for them the use of technology in all that they do.
- ◆ Principals need to change well-established human resources methods for those where technology can, or potentially can, serve them even better.

> *There needs to be balance between technology and person-to-person interaction. Principals need to find that balance.*

INTRODUCTION

The contributions technology can make to educational human resources are just beginning to emerge. The topics covered in this chapter include: job listing systems; résumé scanning; personnel reporting systems; a case example; and both positive and negative features of technology.

LISTING SYSTEMS

A computerized job listing service available on the World Wide Web, *Project Connect*, is basically a paperless employment agency. After registering for the service, districts can enter vacancies by processing them directly into an on-line form. The vacancies are then sent to colleges and universities throughout the United States.

Teachers who are seeking positions can use the service at the Project Gopher site. They are able to search for vacancies nationally as well as internationally. To find vacancies, the teacher candidate would enter the grade level, subject area, and the geographical preference.

The teacher could also use the service's on-line candidate form to send a personal information sheet to school districts. This service is available 24 hours a day.

The features of *Project Connect* are:

♦ On-line search of participating colleges and districts.

♦ School and college profiles on-line.

♦ On-line listserv management. Participants are be able to make and change their listserv connection on-line.

School districts can use the World Wide Web to list openings. One example, the North Slope Borough School District, AK, is shown in Figures 11.1.

Nationally, an applicant can gain information on opening through the National Educators Employment Review, as shown in Figure 11.2.

RÉSUMÉ SCANNING

Screening résumés is a major human resources activity which can benefit from the latest technological innovations including scanners, sorting systems, and on-line data pools. George Carlson, a recruiter for Motorola's Land Mobile Products Division in Ft. Lauderdale, FL, designed a desktop document management system using a Hewlett Packard ScanJet IIcx

FIGURE 11.1. NORTH SLOPE BOROUGH SCHOOL DISTRICT

Welcome to the NSBSD Personnel Office.

Alaska's North Slope Borough covers almost 90,000 square miles of tundra on the northern coastal plain of the Brooks Range and is home to <u>ten schools</u>. <u>Three</u> of these are in Barrow and <u>seven</u> are in the outlying villages. During the 1995-1996 academic year, 2,126 students from Early Childhood Development through twelfth grade are enrolled in this northern-most American district.

Thanks for your interest in the North Slope Borough School District. In order for you to be considered for employment, you **must** be interviewed face-to-face at a job fair. Please see below for a list of the fairs this year. We need the following information to assess your candidacy: (just click on the word that is of interest to you)

© **1996 by the North Slope Borough School District.**

URL: http://www.nsbsd.k12.ak.us

FIGURE 11.2. NATIONAL EDUCATOR EMPLOYMENT REVIEW (EXCERPTS)

National Educators Employment Review

The Only *National* Monthly Publication Featuring K-12 Positions

Hundreds of Employment Opportunities For Teachers, Specialists, and Administrators Nationwide

- Published by Education Professionals with over 20 Years Experience
- Hundreds of Current Job Openings In Each Issue
- Inside You'll Find Special Features with Guest Columnists
- Information on How to Effectively Respond To An Ad
- State to State Listings of Schools and their Contacts
- Instructions on How to Apply For Certification in Your State
- How to take a Successful Interview

EVERY ISSUE OF THE REVIEW FOCUSES ON A PARTICULAR REGION OF THE COUNTRY, PROVIDING CERTIFICATION INFORMATION AND PROCEDURES FOR EACH STATE

Superintendents and Personnel Administrators:

- Gain National Exposure For Your Hard To Fill Positions by Advertising In The Review
- Information on How to List Available Positions in Your School
- Tips on How to Conduct a Successful Interview

Click here to read about other advantages of subscribing to The Review!

Check out our new site: http://www.teacherjobs.com

scanner and PageKeeper document management software from Caere Corp. With this new system résumés received in hard copy format can be scanned into the system. Those received electronically can be easily imported directly into PageKeeper.

IntelliMatch, Inc., of San Jose, CA, has an on-line system which converts résumés from a summary of experiences to a summary of skills. The system searches according to skill level, recency, years of experience, geographic preferences, education, and other specifications set by the employer. Weighted values can also be assigned to the various criteria.

Job seekers can also benefit from another product available on the World Wide Web called Résumé Builder from Resumix Inc. Résumé Builder formats résumés so they can be more easily read by scanners and processing systems.

REPORTING SYSTEMS

An impressive product available for Macintosh or Windows is HR^3, also advertised on the World Wide Web. HR^3 is a Human Resources Tracking system which keeps track of a variety of human resources information. In addition to tracking vacation and sick days, it tracks the date of birth and hire, as well as the "soft" data such as evaluations.

HR^3 also has sorting and reporting capabilities which allow clients to analyze their human resources information. It is possible to produce lists of employees who participate in health programs, receive continuing education credits, as well as those who will need them in the next year.

Custom reports show precisely the information needed to help write reports. The custom reports available include the following:

- Attendance
- Benefits
- COBRA
- Compensation
- EEO
- Employment
- Personal Information

SOUTH KITSAP–AN EXAMPLE OF HUMAN RESOURCES RECORD MANAGEMENT

Sherrie Evans, the Personnel Director of the South Kitsap School District (WA), helped develop a computerized records management system to meet the needs of the school district. The goal was to design an integrated system, linking applicant and employee file data. Since they were already using the Microsoft Access program for their software, they contracted with a local company, AlphaImage, to assist with the project. The database system, "Educational Resource Management," is comprised of four components, Job Position Logs, Applicants, Certificated Employees, and Classified Employees.

The *Job Position Logs* tracks both certified and classified openings. Information related to the job is contained in the database including the date posted, date closed, position title, reason for vacancy, person replaced, and location. Since it is linked to the applicant base it also tracks the candidates who applied for the position, who was hired, and the hire status as to whether it was a rehire, new hire, etc. They have the capability of producing a status report at any time of positions processed as well as on open positions. They can also access reports on a specific position.

The *Applicant* system tracks common applicant information. It is possible to keep track of the positions for which the applicant applies and whether he or she receives an interview. They can also ask for a profile report that was designed to highlight specific information.

The *Certificated Employees* component tracks information on credits, degrees, and experience for the salary schedule. When a candidate is hired, the personal information is carried over from the applicant file to the employee file. They also have additional screens for certificated employees' information such as certificates, hiring checks, degrees, credits, and experience.

The *Classified Employees* component is similiar to that for the certificated employees. Once the candidate is hired, the information in the applicant file is transferred to the employee file, then other data are entered. Union affiliation, start date, salary, hours per day, days per year, annual bonus, and full-time equivalency (F.T.E.) are completed in the employee file screen.

While the system is still a work in progress, the district feels it has made its records management much easier and allows it to provide its employees with much better data more quickly and accurately than ever before (Evans, 1996).

Positive Features of Technology

Principals need to be aware of the positive aspects of technology. There are multiple positive features associated with technology that benefit both the employer and the employee.

- *Improved performance*—The new technologies will allow management a greater potential for information processing, decision making, and problem solving.

- *Increased work discipline*—This allows employees to perform their tasks in a more effective and efficient manner. The increased discipline may also result in minimizing interruptions by others seeking information as they can also access the information via the computer.

- *A reduction in unproductive activities*—This is unproductive time spent in traveling, making telephone calls, leaving messages, and interruptions. By using technologies such as conference calling, e-mail, and voice mail, the amount of time wasted is minimal and allows time for other tasks.

- *Increased efficiency*—There is a reduction in the transformation of written material. The secretarial tasks of dictation, typing, revising, retyping, and searching for documents are diminished or made more efficient.

- *An increase in time and control over retrieval and flow of information*—This will speed up the timeliness of decision making and information dissemination for the user. The system can provide timely, detailed printouts on the status of requested information. The quantity and quality of the user's work will be greatly increased, which may result in either increased productivity or maintaining present levels of productivity and a decrease of workers.

- *Work alternatives and increased quality of work life*—Working at home and being linked to the office or modifying work schedules allows the individual a better quality of life and it reduces the amount of time spent traveling.

- *Electronic screening*—This allows the department to speed up the recruiting process. A desktop document management system may allow a résumé to be scanned and converted to a summary of skills. For the job seeker there is also software that formats résumés to be more easily read by scanners and processing programs. The system will allow the applicant to include more detail than is usually included in a standard résumé. This scanned information can be compared to the profile from the personnel requisition form for a match.

NEGATIVE FEATURES OF TECHNOLOGY

Principals also need to be aware of the possible negative impacts of technology.

- ◆ One of these concerns is *security*. It is advisable to have guidelines and policies for the establishment, maintenance, and utilization of computerized human resources data. Data access must be considered and a method for requesting information through a formal approval process is recommended. Administrators may be restricted to obtaining data on employees associated with their worksite. On-line access, printed material, mailing labels, and datasets which allow the user to manipulate data within the mainframe are all methods of securing information that need to be addressed.

- ◆ There may also be issues of *dependency and stress* for the user. This occurs when the employees' jobs becomes more dependent on technology and thus workers may experience an increased level of stress. This is due to feeling a lack of control and the stress of increased pressure to improve productivity along with new demands placed upon their jobs.

- ◆ *Recruiting on the Internet* through on-line résumé pools is an area of caution for schools. Schools should carefully track applicant information and respond in a timely and appropriate manner. Education is a "people business" and thus relationships and communication with prospective employees is critical. The new technologies that were meant to help reduce the burden on personnel offices can actually result in more record keeping and offend an applicant.

- ◆ Potential boredom, loss of job satisfaction, and a sense of isolation may occur with computerization.

Minimize the Negative Impacts

Too much new technology introduced into the office in too short a time may result in fear, resistance, and even rejection of the new ways. To minimize the impact of these negative areas, consider these five points:

- Elicit workers' input regarding areas and tasks that should be automated. Allow the workers to feel proactive in the change process and they will begin to psychologically prepare themselves for the change and recognize the positive uses for the new technologies.

- Include them in the design of the system, hold frequent staff meetings, provide progress reports, and allow them to meet with the vendors regarding software.

- Allow the workers opportunities to experiment and adapt the new system to their jobs. Provide training to insure comfort and knowledge of the system and its operations.

- Understand that resistance may be met if workers are feeling all or any of the following: loss of control or inadequacy, fear of the unknown or fear of failure, stress, separation from psychological habits that must be broken, and replacement by new procedures and behaviors.

- Computerization has an affect on the communication within an office. There is a dramatic decrease in interpersonal interaction as a result of electronic mail and messaging systems. Staff members can feel isolated.

In the process of transforming to automation, it is generally agreed that three steps should be taken in developing an effective and accepted system.

First, the administrators should analyze the needs of their office and then decide which of these needs can be efficiently fulfilled by computers and prioritize them. Sometimes, it is recommended that a technology advisor be secured to review this information and advise. Once the system is automated, a technology expert should be kept on staff as the system will need to be kept running and updated.

Secondly, hardware and software should be purchased from a dealer who has a good reputation, on-site repair abilities, and is conveniently located. The dealer should have a variety of products and be able to demonstrate these.

Finally, be aware of hidden costs. These will be in time invested to learn the new system by administrators, costs of consultants, maintenance costs, special furniture to accommodate the equipment, insurance, and training of all staff members to use the computer.

CONCLUSION

The "rising tide" of technology is here. Education personnel are grappling with technology as they attempt to maintain pace with industry standards in training students. Now we have to also be cognizant of the impact of technology in the area of human resources. We are witnessing a wave of new teachers and administrators who are confronted with the reality that they must be technologically literate as well as being professionally prepared in the exercise of their teaching. Technology is affecting the recruitment, selection, and training of our school employees. We can "surf" the net for new employees as well as advertise our employment search in the world of cyberspace. Technology will soon replace mundane and repetitive personnel functions, allowing employees instant access to records or changing their medical plans, for example. Regardless of the technological expertise of school employees or the efficiency of the district personnel office, our final outcome is the effect of technology on the education of our students.

Smith (1992) examined the criteria used in hiring "first-time" technology teachers. Interestingly, the results indicated that "when hiring first-time technology teachers, principals are looking for **healthy, outgoing, enthusiastic, confident teachers who know their subject matter, like working with students, and are able to deliver their course content effectively. Administrators are seeking teachers who will use contemporary teaching techniques such as decision making, problem solving, and simulations to instill traditional work values within their students.**"

REFERENCES

Alabama Center for Evaluation (1982). *The administrative use of microcomputers*. Technical Report. Tuscaloosa: Alabama University, College of Education. 1–15.

Barton, C.R., (1996). High-tech help? It's your call. *Nation's Business*, 84 (2).

Bliss, S.W. (1983). Educational budgeting and computer technology. *School Business Affairs*, 49 (5), 54–55.

Boylan, C., and H. Bandy (1994). *Education and training for rural teachers and professionals.* International Conference by the Rural Education Research and Development Centre, Townsville, Queensland, Australia. ED 390603.

Crawford, C.W. (1983). Questions to ask before buying administrative software. *School Business Affairs,* 49 (5), 48.

Egan, T. (1996). A temporary force to be reckoned with: Wanted: High-tech hired guns. *The New York Times,* 145.

Evans, S. (1996). *Records management.* American Association of School Board Personnel Administrators, 4–6.

Geer, C. (1994). For a new job, press #1. *Forbes,* 154 (4).

Halliday, I. (1989) Teacher management and records in the national education system: Resource book for educational administrators. *Commonwealth Secretariat,* London, England.

Hoover, T., and S. Gould (1982). Computerizing the school office: The hidden cost. *NASSP Bulletin,* 66 (455), 87–91.

Licata, B.J. (1984). *New technology implementation and use: Workers' attitudes and behaviors.* Presented at the American Society for Training and Development Conference, 24.

Minnaar, P.C. (May 1992). An integrated decision support system for planning and measuring institutional efficiency. *AIR 1992 Annual Forum Paper,* 20.

Mitchell, R.E. (1982). Tomorrow's school office today. *American School and University,* 54 (8), 30–35.

Ponessa, J. (1996). Demand for technology-savvy workers falling short of supply. *Education Week,* 25 (40).

Rifkin, G. (1996). Leadership: Can it be learned? *Forbes,* 01206337 ProQuest ABI/INFORM.

Sheley, E. (1995). High tech recruiting methods. *HR Magazine,* Society For Human Resource Management, 1–3.

Smith, R.A. (1992). *Criteria for hiring first-time teachers, with an emphasis on technology education,* ED 364682.

Wilkinson, D. (July 1990). *Personnel department automation.* Austin Independent School District, Texas Office of Research and Evaluation, 27.

12

A GLANCE INTO THE FUTURE OF HUMAN RESOURCES

REASONS FOR STUDYING THE FUTURE OF HUMAN RESOURCES

- To be able to anticipate the future will allow us to prepare for it.
- A major element of human resources management is planning. It is critical in planning to know not only where you are, but also the direction you are heading.
- Things change. Those human resources elements that work well now may be only minimally effective in the future.

Tomorrow's problems will be the results of today's solutions.

INTRODUCTION

This chapter points toward the future by identifying trends which may influence the human resources activity as well as the people who are involved in it. The trends generally pertain to the topics discussed in the chapters of the book and are influenced by the discussion in each chapter. However, forecasting the future is difficult if not impossible, so each of these trends ought to be monitored for future viability.

TREND 1: SCHOOL-BASED LEADERSHIP

School-based leadership is one trend that will be gaining prominence. There will be adjustments as to which activities belong with the central office and which ones belong with the school site. The human resources function will continue to gain importance for the building principal. The principal and the site council committee will be making major decisions in this area. The chart below illustrates the topics contained in this text and the respective human resource roles of the principal and the central office:

Elements	Principal	Central Office
Planning	Major	Secondary
Recruitment	Major	Secondary
Selection	Major	Secondary
Supervision/Evaluation	Major	Secondary
Assisting the Marginal Teacher	Major	Secondary
Staff Development	Major	Secondary
Collective Bargaining/Compensation	Secondary	Major
Continuity and Legal Issues	Secondary	Major
Technology	Major	Secondary

TREND 2: PROACTIVE LEADERSHIP BY THE PRINCIPAL

The principal will need to be more proactive in the anticipation of the entire human resources function. An example will indicate the need for being proactive. The central office business department often plays a major role in predicting the enrollment and thus, staffing needs for the next year. Often, in order to maintain a safe budget position, the enrollment estimates are ultraconservative. "We will wait until we see the whites of their eyes," business office dictates. However, when more students arrive on the first day of school than predicted, there are not enough teachers or staff to instruct them. Quickly, the principal begins the search for staff only to find that the number and quality of available candidates is below the spring or early summer level. The principal, under pressure to hire staff, will often make a decision only to regret it later. The point is that the principal must be proactive and persuasive regarding the estimate of enrollment and staffing needs. The district may need to be conservative, but not ultraconservative.

TREND 3: HUMAN RESOURCES DEVELOPMENT EXCEEDS CURRICULUM DEVELOPMENT

Curriculum development is very important and has been for many decades. However, staff development will take on a much greater importance than it has and will surpass the development of curriculum in terms of budget allocation, time, and importance. The birthright of every child will be to have a competent, caring teacher who is well trained.

TREND 4: PRESSURE ON THE PRINCIPAL TO ELIMINATE POOR PERFORMING TEACHERS

There will be more and more pressure to eliminate poor performing teachers. There will be efforts to improve their performance or exit them from the system. Parents and community members will be demanding this action. It will be very important for the principal to have well-developed evaluation and supervision skills first, and then the courage to use those skills to eliminate teachers who are significantly below standard.

TREND 5: INDUCTION WILL BE MORE THAN ORIENTATION

Induction will play a significant role beyond that of two or three days of orientation. The process will be well-planned and year-long in duration. Mentor teachers will also need to be trained specifically to assist the beginning teacher.

TREND 6: DIVERSITY OF THE WORKFORCE WILL BE IMPORTANT FOR SCHOOLS

Although there will be modifications to the affirmative action goals/quotas from a legal standpoint, schools will continue to recruit and select a diverse work force in order to provide role models for students.

TREND 7: COLLABORATION BETWEEN K-12 AND UNIVERSITIES

There will be more collaboration between public school and university schools of education to provide a longer and more intense "student teaching." In addition, more adjunct professors will guest-lecture at universities.

TREND 8: CHILD-CARE PROGRAMS FOR CHILDREN OF STAFF MEMBERS

Schools will provide more benefits for the teaching staff in terms of child care programs. This will encourage teachers to stay in the work force and raise a family rather than choose between the two roles.

TREND 9: TUITION TO BE PAID BY SCHOOL DISTRICT

Schools will direct and thus pay for the continuing education development of the staff. Tuition will also be paid for at public universities as long as the education relates directly to improving the teacher's competency level and improving the instructional program.

TREND 10: THE USE OF TECHNOLOGY WILL SIGNIFICANTLY INCREASE IN THE HUMAN RESOURCES FUNCTION

Technology will play an increasing role in the human resources function. Réumés, letters, and placement files will be scanned by the computer and produce a profile of the teacher. This profile will be matched against the needs of the school and district. Interviews will still play a major role in the selection process but some interviews will be done over two-way video-audio computers for those candidates who are far from the school. In addition, application forms will be done on computer and sent on disk to the applicant.

TREND 11: EMPLOYEE ASSISTANCE (EAP) AND WELLNESS PROGRAMS WILL INCREASE

The school year/day will be extended, thus providing opportunities for teachers to earn substantial pay increases. With this, however, will come increased stress and pressure to provide more extensive employee assistance and wellness programs.

TREND 12: LEGAL COMPLAINTS IN HUMAN RESOURCES WILL ESCALATE

Legal complaints in the human resources arena will mount: sexual harassment for both employee-to-employee and employee-to-student, equal employment/affirmative action challenges, dismissal confrontations, as well as others. The EEOC does not keep a record of how many cases end up in litigation since many are settled out-of-court. Nevertheless, the cost for school districts will be substantial in the legal field.

TREND 13: ACCOMMODATIONS FOR THE DISABLED

The Americans with Disabilities Act will have a significant impact in schools. Schools must be proactive in accommodating coworkers with disabilities. The building modifications are minor compared to the negative attitudes that some administrators hold.

CONCLUSION

The pace of change is escalating and never is it more true than in human resources in education. The trends listed above could come about very soon. Regardless of the pace, it is anticipated that the principal in a site-based leadership role will have to deal with them and deal with them successfully. Teachers, students, parents, communities, and the central office personnel are counting on the principal to be successful in this endeavor.

REFERENCES

Bensimon, H.F. (1994). Violence in the workplace. *Training and Development*, (Jan.) 26–32.

Berry, W.E. (1993). HRIS can improve performance, empower and motivate "knowledge workers." *Employee Relations Today*, (Autumn) 297–303.

Forehand, P. (1993). What cures job stress? *Training*, (Dec.) 32–36.

Hall, F.S. and E.I. Hall (1994). The ADA: Going beyond the law. *The Executive*, 8 (1), 17–34.

Kutscher, R.E. (1992). Outlook 1990–2005: Major trends and issues. *Occupational Outlook Quarterly*, 2–5.

Monford, J. (1993). HIV/AIDS education and the workplace. *SIECUS Report*, 21 (6), 13–16.

INDEX